Cities in Federal Constitutional Theory

Cities in Federal Constitutional Theory

Edited by

ERIKA ARBAN

OXFORD
UNIVERSITY PRESS

OXFORD
UNIVERSITY PRESS

Great Clarendon Street, Oxford, OX2 6DP,
United Kingdom

Oxford University Press is a department of the University of Oxford.
It furthers the University's objective of excellence in research, scholarship,
and education by publishing worldwide. Oxford is a registered trade mark of
Oxford University Press in the UK and in certain other countries

First Edition published in 2022

Impression: 1

Published in the United States of America by Oxford University Press
198 Madison Avenue, New York, NY 10016, United States of America

British Library Cataloguing in Publication Data

Data available

Library of Congress Control Number: 2022938060

ISBN 978–0–19–284327–2

DOI: 10.1093/oso/9780192843272.001.0001

Printed and bound by
CPI Group (UK) Ltd, Croydon, CR0 4YY

Acknowledgements

Completing this volume would not have been possible without the help and support of several people. I first started thinking about this book after convening the aforementioned workshop 'Cities in Federal Theory' in Melbourne in 2019. My sincere thanks go therefore to Gabbi Dalsasso and to all the people who have made that event possible and who have participated as organizers, speakers, discussants, chairs or just audience.

I am deeply grateful to Professor Adrienne Stone at Melbourne Law School for her support for this project and for her mentoring and encouragement during my postdoctoral time at the Centre for Comparative Constitutional Studies.

I am also very grateful to all the authors of this book, who have kindly and enthusiastically accepted to be involved in the project and share their knowledge, insights, and ideas, thus making this publication possible.

A word of thanks goes to Jamie Berezin at OUP for believing in the project since the beginning, to the anonymous reviewers for their constructive feedback, and to the publisher for invaluable assistance during the production stages of the book.

I owe a great debt of gratitude to Joshua Forrest for providing excellent and invaluable support in copy-editing and formatting the chapters.

Finally, I acknowledge the generous support of the Australian Research Council through the Laureate Program in Comparative Constitutional Law 'Balancing Diversity and Social Cohesion in Democratic Constitutions'.

Acknowledgements

Contents

List of Contributors

Erika Arban is Postdoctoral Research Fellow at Melbourne Law School, University of Melbourne; LLB; LLM; PhD; email: erika.arban@unimelb.edu.au.

Richard Briffault is Joseph P Chamberlain Professor of Legislation, School of Law, Columbia University; BA; JD; email: rb34@columbia.edu.

Maria Cahill is Professor of Law, School of Law, University College Cork; LLB; LLM; PhD; email: maria.cahill@ucc.ie.

Ran Hirschl is Professor of Government and Earl E. Sheffield Regents Professor of Law, Department of Government and School of Law, University of Texas, Austin; PhD; MPhil; MA; LLB; BA; email: ran.hirschl@austin.utexas.edu.

Hoi L Kong is Full Professor and the Rt Hon Beverley McLachlin, PC, UBC Professor in Constitutional Law, Peter A. Allard School of Law, University of British Columbia; BA; MA; LLB; BCL; LLM; JSD; email: kong@allard.ubc.ca.

Rebecca Nelson is Associate Professor, Melbourne Law School, University of Melbourne; BE/LLB; JSM; JSD; email: rebecca.nelson@unimelb.edu.au.

Garry O'Sullivan is Research Assistant, School of Law, University College Cork; BCLB; email: 116339721@umail.ucc.ie.

William Partlett is Associate Professor at the Melbourne Law School, University of Melbourne; AB; MPhil; DPhil, JD; email: william.partlett@unimelb.edu.au.

Bilyana Petkova is Professor of Law at the University of Graz, Austria; BA; MA; MSL; PhD; email: bilyana.petkova@uni-graz.at.

Cheryl Saunders is Professor of Law, Melbourne Law School, University of Melbourne; BA; LLB; PhD; email: c.saunders@unimelb.edu.au.

Richard Schragger is Perre Bowen Professor of Law, Martha Lubin Karsh and Bruce A Karsh Bicentennial Professor of Law, School of Law, University of Virginia; BA; MA; JD; email: schragger@law.virginia.edu.

List of Contributors

Introduction

The Growing Importance of Cities and Federal Constitutional Theory

Erika Arban

This edited volume *Cities in Federal Constitutional Theory* takes as its point of departure the increased importance of cities and urbanization in recent decades. In fact, as Hirschl maintains in his latest seminal work, cities are 'both ubiquitous and crucial to today's society, culture, economics, and politics'.[1] Furthermore, today 'the majority of the world's population lives in cities'[2] and it is no accident that the 21st century has been dubbed 'the century of the city'.[3]

The rising importance of cities can be explained by several factors. First, there is an *economic and cultural* factor, as cities—small and large—continue to be the engines of development, innovation, cultural and social interaction, and cohesion.[4] Cities are places of business relations, commerce, trade, as well as cultural and educational centres that provide basic, essential services to citizens.[5] Secondly, there is a *political* factor, as cities are usually more liberal than rural parts of the same country and thus display more progressive political agendas.[6] Thirdly, there is a *demographic* aspect, driving the exponential growth of many cities around the world. This growth has occurred particularly (but not exclusively) in developing countries, thanks to increased natality rates and changed migratory patterns.[7] Fourthly, and relatedly, there is a *diversity* factor: cities attract people from different socio-economic, cultural, ethnic, linguistic, and religious backgrounds.[8]

Thus, cities have become sites of conflict as well as innovation, solidarity as well as the cohabitation of diverse populations. Cities express tensions between

1 Ran Hirschl, *City, State: Constitutionalism and the Megacity* (OUP 2020) 1.
2 ibid.
3 'Report: Century of the City' (*Rockefeller Foundation*, 2006) <https://www.rockefellerfoundation.org/report/century-of-the-city/> accessed 29 October 2021, cited in Hirschl (n 1) 1.
4 Erika Arban, 'Constitutional Law, Federalism, and the City as Unique Socio-economic and Political Space' in Ernst Hirsch Ballin and others (eds), *European Yearbook of Constitutional Law* (Springer 2021) 328.
5 ibid.
6 ibid, 330.
7 Hirschl (n 1) 1ff.
8 ibid, 226.

Erika Arban, *Introduction* In: *Cities in Federal Constitutional Theory*. Edited by: Erika Arban, Oxford University Press.
 DOI: 10.1093/oso/9780192843272.003.0001

diversity and social cohesion.[9] All this, however, poses challenges. These challenges are exacerbated because people living in large cities are often faced with deeper socio-economic divides and inequalities compared to those living in rural (or less urbanized) areas. City dwellers also deal with more serious environmental and criminal problems, social and ethnic tensions, zoning, and housing concerns.[10] Cities play a crucial role as political, economic, and socio-cultural actors in today's society, but they are also unique spaces characterized by deep differences.

Reflecting the complex issues surrounding urban areas, a substantive body of scholarship has blossomed in the past decades—particularly in the social sciences—exploring these multifaceted realities through different epistemological lenses.[11] However, this prolific intellectual production in the social sciences has not been matched by an equally vibrant scholarship in (comparative) constitutional law, where the city as an independent subject of scholarly theorization and investigation has remained largely neglected.[12] Yet, urban agglomeration and the ever-increasing tasks that cities are required to perform represent challenges that constitutional law scholars and drafters can no longer ignore.

Although in recent years some constitutional law theorists have started to discuss more seriously the legal dimension and place of cities, recommending their (re)positioning at the centre of the constitutional debate,[13] the study of cities as autonomous constitutional subjects is still scarce and sporadic, and no solid theoretical foundation has been established yet.[14] This is even more so in federalism theory where, as Hirschl contends, theory remains anchored to '[a]ge-old federalism doctrines predicated on regions or on states as the relevant subunits'.[15] Among the several reasons that help explain this neglect of cities in constitutional theory and federalism, Hirschl suggests that 'we are still captives of constitutional structures, doctrines, perceptions, and expectations that were conceived along with the modern nation-state and germinated through the age of revolution, a historical process that saw the subjugation of the sovereign city'.[16]

In light of the foregoing, in June 2019 I convened a workshop at Melbourne Law School titled 'Cities in Federal Theory'. Its main purpose was to gather junior and senior scholars from around the world to discuss this largely understudied subject in constitutional law and federalism. Being perhaps one of the first academic

[9] Arban (n 4) 323.
[10] Hirschl (n 1) 5.
[11] For example, Jane Jacobs, *The Death and Life of Great American Cities. The Failure of Town Planning* (Penguin 1964); Jane Jacobs, *The Economy of Cities* (Random House 1969); Jane Jacobs, *Cities and the Wealth of Nations* (Penguin 1986); Saskia Sassen, *The Global City: New York, London, Tokyo* (Princeton U P 2001); Max Weber, *The City* (Free P 1968). Part of this rich scholarship is discussed in Hirschl (n 1) 20.
[12] Hirschl (n 1) 1, 28; see also Hirschl, chapter 4 in this volume.
[13] See in particular Richard Schragger, *City Power: Urban Governance in a Global Age* (OUP 2016).
[14] Hirschl (n 1) 1.
[15] ibid, 18. See further Arban and Hirschl, chapters 1 and 4 respectively in this volume.
[16] Hirschl (n 1) 9. See further Arban and Hirschl, chapters 1 and 4 respectively in this volume.

meetings focusing on cities as federal constitutional subjects, the workshop was highly successful, enriching, and stimulating.

The most important message that emerged from the discussion was the need to develop a thicker theoretical framework in which the debate on the role and place of cities in constitutional law and federalism could be situated. More specifically, among the several sub-themes originated by that conversation, the following were considered particularly critical and thus deserving more attention and further investigation:

- Is federalism bad for cities, considering that its purpose is to decentralize and share power? Does it deny cities an adequate role?
- What is the relationship between cities, federalism, and subsidiarity?
- Would the constitutional entrenchment of cities be helpful to expand their role, powers, and visibility? If so, which legal/constitutional role(s) should be granted to them?
- How can the rigidity of many federal constitutions be dealt with, especially older ones, when it comes to changing the role and place of cities (considering that constitutional rigidity is one of the main obstacles to this transformation)?
- How can we define a city for federal constitutional law purposes?
- Last but not least, how can cities deal with the challenges posed by new technologies and environmental changes?

Building upon this thought-provoking conversation and the basic assumption that the constitutional role and place of cities has not been reframed in spite of their continuous rise in prominence, the various chapters in this volume aspire to address some of these questions.

Against this backdrop of general undertheorization (but also misunderstanding) of cities in constitutional theory and federalism, the primary objective of this volume is thus to offer a fresh theoretical account of cities as federalism subjects and introduce the city as a novel constitutional unit of analysis into the discussion. The volume collects contributions from prominent constitutional law and federalism theorists who have been pioneer thinkers in this field. The collection thus represents an opportunity for them to bring together in one place their theoretical reflections, and contribute to enriching the research output in the field of federal constitutional theory.

Because the emerging interest for this topic suggests that there is a need to frame a thicker theoretical account for cities in federal constitutional law, the methodological approach adopted in the book is primarily theoretical. From time to time, this methodology has been coupled with ancillary approaches, including the comparative, normative, and doctrinal analyses of specific jurisdictions: this serves an explicatory purpose and helps develop the theoretical narrative proposed in the book.

The volume has been compiled with a broad readership in mind. The most obvious beneficiaries of the work are scholars of federal constitutional theory: in fact, in offering perhaps the first extensive theorization of cities as (neglected) federal constitutional units of analysis, the book has the potential to become an essential resource for them. At the same time, constitutional drafters and experts involved in constitutional reform processes will also find valuable insights in the book, as the novel perspective on the role and powers of cities, their current limitations and present and future challenges, may provide valuable insights to be considered in drafting or amending a constitutional text. Further still, scholars from other disciplines focused on cities may benefit from viewing the city through an unfamiliar, federal constitutional, lens.

As noted, the book situates the discussion within the discrete theoretical framework of federal constitutional theory. There are several reasons for this choice.

First, there is an opportunity to contribute to the theoretical development of federalism scholarship. As Tierney has observed, federalism, as a field of study, has both been undertheorized and dominated by political scientists. To the extent that legal scholars have engaged with this field, they have done so from an empirical rather than theoretical standpoint.[17] Similarly, Levy has remarked that, in spite of being widely employed in liberal constitutional democracies, 'federalism remains understudied and poorly understood', with theory falling behind practice.[18] There is an opportunity for legal scholars to engage more with federalism, on theoretical terms. This volume seeks to avail itself of that opportunity.

Secondly, and relatedly, federalism is traditionally understood as an ideal mechanism to reconcile diversity and social cohesion through the implementation of a multi-tiered system of government and the combination of 'self-rule' and 'shared rule'. Because it is naturally articulated as comprising different levels, it is a framework within which cities might be readily conceived as a tier of governance.

In any event, although the book is set within the framework of federal constitutional theory, many arguments and claims made here have the potential to be 'exported' to unitary systems as well, thus finding application in constitutional law more generally.

The volume is structured in two parts. Part I sketches the conceptual framework in which the book is situated, by offering an overview of the meaning and scope of federalism as understood in the book, of local governments, and subsidiarity. Part II, on the other hand, focuses on the status of cities as neglected constitutional players and the consequences on several levels, including the centre–periphery relationship (eg in areas such as data protection and privacy, environmental, and

[17] Stephen Tierney, 'Federalism and Constitutional Theory' in Gary Jacobsohn and Miguel Schor (eds), *Comparative Constitutional Theory* (Edward Elgar 2018) 45.

[18] Jacob T Levy, 'Federalism, Liberalism and the Separation of Loyalties' (2007) 101 *Am Pol Sci Rev* 459.

criminal law). The common thread linking the various chapters is that they introduce the city as a constitutional unit of analysis in federalism, and directly address the relationship between cities, federalism, and localism (or subsidiarity). In this way, the book directly responds to some of the concerns raised by Hirschl on the scarcity of innovative theoretical discussion around cities as federal constitutional subjects. While encouraging such intellectual debate, the book also strives to redefine certain accepted concepts and doctrines in the field (eg subsidiarity).

In chapter 1, Erika Arban retraces the intellectual history of federalism, offering an account of federalism from the point of view of constitutional theory. To this end, federalism is presented as a constitutional principle that advocates division of authority and dispersion of powers among different societal groups and organizations. It is also an umbrella term that includes different constitutional experiences, from classic federations like the US or Australia to federal-like systems such as Spain, South Africa, and Italy. In addition to identifying the intellectual milestones of federal history and theory, the chapter delves into the historical treatment (or lack thereof) of cities as federal constitutional entities or 'units'. This commences a broader discussion, continued throughout the volume, on whether certain cities have the required features to become separate federated entities, autonomous from the local governments of which they are usually part.

In chapter 2, Saunders and Arban focus on the constitutional position of local government in federal systems. They consider whether local government ought to be entrenched in federal constitutions throughout the world. The chapter identifies ways in which the local level of government contributes to desirable federal properties: deepening democratic engagement, engaging more closely with local constituencies, and providing opportunities for innovation and experimentation. But it also identifies challenges in formalizing a constitutional role for local government: local government is often territorially small, resource-dependent on other units, and can sit uneasily in a system of shared rule. Unless care is taken, the formalization of a position for local government can have adverse structural and political effects on the federation. After surveying the spectrum of ways in which cities, and local governments, are constitutionally recognized, the chapter suggests a particular method of formal recognition of local government suited to enhancing the role played in a multi-level federal system. It advances a concept of 'partnership' with other levels of government, governed by principles of comity, solidarity, subsidiarity, and equivalence.

In chapter 3, Cahill and O'Sullivan discuss subsidiarity in relation to cities. This is a principle that is often invoked by scholars to justify enhanced formal and material autonomy for cities, and is assumed to offer a presumptive endorsement of city autonomy. The chapter examines the symbiotic interplay between subsidiarity and the city by exploring four types of justifications for increasing city autonomy: (a) the consistency argument; (b) the expertise argument; (c) the stake-holding argument; and (d) the distinctiveness argument. It tests the extent to which these arguments track with four models of subsidiarity: (a) subsidiarity-as-federalism; (b) subsidiarity-as-efficiency; (c) subsidiarity-as-democracy; and (d) subsidiarity-as-respect-for-distinctiveness. The authors suggest that this reflective exploration yields important learning opportunities. For subsidiarity scholars, closer analysis of the concrete example of the case of city autonomy exposes the dangers of eliding the difference between subsidiarity and federalism, on the one hand, or subsidiarity and efficiency, on the other. It also showcases the surprising attractiveness of a model of subsidiarity that focuses on the distinctiveness of the (putative) decision-making level involved. For city scholars, deeper reflection on the challenges that subsidiarity scholarship poses to it will demand, first, greater clarity about how the city is to be defined and, second, greater specificity about the level of autonomy the city should bear.

In chapter 4, Hirschl sketches a comparative framework for the subsequent study of cities. The chapter looks at the phenomenon of urbanization, generally neglected by comparative federalism scholarship. Hirschl considers two questions concerning the constitutional status of cities in federal systems. First, he explores the significance of the federal/unitary distinction in determining the constitutional status of cities. He doubts its significance, identifying the Global North/Global South distinction (particular the tendency towards stagnation in the former versus a tendency towards innovation in the latter) as more significant in assessing the constitutional status of cities. Second, he investigates what national constitutions say about one of the significant contemporary political dynamics: the urban/rural divide. He also explores the significance of the federal/unitary distinction to addressing that challenge. Again, the data suggests that despite the central place of subsidiarity and local autonomy in federalism theory, the constitutions of federal countries are no more likely than the constitutions of unitary states to commit to addressing the urban/rural divide. This in turn raises the possibility that federal constitutional theory's preoccupation with traditional subnational unit boundaries may in fact lead to conceptual rigidity and institutional path dependence when it comes to addressing new spatial challenges such as urban agglomeration, the rise of mega-cities, or the increasing salience of the urban/rural divide. It may also suggest that whether federalism is favourable or unfavourable to cities is merely an auxiliary consideration to other more pertinent considerations such as the Global North/South distinction, constitutional 'newness' or malleability, and concerted political will to constitutionally strengthen cities.

In Chapter 5, Briffault delves into the 'new' doctrine of preemption in the US to reflect upon the apparent conflict between federalism theory (which advances certain values that cities are in a better position to foster) and formal federalism (in which the states are the main units or players). In this regard, recent years have witnessed heightened conflict between American cities and their states, since some cities are actively pursuing progressive agendas while the governments of their states have not only rejected progressive policies at the state level but have preempted progressive city action. Among other things, this new preemption highlights the failure of US federalism to recognize cities apart from their states. It also provides new insight into the tension within the theory of federalism as to whether federalism is about the protection of the specific polities that constitute the federal union or represents a broader commitment to subsidiarity. Although these two theories of federalism are not necessarily at odds, the new preemption illustrates how the two can come into conflict. It also underscores how US federalism, despite the subsidiarity rhetoric often used by the Supreme Court, is really a commitment to the states rather than cities. The new preemption also provides an opportunity to consider the role of subnational constitutions in protecting cities. Beyond the specific US example provided by the author, the chapter reflects upon issues of global relevance: namely, the theory underlying the relationship between federalism, localism (or subsidiarity), and the city; and the question as to whether federalism is bad for cities.

In chapter 6, Kong argues that cities should be understood in light of a specific constitutional theory of federalism. First, he argues for a particular version of republican theory that justifies constitutionally entrenching a division of powers between territorially defined jurisdictions. Next, he contends that cities and their residents have interests and characteristics that can be described and understood in the terms of this republican theory. Focusing then on the Canadian experience, Kong posits that according to a general theory of constitutional change, the Canadian Constitution should be amended to entrench the status of cities. Finally, he shows how entrenchment in the Canadian context might serve republican ends and offers policy prescriptions for achieving entrenchment. The chapter advances both conceptual and normative claims and contributes to an emerging and globally relevant theoretical debate about whether federations should constitutionally entrench the jurisdictional status of their cities.

In chapter 7, Partlett draws on examples from a number of federal jurisdictions to buttress the idea that the intrinsic advantages of federalism and decentralization are rarely explored. He suggests that the diffusion of powers can help generate a more effective criminal justice system. Cities might become important sites to advance the key ends of federalism, thus ensuring that federalism contributes to criminal justice reforms. Federal states are grounded on the idea that decentralization yields important advantages. Federations, however, frequently ignore these built-in advantages when reforming criminal justice systems. This, he suggests, is a mistake: federalism's diffusion of power can make criminal justice systems fairer and more effective. Partlett contends that empowering cities can help to introduce the benefits of federalism to criminal law reform. In particular, urban accountability mechanisms—many of which already exist—provide cities with mechanisms for understanding, debating, and holding accountable the discretionary decision-making of police and prosecutors. Expanding the reach and scope of these urban accountability mechanisms will, he suggests, improve trust between executive law enforcement and the urban community and help to ensure a fairer and more effective criminal justice system. The chapter also addresses the theoretical relationship between federalism, cities, and subsidiarity, with the insight that federalism is not necessarily bad for cities, and that cities can—at least in some areas—foster the innate advantages of federalism.

In chapter 8, Nelson offers an account of the legal mechanisms that could help cities better face environmental issues, particularly considering the impact that climate change will have on the future of cities. Human influence on the environment is now widely considered to be so significant as to constitute a new geological epoch, the Anthropocene. The rapidly accelerating pace, scale, and impact of urbanization makes it a critical driver of that influence, so much so that some prefer the term 'Astycene'—an era altered and characterized by the 'astos', or urban dweller. The widespread adoption of modern constitutional environmental rights provisions speaks to the scale and severity of contemporary environmental threats in general. However, the centrality of cities in causing and experiencing environmental threats, and the corresponding constitutional implications, remain substantively unaddressed by constitutions and their scholars. The chapter applies an environmental lens to the key questions of whether constitutions should recognize cities, and what any such recognition should seek to accomplish. It uses the metaphor of the constitutional stage, first describing the environmental backdrop to that stage in physical and institutional terms. It then argues that although cities can act in the role of both environmental victim and villain, recognizing them in constitutions would help address important environmental problems in both situations. Both situations also support constitutionalizing intergovernmental coordination mechanisms that can adapt to changing circumstances. Finally, the chapter explores what counts as a city for the purposes of an environmentally informed constitutional narrative. In focusing specifically on environmental issues, the chapter contributes—among other things—to the broader theoretical debate on how cities could be better equipped to deal with pressing contemporary challenges.

In chapter 9, Petkova examines the tension between the traditional anonymity of city life, and the 'datafication' of cities. She suggests that the rising economic and political power of cosmopolitan, data-rich cities calls for new understandings of federalism in a digital age. The chapter explores how the link between privacy and big cities translates into both a normative commitment to diversity and varying legal privacy protections in North American and European cities. The complex picture that emerges from such analysis shows how cities undertake two distinctive roles that might come into conflict: that of privacy activists and of data stewards. The chapter further argues that to optimize data privacy (but also data sharing in the public interest) constitutional recognition for city power be accompanied by the mechanism of 'data trusts'—an independent broker between the city and its inhabitants. Similar to the previous chapter by Nelson, this chapter also contributes to the broader theoretical debate on how cities could be better equipped to deal with pressing contemporary challenges, among other things.

Finally, in chapter 10, Schragger offers his concluding remarks by reiterating how cities have been largely absent from the theory and doctrine of federalism. The chapter first considers the mismatch between cities' increasing economic, political, and sociological importance and their relative lack of status in constitutional theory. It then discusses the use and definition of the term 'city'—a threshold issue that drives much subsequent theorizing about it. Finally, it considers the various ways institutional designers might go about empowering the city. These observations lay the groundwork for the broader argument that state-based federalism is bad for cities. The 'old' federalism is based on the theory that sub-national governments are sharply limited in their policy choices by the threat of capital flight, presumed weak and ineffectual cities. It is a presumption that has become self-fulfilling especially in the US, where states have been aggressively reducing and restraining city power. A 'new' federalism would recognize the central role of cities in an urban-based political and economic order and provide them with powers commensurate with that role. As global urbanization continues apace, the urban–rural political divide deepens, and nation-states face repeated crises of legitimacy, the necessity of building the city into our constitutional institutions becomes increasingly apparent.

As with most books and edited collections, this volume does not seek to be fully exhaustive in its intellectual output by addressing all questions and by providing all possible answers. Nonetheless, it aspires to offer a significant contribution to this emerging field of scholarship. It should thus be conceived as just another piece in this jigsaw puzzle that is represented by cities in constitutional law and theory.

PART I
CONCEPTUAL FRAMEWORK

1

An Intellectual History of Federalism

The City and the 'Unit' Question

Erika Arban[*]

I. Introduction

The purpose of this chapter is to briefly retrace the intellectual history of federalism and offer an account of federalism from the point of view of constitutional theory. Federalism is a multifaceted concept that can be explored through several lenses: in fact, it can be studied as a political, historical, philosophical, social, or religious phenomenon. However, because federal principles and doctrines are usually ingrained in written constitutions, federalism should be considered as, first and foremost, a constitutional phenomenon, although interlaced with political, philosophical, or historical aspects.[1] This chapter, as well as the volume in general, will thus privilege a theoretical understanding of federalism from the standpoint of constitutional law. The need to focus on the theoretical aspects of federalism as a constitutional phenomenon stems from the fact that, as a principle, federalism is still largely 'understudied' and 'poorly understood'[2] in constitutional law and it is more common in practice than studied in theory.[3]

Federalism as discussed in this book is also construed as an umbrella term that includes different experiences. In fact, while the federation that emerged in the United States in 1787 is usually regarded as the quintessential 'pure', 'classic', or 'fully fledged' federation, thus inspiring and shaping several other models developed afterwards, in recent years federal principles and elements have been adapted to a variety of situations, blending centripetal and centrifugal forces, federal and non-federal experiences, in a process leading to always novel experimentations. The discussion of cities in federal constitutional theory—which lies at the core of this volume—is a compelling illustration of this recent intellectual evolution in federalism design.

[*] Postdoctoral research fellow, Melbourne Law School.

[1] Stephen Tierney, 'Federalism and Constitutional Theory' in Gary Jacobsohn and Miguel Schor (eds), *Comparative Constitutional Theory* (Edward Elgar 2018) 45.

[2] Jacob T Levy, 'Federalism, Liberalism and the Separation of Loyalties' (2007) 101 *Am Pol Sci Rev* 459, 459.

[3] ibid, 473.

Erika Arban, *An Intellectual History of Federalism* In: *Cities in Federal Constitutional Theory*. Edited by: Erika Arban, Oxford University Press. © Erika Arban 2022. DOI: 10.1093/oso/9780192843272.003.0002

Providing a universally accepted definition of federalism, however, remains challenging. Etymologically speaking, the term derives from the Latin *foedus*, meaning agreement, bargain, covenant, compact, or contract.[4] But *foedus* is also linked to the word *fides*, meaning faith or trust. Federalism could thus be traced back to this idea of agreement or contract based upon reciprocal trust or faith.[5] But while such etymology is uncontested, the practical significance of federalism is more controversial. In this volume, federalism is broadly construed as a constitutional principle that advocates division of authority and dispersion of powers among different societal groups and organizations,[6] to reflect what Elazar dubbed 'self-rule' and 'shared rule'.[7]

A conceptual distinction is also often made between federalism and federation. In fact, building on Burgess, the former can be read as a 'philosophical statement' or 'ideological position' that promotes a form of government where powers are dispersed among various levels of government.[8] In this sense, federalism is the 'animating force' of a federation.[9] Federations, on the other hand, are tangible institutions characterized, as will be explained, by specific features.[10]

While it was with the US Constitution of 1787 that our understanding of modern federalism became clearer, the idea behind federalism exists 'from time immemorial'.[11] The history of federalism is often traced back to the first communities of Israel (3000 BC),[12] as their relationships between individuals and families reflected the biblical covenant that defined the relationship between God and human beings.[13] The first leagues of Greek city-states and the Roman Empire also offered examples of rudimentary federal organizations.[14] Likewise, the Holy Roman Empire is construed by some as a 'federalistic organization'[15] and the Hanseatic League that bound together a number of northern German towns is regarded as a form of 'medieval' federalism.[16] However, no theory of federalism as we presently

[4] Daniel Elazar, *Exploring Federalism* (U Alabama P 1987) 5 (hereafter Elazar, *Exploring Federalism*); Michael Burgess, *Federalism and European Union: The Building of Europe 1950–2000* (Routledge 2000) 13 (hereafter Burgess, *Federalism and European Union*).

[5] Burgess, *Federalism and European Union* (n 4) 13; Robert Schütze, *From Dual to Cooperative Federalism: The Changing Structure of European Law* (OUP 2009) 14.

[6] Burgess, *Federalism and European Union* (n 4) 27.

[7] Elazar, *Exploring Federalism* (n 4) 5, 12.

[8] Burgess, *Federalism and European Union* (n 4) 26.

[9] Michael Burgess, *Comparative Federalism: Theory and Practice* (Routledge 2006) 102 (hereafter Burgess, *Comparative Federalism*).

[10] Burgess, *Federalism and European Union* (n 4) 25.

[11] Burgess, *Comparative Federalism* (n 9) 73.

[12] Ronald Watts, *Comparaison des Régimes Fédéraux* (2nd edn, McGill-Queen's U P 2002) 2; Elazar, *Exploring Federalism* (n 4) 4.

[13] Daniel Elazar, *Federalism and the Way to Peace* (Queen's U P 1994) 21 (hereafter Elazar, *Federalism and the Way to Peace*).

[14] Watts (n 12) 2–3.

[15] Heinz Eulau, 'Theories of Federalism under the Holy Roman Empire' (1941) 35 *Am Pol Sci Rev* 643; Elazar, *Exploring Federalism* (n 4) 4.

[16] Charles McCoy and Wayne J Baker, *Fountainhead of Federalism: Heinrich Bullinger and the Covenantal Tradition* (John Knox P 1991) 15–16 ; John Loughlin, 'Reconfiguring the

understand it was formulated in the ancient or pre-modern world.[17] The current conception of federalism is the product of modern political theory and of the rise of the Westphalian state system.[18] In the pre-modern world there was only one type of federal-like model, the confederation, with sovereign states bound together by a 'perpetual treaty'.[19] The Confederacy that emerged in the United States in 1781 bringing together the first thirteen colonies, can be traced back to this tradition. But this federal-like pact belonged to international law and confederations were in fact international organizations.[20]

The existing literature on federalism and federal theory is truly gigantic and therefore it is impossible to treat it exhaustively in a very limited space. The present chapter will thus identify what I believe are the intellectual milestones of federal history and theory (section II) before delving into the historical treatment (or lack thereof) of cities as federal constitutional entities or 'units' (section III).

II. A (Brief) Intellectual History of Federalism

A. The pre-modern federal tradition: Bullinger and Althusius

Before the emergence of the Westphalian state system in the 17th century and of the first modern federal constitution in the US in the late 18th century, the rudiments of modern federal ideas started to sprout within certain religious circles in European countries like Switzerland, Germany, and Holland at the time of the Reformation (16th century).[21] In fact, at least two of the founding fathers of modern federal thought, Bullinger and Althusius, were theologians who contributed to the debate on the relationship between church, state, and religion. Their philosophical production is important because, through their ideas, they contributed to the development of modern federal thought as well as to the way cities were (and still are) conceived in federal constitutional theory.

The Swiss theologian Heinrich Bullinger (1504–1575) was a leader of the Reformed church of Zurich from 1531 until his death.[22] He is identified as the father of the 'covenantal' theory of federalism, usually associated with the Anglo-American (rather than the European) federal tradition.[23] The latter conceives of

Nation-State: Hybridity vs Uniformity?' in John Loughlin, John Kincaid, and Wilfried Swenden (eds), *Routledge Handbook of Regionalism and Federalism* (Routledge 2013) 5 .

17 Schütze (n 5) 14.
18 Loughlin (n 16) 5.
19 Schütze (n 5) 18.
20 ibid, 15.
21 McCoy and Baker (n 16) 19.
22 ibid, 17.
23 Burgess, *Federalism and European Union* (n 4) 4; McCoy and Baker (n 16) 17.

federal constitutions as a covenant (*foedus*) between the federal government and formerly independent units.

The essence of Bullinger's thought is contained in *The One and Eternal Testament or Covenant of God*, authored in 1534,[24] where he unveiled the meaning behind the pact or covenant concluded by God with Abraham as described in the Bible. For Bullinger, the covenant was conceived as 'the divine framework of human life, both religious and civil, from the beginning of the world until the last judgment'.[25] Being a theologian, Bullinger did not come up with a mature federal political theory as his reflections on the covenant were mainly religious and philosophical. However, he did contribute to planting a seed that would later sprout; in fact his work and ideas were probably taken to the North American colonies by the Puritans and used as the model for their social and political organization.[26]

By contrast, the German Calvinist Johannes Althusius (1563–1638) is often regarded as the intellectual or 'theoretical godfather' of continental European federalism.[27] The gist of his philosophy is sketched in *Politica Methodice Digesta*, first published in 1603[28] and considered the first, systematic articulation of modern federal ideas.[29] Althusius is also considered by some as one of the precursors of the principle of subsidiarity that has mainly informed European federalism.[30] Althusius propounded an idea of politics as the 'art of associating (*consociandi*) men for the purpose of establishing, cultivating, and conserving social life among them'.[31] Althusius then described the many forms of associations in which human beings expressed themselves, operated, and maintained their liberties: (i) families; (ii) collegia; (iii) cities; (iv) provinces; and (v) the commonwealth.[32] Families and collegia were regarded as simple and private associations, while cities, provinces, and the commonwealth were treated as mixed and public ones.[33]

Althusius' work, much like Bullinger's, was interspersed with theological and philosophical (rather than fully fledged political) ideas. However, what was remarkable about his thinking was the new way of conceiving society as a multilayered compound built up from the family as the primordial form of association. In this new conception of multilayered society, it is possible to see an embryonic idea of subsidiarity and federalism.

[24] The original title of the work was *De testamento seu foedere Dei unico et aeterno*. An English translation of this work is contained in McCoy and Baker (n 16) 101–38.

[25] McCoy and Baker (n 16) 20.

[26] ibid, 21–2.

[27] Elazar, *Federalism and the Way to Peace* (n 13) 41.

[28] Johannes Althusius, *Politica* (Frederick Carney ed and tr, Liberty Fund 1995) (abridged and translated version of the original work of 1603).

[29] Burgess, *Federalism and European Union* (n 4) 7; McCoy and Baker (n 16) 62.

[30] On subsidiarity, see further Cahill and O'Sullivan, chapter 3 in this volume.

[31] Althusius (n 28) 17.

[32] ibid, 27, fns 1–3; Elazar, *Federalism and the Way to Peace* (n 13) 41–2.

[33] Althusius (n 28) 27; Elazar, *Federalism and the Way to Peace* (n 13) 41–2.

Althusius's and Bullinger's ideas, however, did not elicit much intellectual interest during their own lives, mainly because they conflicted with the unitary, centralized, and monarchical state theorized by Jean Bodin (1530–1596) in *Les Six Livres de la République* of 1576.[34] Bodin's proposal was based on an 'absolute', 'centralized,' and 'indivisible' authority of the state coupled with a 'supreme' and 'sovereign power' residing in a monarch and responsible only to God and natural law.[35] Bodin's scheme (originally meant for France) was thought to be necessary for the achievement of order, stability, and security in a world that was dangerous and uncertain.[36] Bodin's ideas deeply influenced the works of his contemporaries, such as Hobbes's *Leviathan* and Locke's *Treatise on Civil Government*.[37] The Westphalian state that emerged in the 17th century and that still shapes our idea of state was mainly premised on Bodin's thought.

B. The Anglo-American federal tradition and the US Constitution as the first federal model

After declaring their independence from the British Empire in 1776, most of the thirteen American colonies drafted their own constitutions,[38] which eventually served as the basis for the Articles of Confederation of 1777 and later for the (federal) Constitution of 1787.[39] Earlier that year, a conference was called in Philadelphia to discuss traditional views of the (con)federation as an agreement among sovereign states under international law.[40] As is well known, however, the Philadelphia conference led to the proposal of a new constitutional arrangement whose essence was distilled in the *Federalist Papers* authored by Alexander Hamilton, John Jay, and James Madison under the pseudonym *Publius*[41] to persuade the delegates to the convention to ratify the new US Constitution and replace the Articles of Confederation.[42] The Philadelphia compromise placed the United States in a position between an international and a national structure[43] where sovereignty was shared between the Union and the states who joined all together the federal covenant as partners on equal standing.[44] Among the novelties introduced

34 Burgess, *Federalism and European Union* (n 4) 2.
35 ibid, 2.
36 ibid, 2.
37 ibid, 3.
38 John J Dinan, 'State Constitutions and American Political Development' in Michael Burgess and G Alan Tarr (eds), *Constitutional Dynamics in Federal Systems: Sub-National Perspectives* (McGill-Queen's U P 2012) 48.
39 Burgess, *Comparative Federalism* (n 9) 53; Dinan (n 38) 48.
40 Burgess, *Comparative Federalism* (n 9) 54–5.
41 ibid, 55.
42 Alexander Hamilton, James Madison, and John Jay, *The Federalist Papers* (Pocket Books 2004) vii.
43 Schütze (n 5) 23.
44 ibid, 27–8.

by this Constitution was the proposal of a union not only of states but of citizens as well. In fact, the federal government would represent states in the Senate (the 'federal' element), while citizens would be represented in the House of Representatives (the 'national' element).[45] Also, the new Constitution was ratified by the people of the several states, rather than by the aggregate American people.[46] By drawing a system of government based on popular sovereignty, embedded in a written constitution, with a political authority divided and shared 'between different levels of government in separate territorial spheres', the US Constitution of 1787 quickly became the 'archetypical model' of the modern federation.[47]

C. Federalism in contemporary times and the European federal tradition

Because of its innovative features, the federal model that emerged in Philadelphia in 1787 greatly inspired other constitutional experiences across the globe. For example, the federal models implemented in Latin America in the 19th century (Mexico, Argentina, Brazil, Venezuela) were all moulded on the US Constitution. In those same years, federal constitutions were adopted also in Switzerland and Canada, and this trend continued throughout the 20th century: Australia became a federation in 1901, Austria in 1920, Germany in 1949. Federalism also informed the European integration process started in the 1950s.

Unlike the US tradition (which clearly built on Bullinger's covenantal idea), however, the European federal tradition was influenced mainly by Althusius (who was rediscovered in the late 19th century by Otto von Gierke) and by other philosophical and theoretical strands, in particular Roman Catholic social theory, whose core tenets were spelled out in a series of papal encyclicals written between the 1880s and the 1960s.[48] In particular, *Rerum Novarum* was authored by Pope Leo XIII in 1891[49] to defend the interests and conditions of the working classes[50] and to protect private property. Leo XIII defined families as true societies 'older than any State' with rights and duties 'quite independent of the State'[51] and which were 'prior to those of the community'.[52] The state should intervene only when a family found itself in 'exceeding distress'; then, public aid should help to meet their

[45] ibid, 25–6.
[46] Ibid, 24.
[47] Burgess, *Comparative Federalism* (n 9) 185; Kenneth Wheare, *Federal Government* (OUP 1947) 1.
[48] Burgess, *Comparative Federalism* (n 9) 174.
[49] *Rerum Novarum: Encyclical of Pope Leo XIII on Capital and Labor* (*Vatican Library*) <http://www.vatican.va/holy_father/leo_xiii/encyclicals/documents/hf_l-xiii_enc_15051891_rerum-novarum_en.html> accessed 25 August 2021).
[50] ibid, § 2.
[51] ibid, § 12.
[52] ibid, § 13.

needs.[53] In other words, following Althusius, Leo XIII reaffirmed the relevance of the family as the very basic component of a society, with state institutions playing the role of promoting the common good.[54] This relationship between families and state institutions seems to anticipate the idea of 'vertical' subsidiarity cemented in subsequent encyclicals. In 1931, Pope Pius XI wrote *Quadrigesimo Anno*[55] which confirmed many positions on ownership and private property, socialism, and social order in general as sketched in the previous encyclical. Its importance rests on the fact that it explicitly called upon the principle of subsidiarity to rein in the excessive centralism of the state.[56] Subsidiarity keeps decision-making processes as close as possible to citizens; it thus means that responsibility for implementing any law should rest, whenever possible, with the lowest level of government, since a higher level of government should come into play only when the lowest level is not in a position to carry out the task.[57] Finally, *Pacem in Terris* by Pope John XXIII of 1963[58] 'elevated' subsidiarity to a 'universal' principle to be adopted in international relations and the world order as well.[59]

D. The modern understanding of federalism

At least for the oldest federations moulded on the US model, several reasons help explain the recourse to federalism as a form of coming together of different polities: from the need for common defence to economic benefits, from geographical continuity to desire to be independent from foreign power.[60] In certain contexts, common language or common nationality has also contributed to a desire for unity.[61] Geographical factors also played a role, not only in the US but also in Canada and Australia, where distance among different communities and a sense of isolation contributed to developing a 'regional consciousness' while in places like Switzerland, isolation of communities was caused by the natural barriers created by mountains.[62] By skilfully combining 'self-rule' (the delegation of powers from the centre to the periphery) and 'shared rule' (peripheral governments participating

[53] ibid, § 14.
[54] ibid, § 32.
[55] *Quadragesimo Anno: Encyclical of Pope Pius XI on Reconstruction of the Social Order* (*Vatican Library*) <http://www.vatican.va/holy_father/pius_xi/encyclicals/documents/hf_p-xi_enc_19310515_quadragesimo-anno_en.html> accessed 25 August 2021).
[56] Burgess, *Comparative Federalism* (n 9) 175–6.
[57] Ugo M Amoretti, 'A New Look at Federalism: Italy Decentralizes' (2002) 13 *J Democracy* 127.
[58] *Pacem in Terris: Encyclical of Pope John XXIII on Establishing Universal Peace in Truth, Justice, Charity and Liberty* (*Vatican Library*) <http://www.vatican.va/holy_father/john_xxiii/encyclicals/documents/hf_j-xxiii_enc_11041963_pacem_en.html> accessed 25 August 2021.
[59] Burgess, *Comparative Federalism* (n 9) 176.
[60] Wheare (n 47) 37.
[61] ibid, 38.
[62] ibid, 41.

and having a role in central politics),[63] federalism has been increasingly employed to reconcile unity and diversity, and also to foster peace, democracy, flexibility, and experimentation, thanks to the possibility of adapting federal ideas to the specific historical, socio-economic, and political context in which they are employed.[64] Federated units especially are often perceived as 'laboratories of democracy.'[65] For this reason, federalism is both a simple and a multifaceted concept that includes profoundly different experiences, and whose essence is always enriched by new approaches and experiments. In fact, as an ideological concept, federalism implies a division of authority and a dispersion of powers among different social groups.[66] Yet, this relatively basic idea of power dispersion and authority distribution has been articulated into a variety of elaborate legal frameworks and constitutional arrangements. Federal states are thus complex entities characterized by some common features and developing trends, as I will briefly outline in the next sections.

1. Common elements of federations

First, a federal state is distinguishable from other legal models because it presents a constitutionally embedded division of legislative powers between the central government of the state as a whole, typically for purposes of common interest, and a number of constituent units variously labelled (states, provinces, regions, cantons, *Länder*) for purposes of local autonomy.[67] Constitutions are central to federal systems: traditionally, they were construed as covenants among the two tiers of government that came together as equal partners to constitute the federation. Furthermore, they were (and still are) written, supreme, and amendable (at least ideally) only with the approval of both federal and state/local units. Also, in a federal system, both the federal government and the governments of the federated entities are autonomous in their own spheres of power. This means that there should be no subordination between them as they are both 'partners' of the *foedus*: consequently, federated entities or units are not delegates of the federal government,[68] but they enjoy all the law-making and other powers attributed to them by the constitution.[69] A federal constitution might also delineate the division of revenues between the various tiers of government, since fiscal independence contributes to making each level of government autonomous from the other. Building on the US federal constitution, federal systems are also characterized by a second,

63 Elazar, *Exploring Federalism* (n 4) 5, 12.

64 Loren King, 'Cities, Subsidiarity, and Federalism' in James E Fleming and Jacob T Levy (eds), *Federalism and Subsidiarity* (New York U P 2014) 292.

65 Levy (n 2) 460.

66 Burgess, *Federalism and European Union* (n 4) 27.

67 Burgess, *Comparative Federalism* (n 9) 136.

68 Hugo Cyr, 'Autonomy, Subsidiarity, Solidarity: Foundations of Cooperative Federalism' (2014) 23 *Constitutional Forum Constitutionnel* 21.

69 ibid.

or upper, chamber (usually called the federal senate) which represents the interests of the constituent units at federal level, thus giving them a forum to advance their claims at the centre and participate in federal legislation.[70] Federations also contemplate an umpire (in the form of a constitutional or supreme court) to settle disputes on division of powers between the two tiers of government.

While most federations fall one way or the other within the description outlined above, there is no uniformity among them, as geographical, historical, economic, linguistic, cultural, intellectual, demographic, international, or security factors may deeply impact the way a federation is shaped.[71] One consequence is that the way that powers are divided between the various levels of government varies on a case-by-case basis, with some federations being more (de)centralized than others, and powers assigned exclusively or concurrently to each level of government. Federations also vary depending on how representation is framed in the federal senate: sometimes senators are directly elected by citizens, while at other times they are appointed by the executive; furthermore, representation in the senate can be based on equal representation (where each sub-entity has the same number of senators regardless of population, like in the US) or on population (where the number of senators for each sub-entity depends on its population size, like in Germany). The number and size of the federated units may also have an impact on the way each federation is engineered, as the use of common law, civil law, or a mix of both traditions can affect the way federalism is interpreted.[72]

2. New federal-like arrangements

From a historical perspective, the mid-1950s were momentous for federalism: in fact, after WWII new models of federal arrangements developed across the world. Consequently, in addition to classic federations such as the US, Canada, Switzerland, and Australia, new paradigms have emerged, which Elazar classified into the following categories:[73] (a) *federacies*, characterized by an asymmetrical link in a federal pact (that can be dissolved by mutual agreement) between a larger power and smaller polity, whereby the latter has greater autonomy compared to the component units of the larger power but a reduced role in the government of the larger polity; (b) *associated states*, which are similar to a federacy but can be dissolved unilaterally;[74] (c) *common markets*, referring to models that mainly focus on shared economic (rather than political) functions among members;[75] (d) *consociational polities*, whereby non-territorial federations are divided

[70] Henry Brun, Guy Tremblay, and Eugénie Brouillet, *Droit Constitutionnel* (5th edn, Yvon Blais 2008) 407.

[71] Watts (n 12) 37.

[72] Ronald L Watts, 'Typologies of Federalism' in John Loughlin, John Kincaid, and Wilfried Swenden (eds), *Routledge Handbook of Regionalism and Federalism* (Routledge 2013) 30–1.

[73] Elazar, *Federalism and the Way to Peace* (n 13) 22–3.

[74] ibid.

[75] ibid.

into religious, cultural, ethnic, or ideological groups;[76] (e) *unions*, or compounded polities where the constituent units maintain their integrity through the common organs of the general government, usually with some degree of devolution granted by the general government;[77] (f) *leagues*, or associations of independent polities for specific purposes, often functioning through a common secretariat, and allowing the unilateral withdrawal of member states;[78] and (g) *regional states*, or arrangements based on the same theoretical foundations as federalism without creating a fully fledged federation.[79] More recent scholarship has also coined the expression *multilevel governance* as an 'umbrella term' which embraces all decentralized forms of government. Originally, the term was devised for the supranational EU scheme, but it was later extended to all types of models characterized by the presence of multiple levels of government.'[80]

3. Asymmetrical and multinational federations

Within the same federation, the level of homogeneity among the federated units might differ due to economic, social, linguistic, or religious disparities. Scholars have identified these situations as examples of 'asymmetrical federalism'.[81] Political or *de facto* asymmetry typically refers to the various cultural, economic, social, and political conditions that distinguish one sub-unit from the other, while constitutional or *de jure* asymmetry refers to the non-uniform way in which powers are attributed by constitution to the federal sub-units.[82] Asymmetrical solutions are often conceived as a good way to manage conflicts within democratic federal countries.[83]

Within the constellation of federal possibilities, another classification is between 'single-nation' federations and 'multinational' federations. The term *nation* refers to people who 'share the same culture, [being] a system of ideas and signs and associations and ways of behaving and communicating', and who recognize 'each other as belonging to the same nation'; nations see themselves as distinct societies and demand various forms of autonomy or self-government to ensure their survival as distinct societies.[84] In the case of a single-nation federation, none of the federated

[76] Arend Lijphart, *Democracy in Plural Societies: A Comparative Exploration* (Yale U P 1977).

[77] Watts (n 72) 21; Elazar, *Federalism and the Way to Peace* (n 13) 22.

[78] Elazar, *Federalism and the Way to Peace* (n 13) 22–3.

[79] ibid, 23.

[80] See Loughlin (n 16) 13; Liesbet Hooghe and Gary Marks, *Multi-level Governance and European Integration* (Rowman & Littlefield 2001) xi.

[81] Charles D Tarlton, 'Symmetry and Asymmetry as Elements of Federalism: A Theoretical Speculation' (1965) 27 *J of Politics* 861.

[82] Watts (n 12) 65.

[83] Alain-G Gagnon, 'The Moral Foundations of Asymmetrical Federalism: A Normative Exploration of the Case of Quebec and Canada' in Alain-G Gagnon and James Tully (eds), *Multinational Democracies* (CUP 2001) 322.

[84] John Pinder, 'Introduction: Multinational Federations' in Michael Burgess and John Pinder (eds), *Multinational Federations* (Routledge 2007) 3–4.

units show an interest in external sovereignty,[85] while within multinational federations there is at least one sub-unit that can be identified as a 'distinctive nation' that demands various forms of self-government;[86] furthermore, it often happens that nations within a federation see themselves as co-founders of the federal state.[87] Ethnofederalism is a variant of multinational federations, in the sense that there is at least one component territorial governance unit that is associated with 'specific ethnic categories'.[88] Ethnofederal solutions have been recommended particularly in 'countries torn by ethnic conflict'[89] such as Ethiopia, although federalism has not always been successful in these complex scenarios. In any event, in both multinational and ethnic federations, the federal paradigm has been suggested or implemented as a way to reduce internal conflict, to implement some stable development across the various territories of the polity, to increase democratic participation in governance (especially of representatives of marginalized groups), and at the same time to limit centralized rule especially when this is the source of discrimination, exclusion, and other forms of inequality.[90]

E. Conclusion

In conclusion, federalism as a philosophical idea was born in Europe at the beginning of the 17th century, but it was with the American Constitution that these ideas were translated and adapted into a fully functioning constitutional system. Nowadays, thanks to their elasticity and adaptability, federal solutions are praised as an ideal way to foster democratic participation and reconcile diversity (whatever form it takes) and social cohesion.[91] Because the federal experience has been enriched by new models and experiments over the centuries, this book will adopt a broad understanding of federalism, targeting both pure federations and *quasi-federal* arrangements, the latter being polities which offer some sort of constitutionally embedded division of legislative powers or other forms of constitutionally recognized autonomy between the centre and the periphery inspired by federal ideas, but which cannot be entirely identified with a fully fledged federation.

[85] ibid, 6.

[86] ibid, 4.

[87] John McGarry and Brendan O'Leary, 'Federation and Managing Nations' in Michael Burgess and John Pinder (eds), *Multinational Federations* (Routledge 2007) 181.

[88] Henry E Hale, 'Divided We Stand: Institutional Sources of Ethnofederal State Survival and Collapse' (2004) 56 *World Pol* 165.

[89] ibid.

[90] Michael G Breen and Iain Payne, 'The Concept and uses of "Hourglass Federalism"' (*SSRN*, March 2021) <https://papers.ssrn.com/sol3/papers.cfm?abstract_id=3826079> accessed 18 September 2021.

[91] Elazar, *Federalism and the Way to Peace* (n 13) 17, 31.

III. Cities and Federalism: The 'Unit' Question

A. In general

As indicated in section II earlier, federalism has historically emerged and evolved as a pact or covenant (*foedus*) between a central (federal) government and the various federated units or entities, however called, which were often independent at the time they joined the *foedus* as partners of the federal government. For this reason, older federal systems are considered examples of 'coming together' federations, commonly premised on two tiers of government both enjoying constitutionally embedded law-making powers in specific areas, as well as other privileges. Although other units (like local governments) existed, they were not considered partners in the federation; they lacked constitutional status and/or were deemed mere creatures of the states.[92] The same is true for cities. As King, among others, aptly observed, cities were not taken into account in older federal arrangements and rarely appeared 'in scholarly treatments of either federalism or subsidiarity'.[93]

One reason that helps explain such neglect is that older federal systems evolved at a time when the territory was mostly rural: consequently, cities were small and 'subordinated to the purposes of an agricultural society or agriculturally-based commerce'.[94] Federated entities, in other words, were mainly rural territories, and urbanization was not the significant phenomenon that it is today.[95] What is paradoxical, however, is that the advent of urbanization has not changed the picture, and many federal constitutions continue to disregard the increased role of cities, remaining anchored to the traditional idea of federated units as formerly state-size autonomous entities.

Other reasons exist that help explain the neglect of cities as autonomous federalism units. Constitutional rigidity is certainly important, especially in older jurisdictions like the US, Canada, and Australia where constitutional amendment is difficult, if not impossible, thus making it problematic to embed cities as autonomous constitutional entities despite increasing urbanization.[96] In addition, cities can be considered as potential threats to state hegemony and as competitors of the state, which thus becomes reluctant to empower them.[97] As a result of this concatenation of causes, the theory and practice of federalism—and constitutional law more generally—tends to exclude cities.[98] This neglect for cities in federalism scholarship stands in sharp contrast with other disciplines in the social

[92] See further Hirschl, Briffault, and Kong, chapters 4, 5, and 6 respectively in this volume.
[93] King (n 64) 293.
[94] Elazar, *Exploring Federalism* (n 4) 255.
[95] ibid.
[96] Ran Hirschl, *City, State: Constitutionalism and the Megacity* (OUP 2020) 51–2.
[97] ibid, 19.
[98] ibid, 31.

sciences which have devoted time and resources to the study of urbanization, city growth, etc.[99]

The historical neglect for cities in federal theory and design, however, is curious for at least two reasons: first, cities were not entirely absent from the first theorizations of federalism and, second, there are examples of cities that are entrenched in federal constitutions. This suggests that there are both historical and practical foundations to justify a more substantive role for cities in federal systems. The next sections will briefly illustrate both aspects.

B. The city and Johannes Althusius

In section II above, Althusius is presented as one of the godfathers of the European strand of modern federalism.[100] As noted, the originality of his thinking was that he conceived of a multilayered society built up from below, where cities were one of the several rings of the societal chain along with families, collegia, provinces, and the commonwealth. In other words, in his *Politica*, Althusius had already espoused a rather inclusive idea of a compound society with cities as key players.

Althusius presented the city (or *civitas*) as an urban community composed of 'those who practice industrial functions and pursuits while living an urban life'.[101] He described the city as

> a large number of hamlets and villages associated by a special legal order (*jus*) for the advancement of the citizens, and guarded and fortified against external violence by a common moat, fortress, and wall ... [102]

Althusius further characterized the city as a 'community of citizens dwelling in the same urban area (*urbs*), and content with the same communication and government (*jus imperii*)'.[103] In terms of city governance, each city had to be administered by a 'prefect' or 'superior' (sometimes also referred to as 'consul') assisted by 'counsellors' and 'senators' constituting the 'senatorial collegium', whose legitimate decrees had to be observed by citizens.[104] The senate was composed of 'wise and honest select men' entrusted with the 'care and administration of the affairs

[99] King (n 64) 294; Hirschl (n 96) 31.

[100] This section builds on Erika Arban, 'Constitutional Law, Federalism and the City as a Unique Socio-economic and Political Space' in Ernst Hirsch Ballin and others (eds), *European Yearbook of Constitutional Law. Vol 2: The City in Constitutional Law* (Springer 2021) 333 (hereafter Arban, 'Constitutional Law, Federalism and the City') and on Erika Arban, 'Metropolitan Cities, Federalism and Socio-economic Challenges' (2019) 1 *Rivista Di Dritti Comparati* (Special Issue) 226, 235 (hereafter Arban, 'Metropolitan Cities').

[101] Althusius (n 28) 42.

[102] ibid.

[103] ibid.

[104] ibid.

of the city' and representing the entire city.[105] The senatorial collegium controlled a variety of functions, including 'the power of managing and executing the business of the community and so of knowing and judging all that pertains to the community'.[106]

For Althusius, there were at least four types of city.[107] First, the free city, which was 'free from the rule of other princes, dukes, and counts' and which recognized 'as its immediate superior the supreme magistrate'.[108] Second, municipal or provincial cities, which were 'subject to a territorial lord' and which recognized 'a superior other than the supreme magistrate'.[109] Third, a mixed city, which recognized 'partly the emperor and partly a duke or count as its superior' and which enjoyed 'imperial and provincial privileges'.[110] Finally, a metropolitan city (or metropolis), which was defined as

> the mother of other cities that it brings forth as colonies, or because it is preeminent among them and is recognized by them as a mother by whom they are ruled and defended as children. The metropolis is therefore a large and populous city. Other cities and towns of the realm follow its example because of its size, population, rank, houses of religion and justice, and temples of piety and law . . . It also cultivates men distinguished in piety, doctrine, and life that others are able to consult in cases of doubt and perplexity . . . [111]

Lastly, every city was 'able to establish statutes concerning those things that pertain to the administration of its own matters, that belong to its trade and profession, and that relate to the private functions of the community . . . '[112]

From a historical standpoint, the recognition that Althusius's *Politica* dedicated to different types of cities as part of a multilayered society, to endow them with autonomous powers and governing bodies, is compelling. It showed an existing vision of cities as autonomous subjects. At the same time, however, it mirrored a specific, pre-modern society where cities were still relevant economically and politically, since the Westphalian nation state was still in formation. Unfortunately, its impact on actual (federal) constitutional design was basically inconsequential. In fact, the US Constitution as the first federal constitution, and all the other federal constitutions drafted thereafter did not contain any reference to cities as autonomous units, premised as they were on federated entities as previously independent

[105] ibid, 43
[106] ibid, 50.
[107] ibid, 45.
[108] ibid.
[109] ibid.
[110] ibid.
[111] ibid, 45–6.
[112] Ibid, 49.

Westphalian state-centred units. I will elaborate more on this aspect later in the chapter.

C. Federal capital cities and cities having a special status

Some old and new federations give a special constitutional status to their capital cities.[113] Examples include Washington, DC in the US, Canberra in Australia, Brasilia in Brazil, and Abuja in Nigeria. In these cases, the special treatment granted to these cities relates to their status and role as federal capitals. At times, these cities have no history of their own, but have been created ad hoc to serve the specific purpose of being a capital city and thus avoiding rivalries between other equally powerful cities (as is the case of Canberra in Australia). In other instances, the capital city of a federal state does coincide with its most important urban area, as is the case with Buenos Aires, Mexico City, and Addis Ababa: here, the special constitutional status is reserved for the city that is not only the capital but also the most populated and economically advanced.

Besides federal capitals, other examples of cities in federal systems having a special legal status include three German city-*Länder* (the *Länder* of Berlin, Hamburg, and Bremen are actually city-states due to historical reasons) and Brussels in Belgium, which enjoys a unique asymmetrical status as a region reflective of the multinational and multilingual nature of the state.

More recently, Italy has included metropolitan cities in the constitution, as one of the tiers that compose its asymmetrical regional system. Likewise, in the United Kingdom, the city of London enjoys special status.[114]

Similarly to the historical foundation of city empowerment in the work of Althusius, the examples just sketched suggest that, although exceptional, constitutional entrenchment of cities has been tried and exists, and it may be used as model for a successful empowerment of cities as autonomous federated units.

D. Constitutional entrenchment of local governments

The most recent wave of constitutional drafting in federal and quasi-federal systems has turned its attention to the local/municipal sphere (of which cities are part), often elevating this tier of government to constitutionally protected status.

[113] This section extensively builds on Arban, 'Constitutional Law, Federalism and the City' (n 100) 335 and Arban, 'Metropolitan Cities' (n 100) 237.

[114] For a more substantive comparative overview of cities in federations and constitutional law, see Hirschl, chapter 4 in this volume.

Examples include—but are not limited to—Brazil, Germany, India, Italy, Nepal, South Africa, Spain, and Switzerland.[115]

The main problem with the existing model of local governance is that the legal tools available to municipalities in general—and to cities in particular—do not always serve the 'real dimensions of contemporary urban entities'.[116] Specifically, the fiscal and financial powers of cities continue to reduce while their challenges have increased and the tasks they are called to perform have multiplied.[117] Furthermore, many states or national constitutions provide for specific constraints (such as balanced budget requirements, use of public money only for public purposes, limitations on the acquisition of debts, etc)[118] which limit the way in which cities qua local governments can spend and raise money.[119] Such constraints reduce the ability of localities to respond to changes in economic circumstances,[120] thus forcing them to either find indirect ways to fund their services or to depend on transfers coming from the centre.[121] Consequently, traditional local institutions such as municipalities might be 'ill-adapted to the real size of urban issues . . . '.[122]

E. Cities, federalism, and the unit question

As observed, with few exceptions the city as an autonomous subject is practically 'non-existent' in federalism theory and scholarship.[123] We also noted how this neglect for cities can be explained by a variety of factors, including specific trajectories of state formation and constitutional rigidity. More generally, however, the scarce relevance of cities in federal constitutional theory has also to do with the little attention that political and constitutional theory has devoted to what Hirschl has labelled the 'unit' question, and the related dominance of state-sized, sub-national units.[124]

In other words, for Hirschl the broader demise of the city as a constitutional entity coincided with the historical rise of the modern Westphalian state leading, at least in Europe, to 'the subjugation of the medieval city'.[125] Influenced also by

[115] For a more detailed illustration of local governments in federations, see further Saunders and Arban, chapter 2 in this volume.
[116] Jean-Bernard Auby, 'Droit de la Ville: An Introduction' (2013) *Ital J of Pub L* 304.
[117] Lea Scheurer and Annegret Haase, 'Diversity and Social Cohesion in European Cities: Making Sense of Today's European Union-Urban Nexus with Cohesion Policy' (2018) 25 *Eur Urban & Regional Stud* 340.
[118] Richard Schragger, *City Power: Urban Governance in a Global Age* (OUP 2016) 220. Schragger mainly refers to the US, but similar considerations can be made for other jurisdictions
[119] ibid.
[120] ibid.
[121] ibid.
[122] Auby (n 116) 305.
[123] Hirschl (n 96) 29.
[124] ibid., 34; see also Levy (n 2).
[125] Hirschl (n 96) 31.

the idea of a strong, centralized state as envisioned by Bodin, the powers of the medieval city-states were progressively subordinated to the authority of the early-modern state.[126] Although this process occurred differently in different places, cities were rapidly turned into mere components of the nation-state, with no autonomy and with powers reduced to adapt to a 'state-centered conception of sovereignty and spatiality'.[127] Hirschl further maintains that this is the reason 'we are still captives of constitutional structures, doctrines, perceptions, and expectations that were conceived along with the modern nation-state ...'[128] In other words, the neglect of cities in constitutional law and federalism scholarship is a reflection of what Hirschl and Shachar dubbed *spatial statism*:[129] according to this view, the state is able to maintain 'a statist grip' over its territory and boundaries.[130] Consequently, '[c]ore aspects of public law remain largely statist'[131] especially those focused on territoriality, of which the city is an example.[132] Consequently, according to Hirschl, in modern federations 'the near-exclusively applied "unit" of federalism is the state and its equivalents (provinces, *Länder*, cantons, regions, emirates, etc.)' since the Westphalian model 'continues to dominate the theory and practice of federalism, with its notion of sovereign territorial states divided along ethnic, religious, and linguistic cleavages and reflecting conventional notions of nationhood, peoplehood, and/or historical patterns of conquest and settlement' thus leaving no space for cities.[133] The existing conversation about sub-units is thus 'limited to centuries-old ideas about the supposedly proper units of federalism and subsidiarity ... '[134]

Similarly, Levy also laments that most existing federated entities are too large, since they are 'the size of *ancien régime* French provinces ....'[135] Against this backdrop, Levy continues, jurisdictional competition would 'proceed better if the jurisdictions were municipalities or metropolitan regions'.[136] Furthermore, Levy observes that 'there are *so few* states or provinces in any given federation[]'[137] and contends that in many federations 'it is routine for one or more of the component provinces to be understood as the province of an ethnic, cultural, or linguistic minority ...'[138] Consequently, very little competition exists among federated

[126] ibid.
[127] ibid.
[128] ibid, 9; see also King (n 64) 296.
[129] The concept of *spatial statism* is exposed in Ran Hirschl and Ayelet Shachar, 'Spatial Statism' (2019) 17 *Int J Const L* 387.
[130] ibid, 391.
[131] ibid, 393.
[132] ibid, 437.
[133] Hirschl (n 96) 33.
[134] ibid, 29.
[135] Levy (n 2) 461.
[136] ibid.
[137] ibid.
[138] ibid.

entities,[139] and discussion has occurred around the idea of whether cities (or at least some of them) have the necessary or required characteristics to become federated units,[140] or whether they can be considered as a distinct level of government with autonomy to legislate and collect taxes.[141]

In the past, some prominent federalism scholars have devoted some thoughts to the 'unit' question. Wheare, for example, suggested the features of an ideal federal unit, contending that, despite inevitable divergences in size, '[i]t is undesirable that one or two units should be so powerful that they can overrule the others and bend the will of the federal government to themselves'.[142] Consequently, for a properly working federal government, a balance and harmonization between the 'conflicting interests of these differing units' should be found.[143] This means that '[t]he size of the units concerned—in wealth, area and population—is … of prime importance' and it is the responsibility of 'those who frame and work a federal government to see that no unit shall be too large, and, equally important, none too small'.[144] He further contended that adequate economic resources are important to form a federal union, and states 'must possess sufficient economic resources to support both an independent general government and independent regional governments'.[145] Also, a small population is not capable of supplying the workforce of a larger population, so the size of a unit affects 'its capacity to form part of a federal union'.[146] This means that sufficient economic resources are necessary both for subunits and the federal government so that they can be 'financially independent'.[147] In discussing the changes brought about by urbanization, Elazar further observed how '[t]he development of urbanized regions often crossing the boundaries of the constituent polities has led to problems arising from political boundaries that bear little relation to the patterns of regional economic interaction …'[148] He also suggested that urbanization has exacerbated those typical 'federal' tensions that can be more easily controlled in less densely populated or more rural realities: for example, ethnic or racial tensions are more easily manageable in a rural than in an urban setting.[149]

I argue that the way in which federal systems have emerged tells a lot about units. In fact, historically speaking, the covenantal tradition of federalism as unfolded in the Anglo-American tradition as sketched above has been particularly

[139] ibid.
[140] Daniel Weinstock, 'Cities and Federalism' in James E Fleming and Jacob T Levy (eds), *Federalism and Subsidiarity* (New York U P 2014).
[141] King (n 64) 295.
[142] Wheare (n 47) 52.
[143] ibid.
[144] ibid, 52–3.
[145] ibid, 53.
[146] ibid.
[147] ibid, 54.
[148] Elazar, *Exploring Federalism* (n 4) 255.
[149] ibid, 255–6.

influential in the way we discuss federated 'units'. Specifically, the distinction is between 'coming together' and 'holding together' federations, or, to use another expression, between *aggregative* (or integrative) and *devolutionary* federal systems.[150] Coming together federations reflect the 'older' manner in which federal systems have formed, with previously independent states or units joining into a federal compact, as was the case with the US, Switzerland, Canada, and Australia: here, the pre-existing units were independent states or enjoyed a high degree of autonomy before joining the federal structure.[151] There was little discussion on the size, dimensions, and other features of the entities, as they had become by default the partners in the federal covenant in that they already enjoyed sovereignty. In fact, as Gerken writes, for the US, the fact that federalism discussions focus mainly on states is due to the fact that they represented the only subnational units that were sovereign at the time they entered the *foedus*.[152]

Holding together or devolutionary systems, on the other hand, are those in which a unitary state progressively devolves powers to specific sub-units to control centrifugal forces and tame secession aspirations (such as Spain, Belgium, Italy, and South Africa).[153] In comparative perspective, they have become more common and they have contributed to changing the picture. In such schemes, it is not unusual to see the entrenchment of a third level of government—the municipal sphere—and sometimes also of cities.

Furthermore, in multinational federations, units are sometimes carved out of specific ethno-linguistic cleavages, regardless of size and population. Oftentimes, the boundaries of such units are drawn on paper, or are imposed from the top, and are designed at central level, regardless of any pre-existing sovereignty. Such units can be mono-ethnic or pluri-ethnic but, since such demarcation comes from the top, it is often contested and triggers conflicts. In any event, even in multinational and ethnic federations, cities are rarely, if ever, taken into account for purposes of unit design.

In any event, Hirschl and Levy are right when they contend that contemporary federalism theory and practice do not devote enough time to discussing the 'unit' question. If some literature exists, this is sporadic and not systematic. Yet, in light of the evolution of federal models, and of the changes brought by the economic, demographic, social, and ethnic development to the boundaries of federated entities, it would be desirable to return to a discussion on federal units. Cities are an interesting development in this sense.

150 Francesco Palermo and Karl Kössler, *Comparative Federalism: Constitutional Arrangements and Case Law* (Hart P 2017) 45–6.

151 ibid.

152 Heather Gerken, 'Foreword: Federalism All the Way Down' (2010) 125 *Harv L Rev* 4, 21, as cited in Hirschl (n 96) 33.

153 Palermo and Kössler (n 150) 45–6.

IV. Conclusion

In this chapter, I have briefly retraced the intellectual history of federalism to explain how federalism is construed in this volume, thus setting the scene for the chapters that follow. I have observed how federalism shall be understood as a constitutional principle and as an umbrella term that encompasses various experiments, from pure federations to quasi-federal, multinational and asymmetrical systems. I have also emphasized the covenantal theory of federal state formation, as I believe it has influenced and shaped the way cities are (not) present in federalism debates, in spite of increasing urbanization and historical and practical exceptions. Finally, building on Levy and Hirschl, I have suggested that this neglect of cities in federal constitutional theory is part and parcel of a lack of discussion among theorists on the 'unit' question, or what would be the traits (in terms of size, population, socio-economic, and political features, etc.) of an ideal federated unit or entity. The question is whether cities could be considered meaningful players and federated units and, if so, under which terms. Some of the chapters in the remainder of the book will try to shed light on the extent to which cities have the potential to become units in federal systems.

2

Federalism and Local Governments

Cheryl Saunders and Erika Arban

I. Introduction

There is an ongoing fascination with the place of local government in federal-type systems. That it has a place is undeniable. Local structures of government were an early form of organised government, well before the modern state emerged.[1] As states expanded control, local governments were absorbed, with inevitable loss of autonomy. Even so, local government remained a distinct phenomenon, even in otherwise centralised states. One or more levels of localised government also exist in federal and regional states. In this context, however, additional questions arise about the degree of autonomy of local government, its relationship with each of the other levels of government, and its place in the constitutional framework. These questions are answered differently in different federal systems.

Many early federations had 'coming together' characteristics in which large established polities, each with systems of local government of their own, became constituent units in federations with considerable legislative, executive, and sometimes judicial authority in their own right.[2] Some also had, and retained, their own constitutions, subject to the overarching federal constitution. In these conditions, constituent units had the primary responsibility for local government, whatever form that relationship took. In some instances, either initially or over time, local government became entrenched in the constitutions of the constituent units.[3]

By contrast, over the course of the 20th century, as most federations were formed by disaggregation of a previously highly centralised state, the design of federal constitutions typically incorporated local government in some form. In some federations, of which Germany is an example and India came to be another, the federal constitution gave local government some systemic protection but left much of the detail to the control of constituent units. In some more recent federations, of which Brazil, South Africa, and Nepal are examples, local government is entrenched in

[1] Keebet von Benda-Beckmann and Bertram Turner, 'Anthropological Roots of Global Legal Pluralism' in Paul Schiff Berman (ed), *The Oxford Handbook of Global Legal Pluralism* (OUP 2020) 67, 70.

[2] Brian P Janiskee, *Local Government in Early America: The Colonial Experience and Lessons from the Founders* (Rowman & Littlefield 2010).

[3] Both the United States and Australia are in this category.

Cheryl Saunders and Erika Arban, *Federalism and Local Governments* In: *Cities in Federal Constitutional Theory*.
Edited by: Erika Arban, Oxford University Press. © Cheryl Saunders and Erika Arban 2022.
DOI: 10.1093/oso/9780192843272.003.0003

the federal constitution as a third tier of government and draws its powers and even its institutional arrangements directly from the federal constitution itself. Whether this trend in the manner in which the role of local government is formalised is attributable solely to evolving fashions in federal constitutional design, or whether it is linked to a wider range of factors, is a question that is explored in this chapter.

In any event, by the third decade of 21st century, the treatment of local government in the design and operation of federal constitutional arrangements differs significantly across the world.[4] A comparative study of the kind undertaken in this chapter has both descriptive and normative dimensions. The descriptive dimension seeks to understand how and why these differences emerged and the relevance of the contexts in which different approaches are found. The normative dimension considers whether there is a generalizable ideal state for the position of local government in federal-type systems to which existing federations might aspire and that can and should guide the design of new federations. Such an ideal might correspond with the familiar assumption that the desirable end point of the development of local government is its incorporation in the federal constitution as a formally recognised third tier of government. Even that assumption requires elaboration, however, to identify both the degree of de jure autonomy constitutionally conferred on local government in these circumstances and the effectiveness of the operation of such a federation in practice. Alternatively, the generalizable ideal might refer more substantively to the quality of the relationship of local government with other levels of government in a federalised system, which might be formalised in the federal constitution or in other ways, including through intergovernmental arrangements. This possibility is explored further in this chapter under the rubric of 'partnership'.

The ambitions of this chapter are complicated by variations in the configuration, classification, and properties of local government itself, even if local governing entities established for limited specialist purposes are left out of account, as we propose to do.[5] Within any federation or, for that matter, within any constituent unit within a federation, local government may comprise both small rural communities and large urban conglomerates, of which more below. Variations in the characteristics of local government between federations also are extensive and significant for present purposes. Local government may have multiple tiers as in, for example, Italy. There may be multiple designations for different kinds of local government entities within the same tier, as in parts of Australia. Local government may vary in territorial or demographic size from the vast local government zones in northern and western Australia to the smallest municipalities in Switzerland. All such

[4] Nico Steytler (ed), *Local Government and Metropolitan Regions in Federal Systems* (McGill-Queen's U P 2009).

[5] Local Water Boards, for example, provided a form of local government for the provision and protection of water resources in many countries, federal and unitary alike.

differences have implications for capability, responsiveness, and, potentially, institutional design. Expectations of local government also differ with context and may be further differentiated by the characteristics of the communities they serve. Local government areas that serve sizable Indigenous communities are a case in point.[6]

The challenge of examining the constitutional status of local government is complicated further still when the position of cities is added to the mix. Whether and, if so, how cities should receive specific attention in constitutions is the subject of a burgeoning literature, as this volume demonstrates. This developing interest reflects the size and significance of many cities assessed by reference to, for example, their contribution to economic prosperity and their capacity to generate innovation and ideas and, conversely, to the serious problems that cities often face. Typically, they are treated as a component of local government. In considering formalisation of local government, however, whether generally or in the context of federations, there is inevitably a question about whether cities require distinctive treatment in their own right.

Whatever the answer, it must deal with variations in the size, organisation, and nomenclature used for cities both within and between federated states. The designation 'city' may extend from smallish regional but nevertheless urban structures to large international cities with vast populations and a significant global presence. The relations between cities and their hinterland may vary, with demography and geography. Major cities may or may not be governed as a single unit. In the context of particular federations, moreover, some cities are designated as constituent units, reflecting either their status as the federal capital or considerations of other kinds. These realities must also be taken into account in analysing and reaching conclusions about the role of local government, and of cities, in federations.

The chapter contributes, at least indirectly, to some of the broad theoretical questions that this volume seeks to explore, such as the relationship between cities, local governments, and federalism and the values local governments foster in federations. It is structured as follows. The next section explores the strengths of local government as a tier of government and the challenges of determining its formal role in a federal system. To this end, it necessarily considers the purposes of both local government and federalisation and the ways in which they can reinforce each other. A final segment of this section canvasses the distinctive position of cities, through the same lens. Section III of the chapter examines the comparative similarities and differences in the contexts in which local governments operate in federal systems and explores their significance for any normative conclusions. Section IV identifies the options for formalisation of the position of local government in federations and develops the concept of partnership, in theory and practice. Section

[6] For insights, see *Collaborate New South Wales* <http://collaboratensw.org/> accessed 26 October 2021.

V draws together the threads of the argument and indicates directions for future research.

II. Strengths and Challenges of Local Government in a Federal Context

A. Strengths

The existence of many federations can be explained by reference to historical factors.[7] In some cases these relate to the manner in which the state was formed, by bringing together previously separate but established polities, as in the United States or Australia. In other cases, a federation was formed to resolve internal divisions involving or threatening violent conflict, as in South Sudan or Nepal. Every federation has a unique story that can explain its formation. Despite earlier doubts about whether a federal form of state was an end point, or only a transitional stage towards a unitary system, by the 21st century, if not before, it was accepted that federalisation has substantive advantages in its own right.[8]

These might be summarised under three broad headings. The first is the contribution that a properly working federation makes to the quality and depth of democracy, by providing an additional layer of elected governments, each of which has particular responsibilities in relation to a section of the people to whom it is democratically accountable. From this perspective, a federation also offers additional opportunities to participate in public life. Secondly, federations can be conducive to better government, informed by and responsive to local conditions and offering a formal structure to put the principle of subsidiarity into practical effect.[9] Insofar as sub-national jurisdictions are smaller and more compact, moreover, they may encourage innovation and experimentation that eludes the diversity of interests and views for which the state itself must cater. Thirdly, federalism disperses power and so contributes to checks and balances in the overall system of government in a way that also provides a framework for the more equitable treatment of communities, territorially organised. These advantages of federation apply irrespective of ethnic and cultural diversity. They have particular application in states that are deeply divided, however, where they offer a form of self-determination, within the framework of the state, and a means of enhancing community cultural life.

A local level of government contributes to the furtherance of these desirable properties of federation in various ways. Most obviously, it assists in the project of

[7] See further Arban, chapter 1 in this volume.

[8] Earlier attitudes to federalism are reflected in, eg, Gordon Greenwood, *The Future of Australian Federalism: A Commentary on the Working of the Constitution* (Melbourne U P 1976).

[9] See further Cahill and O'Sullivan, chapter 3 in this volume.

deepening democracy, not only by providing additional opportunities for democratic engagement and inclusion but also because of the distinctive relationship of local government to the people, whom democracy seeks to serve. This familiar truism that local government is 'closer to the people' than other levels of government is largely a reflection of the scale on which many local governments operate and the functions that, in consequence, they perform. A local government typically represents a relatively smaller number of people over a relatively smaller geographical area and carries out functions that affect the daily lives of communities. In these circumstances, there is potential for closer contact between people and their elected representatives and a greater chance that individual preferences will influence outcomes. Local government offers people an opportunity to seek elected office while continuing to live and work in their own communities. Locally elected representatives lead relatively normal lives, in constant contact with the people they represent. Of course, there are potential downsides of these characteristics as well, in terms of the susceptibility of lower levels of government to capture by vested interests and other factions. This is a risk to be managed, however, and does not negate the democratic advantages that local government can bring.

The scale of local government also underpins its potential to enhance the quality of governance. The knowledge that local government naturally possesses about local conditions and preferences can make both policy-making and service delivery more responsive. The relatively greater ease of developing consensus, in smaller political communities, increases the potential for innovation. If a function can be exercised at the local level, consistently with the principle of subsidiarity, these characteristics of local government can lead to outcomes that are locally owned, underpinning satisfaction with and trust in democratic government.

By definition, a level of local government, exercising governing authority under law, also contributes to the dispersal of power. The extent to which this attribute of local government significantly furthers the federal project, however, depends on both the extent of power exercisable by local government and the degree of autonomy that it enjoys. Local government does not necessarily have the clout, individually or even collectively, to check the power of the central or regional levels of government. On any view, however, an organised level of local government ensures that there are elected representatives at grass-roots level throughout the federation with specific responsibilities for advancing their own communities and, to this extent, exerting a centrifugal pull away from the established centres of power.

B. Challenges

The previous section shows that local government is compatible with the values of federalism and can make a critical contribution to its goals. It is less evident how the role of local government is best formalised within a federal framework, however, so as to derive maximum advantage from it, generally and in particular cases. Federalism offers a distinctive approach to the organisation of a state, which relies for its effectiveness on a constitutionally entrenched division of public power, including primary legislative power, between polities with the legitimacy and capacity to exercise their power effectively, in their own right. The sub-national polities also influence central policies through participation in central institutions, as a formal design feature of the federation and also, sometimes, through less formal arrangements for intergovernmental collaboration. This combination of unity and diversity is sometimes captured in the rubric of shared rule and self-rule.[10] The very characteristics of local government that underpin its potential contribution to the values and goals of a federal form of government present challenges to formalising it in structural terms.

Some of the challenges are connected to size. The considerations of territorial scale canvassed in the earlier section limit the extent to which authority to develop policy can be conferred on at least some local government units, particularly if it requires the exercise of primary legislative power. One consequence is that the exercise of power by local government may be subject to supervision by one or more of the other levels of government, to a greater degree than would normally be compatible with federalism. For reasons also attributable to scale, local government own-source revenues are unlikely to meet local expenditure needs, making it almost inevitable that local government will be financially reliant on other levels of government, with concomitant blurring of lines of accountability. Of course, problems of spillover and resources affect the constituent units as well, but by an order of magnitude that is considerably less.

Formalisation of the position of local government in federations faces challenges from the perspective of shared rule, as well. Shared rule has both symbolic and practical functions. At its best, it is a vehicle whereby understanding of more localised conditions can influence collective outcomes including, most obviously, decision-making in central institutions. In most federations, shared rule formally occurs through a second chamber of a central legislature, with symbolic and degrees of substantive effect.[11] It may occur in other central institutions as well, including the composition of the government, the support base for an elected President, or the composition of the apex court.[12] In addition, in many federations, there are at least intermittent meetings of members of central and constituent unit governments to coordinate actions on matters of mutual interest.[13]

[10] See further Arban, chapter 1 in this volume.

[11] Cheryl Saunders, 'The Possibilities and Pitfalls of Bicameralism in Federal Democracies' in Alain-G Gagnon and Johanne Poirier (eds), *Canadian Federalism and its Future: Actors and Institutions* (McGill-Queen's U P 2020) 27.

[12] Australia, Nigeria, and Canada respectively offer examples.

[13] Johanne Poirier, Cheryl Saunders, and John Kincaid (eds), *Intergovernmental Relations in Federal Systems: Comparative Structures and Dynamics* (OUP 2015).

The number and variety of local governments make shared rule impossible in the same way that it applies to constituent units, whether through participation in central institutions or through cooperative arrangements. The problem is sometimes met by involving one or more peak local government associations in intergovernmental meetings, or in a second chamber with a redefined role.[14] These are only partial solutions, however. Involving one or more representatives of such a multifarious level of government in arrangements for shared rule provides a local government perspective and may have some symbolic value but cannot capture the advantages of local involvement and local endorsement that shared rule is expected to bring.

These considerations suggest that formalisation of the position of local government in a federation can risk the operation of the federation itself, unless care is taken. The risk takes several forms, some structural and some political. In terms of structure, the difficulty of endowing local government with significant legislative power, to be exercised independently of the other two levels of government, risks compromising the authority and autonomy of the constituent units, if the two levels of government are treated on a par. The result is sometimes described as 'hourglass federalism', with strong federal and apparently strong local institutions but with a weak state/provincial level in the middle.[15] In terms of politics, there can be a temptation for the centre to liaise with local government, as the weaker level of government, to squeeze the authority of the constituent units. Either offers a recipe for centralisation, counterintuitive as that may seem. This is not an argument against formalisation, but in favour of greater creativity in crafting a systemic role for local government that maximises its contributions in ways that are compatible with the remainder of the federal framework. We develop such a role in section IV of this chapter, in terms of a concept of federal partnership, which may take different forms in different contexts.

C. Cities

Consideration of the position of cities in federal-type systems present a different set of opportunities and challenges, which are further complicated by the diversity of the genre. To be categorised as a 'city' an urban community is likely to be large in comparison with other local areas. Cities nevertheless vary tremendously, in terms of territorial and population size. In the state of Victoria in the federation of Australia, for example, the range lies between the City of Portland with nearly

[14] In Australia, as an example of the first approach, a representative of the Australian Local Government Association was a regular member of the Council of Australian Governments (COAG) until it was dissolved in 2020. The second chamber of the Parliament of Nepal, the National Assembly, is an example of the latter approach: Constitution of Nepal 2015 s 86(2).

[15] Nico Steytler, 'Comparative conclusions' in Steytler (n 4) 433.

11,000 inhabitants and the City of Melbourne with almost 5 million inhabitants. Outside Australia, the range widens further still to include, for example, Delhi in India with a population of nearly 19 million people and Sao Paulo in Brazil with a population of 12.33 million people.

Cities are significant territorial entities, raising obvious questions about how they are best accommodated in multi-level governments. Some cities may be larger, in terms of population, than some constituent units, even within the same federation. Cities are a magnet for art, culture, and commerce and may be the economic engines of a state. The density of cities encourages the interchange of ideas and creativity. Cities have distinctive governance needs and, often, distinctive social, economic, and infrastructure problems that require government attention.[16]

The need to formalise the position of cities in states with multi-level governments is clear. Once again, however, the challenge is determining how. In most federations, cities are part of the vastly diverse network of local government entities although in some, of which Germany is an example, a few cities have the status of constituent units.[17] This arrangement allows new cities to evolve, through growth from various causes, and others to diminish in status and size. Within the category of local government, it is possible to provide special treatment for cities, insofar as they are distinguished from other local entities. In recognition of their significance, it would also be possible, in principle, for cities to be singled out for recognition as components of a federation in their own right. This has challenges too, however. As has been seen, the category of cities, itself, may be highly diverse. Not all cities are treated as a whole for the purposes of governance, moreover; some are divided into segments, each of which may also be designated a city.[18] Typically, the boundaries of cities are not fixed in the same way as those of constituent units, reflecting their historic and continuing organic growth over time. Many cities in any event have a close relationship with their hinterland, which would also need to be taken into account in determining a special place for them in a federal structure. Cities thus present a similar problem to that raised by local government as a whole: how to craft a place for them, in a federated state, that acknowledges their significance but is also compatible with the rest of the federal design?

[16] For a thorough treatment of the unique traits of cities worldwide, see Ran Hirschl, *City State: Constitutionalism and the Megacity* (OUP 2020).

[17] There are three such city states (as opposed to 'area states') in Germany: Berlin, Hamburg, and Bremen: see 'Federal States of Germany' (*Deutschland*, 29 September 2020) <https://www.deutschland.de/en/topic/politics/germany-europe/federal-states> accessed 26 October 2021.

[18] The 'Sydney area', in Australia, for example, comprises around thirty-five local government units, some of which are themselves designated cities: Parliament of New South Wales, 'The Roles and Responsibilities of Federal, State and Local Governments' <https://www.parliament.nsw.gov.au/about/Pages/The-Roles-and-Responsibilities-of-Federal-State-a.aspx> accessed at 26 October 2021.

III. Comparative Analysis

Any account of the place of local government in the formal structure of federations must take into account the diversity of current arrangements. In this section, we examine similarities and differences in the contexts in which local governments operate in federal systems and explore their significance for any normative conclusions. We will do so by considering the logistics of federations, including questions of size; the design of federations, including the manner in which power is allocated; and the implications of culture. A final segment of this section offers an overview of the status and role of local governments in contemporary federations.

A. Logistics

Federal-type systems greatly vary when it comes to geographic size, topography, the size and distribution of the population, and the number of constituent units. Although each federal-type system has some common features each is also shaped to a degree by the practical context in which it operates.[19]

Most obviously, some federations are exceptionally large in terms of territory (consider, for instance, the US, Australia, Canada, India, Nigeria, Argentina, and Brazil), while other federal systems have a much smaller land mass (think of Austria, Belgium, and Switzerland). There are also differences in the number of federated entities or units, ranging from the fifty states in the United States to the six states and two mainland territories in Australia. These differences do not necessarily map on to territorial size, as the example of twenty-six cantons in Switzerland shows. Nevertheless, at least some of the constituent units in federations of large geographical size may themselves cover extensive territory, in ways that have implications for the organisation of local government.

Layered over differences in territorial size are other differences that merit consideration. The population may be distributed relatively evenly across the federation as in, for example, Belgium or there may be great swathes of land with isolated pockets of population, as in Canada and Australia. Communities may be separated from each other by topographical features such as mountains or sea areas, as in Switzerland and the Federated States of Micronesia respectively, or communities may co-exist across more accessible terrain, as in South Africa and Italy. Communities may develop around economic activities of different kinds, some of which are relatively stable, while others prove to be transient, causing communities to shrink or disappear altogether. Mining is an example of such an activity, to

[19] See further Arban, chapter 1 in this volume.

which small or abandoned mining towns across the world attest. Agriculture potentially is another.

These and other similar features have implications for the configuration of local government that need consideration in formalising its role in federal-type systems. In densely populated states, of which Italy and Spain are examples, it may lead to multiple levels of local government, with a larger local level interspersed between municipalities and regions or constituent units.[20] In unevenly populated states such as Canada and Australia, there may be different categories of local government with different capabilities and different assignment of functions. Parts of the country may be organised in Indigenous communities; parts may not have organised local government at all. Where there is obvious potential for significant population shifts it is necessary to retain some flexibility in the delineation of local government communities and the organisation of local government around them. These considerations may feed into the assignment of resources and functions as well; an issue that is taken up in the next section.

Another logistical feature of a different kind, with particular relevance to consideration of the place of cities in federations, concerns the location of the capitals, both of the federation and of the constituent units. In some federations, the national capital is given a status of its own, so that it is not dependent on or unduly associated with a particular constituent unit. This is done in various ways: the German capital, Berlin, is a Land in its own right; Buenos Aires is an autonomous district within the federation of Argentina; Canberra is the capital of Australia, within a self-governing Australian Capital Territory. By contrast, in Canada, the National Capital Region within which the capital, Ottawa, is located, constitutes part of the surrounding provinces of Ontario and Quebec and is not a separate political entity. There are also differences in the treatment of the capitals of constituent units, which have relevant flow-on effects. In some federations, of which the United States is an example, state capitals typically are located outside large cities where so much economic power is located. Thus, the capital of the state of New York is in Albany, presenting a challenge for co-existence with the megacity of New York. In other federations, however, of which Australia is an example, the largest city in each state, home to the vast majority of people, is also the state capital, requiring a different kind of accommodation between the state and local government leaders.

[20] See, eg, art 114(1) of the Constitution of Italy 1947, which mandates that the Republic comprises municipalities, metropolitan cities, provinces, regions, and the state. Similarly, art 137 of the Constitution of Spain 1978 provides for a level of 'provinces' between municipalities and self-governing communities.

B. Design

There are aspects of the design of a federation that are likely to have some effect on formalisation of the position of local government. Three are canvassed in this section: the distribution of powers; the source of authority to regulate local government; and the design of the public sector.

All federations divide primary legislative power between the centre and the constituent units. Spillover effects are inevitable, but their significance depends on the size and distribution of constituent units, can be mitigated by careful attention to subsidiarity, and can be managed through intergovernmental relations. The problem of spillover is exacerbated, however, if primary legislative power is also allocated to local government, unless its scope is carefully curtailed.

In some federations it is assumed that legislation made in the exercise of primary legislative power will be implemented by the jurisdiction concerned, which may provide for adjudication as well. In federations of this kind, of which the United States, Canada, and Australia are examples, it is common to find a full set of institutions including, sometimes, courts, in each jurisdiction. Other federations operate differently, however. They depart from the assumption that each jurisdiction must administer its own legislation by enabling or requiring constituent units to administer some central legislation. Integrated federations of this kind, of which Germany is an example, may centralise legislative power to a greater degree than the dualist federations that link legislative and executive power. A quid pro quo, however, in these circumstances, is that constituent units have significant autonomy in the manner in which they apply legislation in their own jurisdictions, to fit local context. Arrangements for supervision of the implementation of legislation respect constituent unit autonomy, particularly in areas in which they implement legislation as a matter of constitutional right. This manner of dividing power in a federation fits the capabilities of local government somewhat better than a dualist approach. It enables local government to implement some legislation of both the federation and the constituent unit in which it is situated, adapting the legislation to the local area, with less significant spillover effects. Relevantly, however, for these arrangements to work effectively, lower levels of government must have significant administrative competence, which may suggest a degree of integration of the public service.

A second issue for design affecting formalisation of the position of local government concerns the location of regulatory responsibility for local government. Even if local government is entrenched in the federal constitution, an issue that is taken up in the next section, supporting legislation on the part of one of the other levels of government is likely to be necessary for some purposes. Such legislation might, for example, deal with boundary changes for local government, provide mechanisms for financial accountability, including audit, or deal with other functional matters for which the constitution itself does not provide.

This is an issue for the federal division of powers. Even if local government is entrenched in the constitution, competence to legislate for local government may be conferred on the constituent units, as the examples of Germany and India show. Where local government is not constitutionalised, it is even more likely to be a constituent unit competence, consistently with the principle of subsidiarity. Inevitably, in these circumstances, the boundaries of local government units will be contained within the boundaries of the constituent unit responsible for them, further reinforcing the role of constituent units and creating the possibility that local government may be organised differently in different parts of the federation, in response to contextual differences, or for some other reason.

A third, related, design issue concerns the structure of the administration. This is an important issue in all federations, which too often is overlooked. The issue applies, most obviously, to the general administration, but potentially includes independent institutions, sometimes labelled the 'fourth branch' as well.[21] In some federal-type systems, the administration is largely integrated across the levels of government, and independent institutions are largely organised at the central level, servicing all levels of government. Such a model may assist to ensure the quality of service provision at the local level, although at possible cost to local responsiveness and accountability. Where the administration is separately organised at central and constituent unit levels, as typically is the case in dualist federations, there is a question about whether local government does the same. Big and even medium-sized cities manage this well, facilitating innovation in local public administration. It is more difficult for smaller local governments, in terms of both resources and expertise. In some federations, including Australia, this has been a catalyst for amalgamation, increasing the efficiency of local government, at cost to its proximity to the communities that it serves.[22]

C. Culture

As we noted earlier, some local government bodies have deep roots in all federations. The cultural understandings, attitudes, and practices that have developed over time vary, however. For example, in European jurisdictions there is a longstanding tradition of local governance: since ancient times, the Middle Ages and throughout the modern era, prior to the formation of the Westphalian nation state, Europe developed around cities and communes (or municipalities) as the centres

[21] Tarunabh Khaitan, 'Guarantor Institutions' (2021) *Asian Journal of Comparative Law* (forthcoming) <https://papers.ssrn.com/sol3/papers.cfm?abstract_id=3766137> accessed 26 October 2021.

[22] In relation to Australia, see Brian Dollery, 'Local Government Amalgamation' (2009) Centre for Local Government, University of New England Working Paper Series 02-2009, <https://www.researchgate.net/publication/242568973_Local_Government_Amalgamation> accessed 26 October 2021.

of trade, commerce, religion, art and culture, education, and more.[23] Most of these cities were enclosed by walls, but even the countryside villages that existed outside of these walls gravitated towards the main city or commune. It does not come as a surprise, therefore, that the historical significance of such cities and communes has been perpetuated in European federal-type systems in spite of the emergence of the Westphalian nation state. To this day, in countries like Italy and Spain, the local identity and sense of belonging to the local commune remains very strong, something that is confirmed by the elevated number of municipalities existing in each country. This provides local government with considerable de facto protection and local governments tend to occupy a prominent place in European federal-type systems. This is reflected in the trajectory of the principle of subsidiarity in Europe. The culture of local government in Europe is also reflected in the European Charter of Local Self-Government and the principles of autonomy that it espouses.

In federations elsewhere, there may be different cultural assumptions that have a bearing on local government. In federations such as Nepal, villages are the traditional source of community for much of the population, but not necessarily in the statist form assumed by federalisation. In other federations, including those in the Anglo-American tradition, local government has typically been viewed through a functional lens, as a tool for effective government, to be shaped to perceptions of contemporary needs by other levels of government. As always in considering culture, none of these assumptions is necessarily permanent or universally held. Cultural assumptions may run deep, however. They need to be taken into account in comparative reflections on the status quo and development of normative positions. They do not preclude transplantation of approaches to the place of local government in federal-type systems, but they may affect the outcomes that are achieved.

D. Roles and status of local government

The earlier segments of this section provide useful background against which differences in the role and status of local government in federations around the world can be understood.

Although a three-level system of government is common to all federal systems, the manner in which this is reflected in the constitution varies markedly.[24]At one end of the spectrum, are federations in which there is no substantive mention of local government in the federal constitution. As noted in the introduction, many

[23] Erika Arban, 'Constitutional Law, Federalism and the City as a Unique Socio-Economic and Political Space' in Ernst Hirsch Ballin and others (eds), *European Yearbook of Constitutional Law 2020: The City in International Law* (Springer 2020) 326.

[24] Nico Steytler, 'Introduction' in Nico Steytler (ed), *The Place and Role of Local Government in Federal Systems* (Konrad-Adenauer-Stiftung 2005) 1.

of the federations in this category are older federations: the United States, Canada, and Australia. All three are also dualist federations, in the Anglo-American tradition. In all these instances, local government is a competence of the constituent units, as an aspect of the residual power in the United States and Australia and as an exclusive head of provincial jurisdiction in Canada.[25] In both the US and Australia, sub-national jurisdictions have constitutions of their own, most of which recognise local government in some way and may provide a measure of protection for it. The powers actually exercisable by local government vary across these federations, ranging from the extensive functions of local government in the US, which typically include public schools, to the much more limited functions of local government in Australia, where local government has no role at all in schooling.

Many other federations recognise local government in the federal constitution in some way. Even here, however, there are differences. In some instances entrenchment is light: local governments are formally acknowledged in the constitution, but do not enjoy specifically constitutionally protected powers or institutions. This is the case in many of the continental European federations. In Germany, for instance, local government is a competence of the Länder, but art 28(2) of the *Grundgesetz* guarantees that the 'constitutional order' of the Länder will recognise the right of municipalities to regulate local affairs and to enjoy self-government within limits prescribed by Länd law. Likewise, in Switzerland, art 50(1) of the Constitution guarantees the autonomy of communes in accordance with cantonal law. In Austria, art 116(1) of the Constitution postulates that municipalities are 'entitled to self-administration' while art 116(2) provides that municipalities are independent economic entities. In Spain, art 137 of the Constitution posits that municipalities and provinces (along with autonomous communities) 'enjoy self-government for the management of their respective interests'.

Light entrenchment of local government is found in federations outside Europe as well. In India, for example, where the Constitution originally offered no special recognition of local government, amendments in 1992 specifically recognised both panchayats and municipalities, providing some protection for their composition, but leaving their powers to laws of the constituent units.[26] Similarly in Malaysia, where the original Constitution conferred exclusive competence on the constituent units in relation to local government, subsequent amendments have extended federal power over local government in a way that also serves to recognise local government indirectly. Under current arrangements, which do not apply in Sabah and Sarawak, the federation may make laws for local government 'for the purpose only of ensuring uniformity of law and policy'[27] and the federation also chairs a 'National Council for Local Government' which operates as an intergovernmental

[25] Constitution Act 1867 s 92(8).
[26] Constitution of India (1950) pts IX, IXA.
[27] Constitution of Malaysia (1957) art 76(4).

body to coordinate local government law and policy.[28] In Nigeria, also, the federal Constitution provides for a system of local government and requires the constituent units to 'secure their existence under a Law'.[29]

At the other end of the spectrum are federations in which the constitutions not only recognise local government as a level of government, but also assign specific powers to them, structuring their institutions and assimilating them to a greater degree to the constituent units. In South Africa, for example, art 40 of the Constitution, contained in a chapter on 'Co-operative Government', identifies the three spheres of government as 'distinctive, interdependent and interrelated,' and chapter 7 of the Constitution deals entirely with local government. In Brazil, art 18 of the Constitution provides that the federation is composed of the Union, the states, the federal district, and the counties, further specifying that all these levels are autonomous. As in South Africa, the powers of local government are listed in a chapter dealing specifically with the counties.[30] Even more notably, in Nepal, the Constitution recognises three levels of government, and mandates relations 'based on the principles of co-operation, coexistence and coordination';[31] provides lists of concurrent and exclusive local government powers;[32] and specifies in some detail the institutional arrangements for local government.[33] Local government also has a role in the choice of members for the second chamber in the national legislature.[34] The effect is to assimilate the position of local government in Nepal more closely to that of the constituent units in other federations.

As these varied examples show, some constitutional recognition of local government does not always translate into genuinely three-tiered systems in which local government plays an autonomous role.

In the 21st century, local governments across the world all share similar challenges.[35] As has been seen, very few constitutions entrench specific powers for local governments and, even when this occurs, these powers may be supplemented by delegation. In most federations, local government is empowered entirely by legislation or delegation from other levels of government. Significant delegated responsibility may place a heavy burden on local administrations that already are stretched and impede their ability to carry out core local government functions.

In a related point, local government invariably is affected by limited financial resources, impeding whatever constitutional autonomy is formally assigned to it. Most local governments rely on transfers of some kind from other levels of

[28] Ibid, art 95A.
[29] Constitution of Nigeria (1999) s 7.
[30] Constitution of Brazil (1988) title III, ch IV.
[31] Constitution of Nepal s 232(1).
[32] ibid, schs 8 and 9.
[33] ibid, pts 17 and 18.
[34] ibid, s 86.
[35] Francesco Palermo and Karl Kössler, *Comparative Federalism: Constitutional Arrangements and Case Law* (Hart P 2017) 315.

government. The problem is exacerbated by unfunded mandates, when powers are delegated to local government with insufficient transfer of resources.[36] In addition, local government is likely to be subject to significant supervision by the level of government with primary responsibility for it, further reducing the reality of autonomy in practice.[37]

At least some of these challenges are the product of assuming that local government, with its distinctive characteristics, can be equated with the other two levels of government consistently with the formula of self-rule and shared rule. It may be that a more effective answer lies in a concept of partnership in multi-level government, geared to maximise the opportunities that multi-level government offers and structured to fit with the practical and financial realities in a given constitutional context. The next section seeks to open a discussion on what such a partnership might look like.

IV. Theorising Partnership

In the earlier sections of this chapter, we identified the advantages of local government and foreshadowed the need to formalise a role for local government to enable these advantages to be seized. We also noted the characteristics of local government as a level of government, which differentiate it from the intermediate tier of constituent units and present challenges for the ways in which the place of local government is formalised. The variety of federal contexts in which local government presently operates, canvassed in section III of the chapter, present a further challenge to any generic answer about the formal role of local government in federal-type systems. One dimension of this variety is the different approaches that federal systems presently take to the entrenchment of local government in the federal constitution. Constitutionalization is sometimes advanced as an appropriate way of acknowledging what local government has to offer. Current experience suggests, however, that constitutionalization is not necessarily a panacea. On the contrary, whether constitutionalised or not, local government is often treated as something of a poor cousin in federations across the world.

This section of the chapter considers what a more holistic solution might look like. Moving beyond the rhetoric of 'three tiers' it seeks to open up discussion of a concept of 'partnership', both in theory and practice. Partnership would pay close attention to the substantive role of local government and the conditions in which it operates, as a foundation on which formalisation of its role can build. It is also a notion that can be developed further, to understand the relationship between all levels of government in a federation.

36 See Briffault, chapter 5 in this volume, and Schragger, chapter 10 in this volume.
37 Palermo and Kössler (n 35) 295.

To some extent the foundations already are laid. Early understandings of federation treated the central level of government and the constituent units as partners in the *foedus*.[38] Each was tasked with different functions but they enjoyed a form of equality, reflected in autonomy and respect, and premised on such principles as comity, loyal collaboration, or (federal) solidarity. The challenge is to develop this concept for contemporary conditions and to be innovative in the ways that it applies. In the remainder of this section we explore these issues by examining principles and processes, before returning to constitutionalization.

A. Principles

This section examines the principles that might provide a foundation for a partnership approach to relations between levels of government in a federation, with particular, although not exclusive, reference to local government. It identifies four such principles: comity or mutual respect; solidarity or mutual consideration; subsidiarity; and equivalence.

Comity stems from mutual respect. Such respect is due between levels of government in a multi-level democracy, in recognition of the legitimacy of representatives chosen democratically by the people or a segment of the people to carry out particular public functions on their behalf. Comity understood as mutual respect also involves recognition of what each level of government contributes to effective governance. In the case of local government, as explained earlier, the contribution potentially includes deep local knowledge and an understanding of whether policies and practices are likely to work on the ground. Understood through this lens, respect might be reflected in the autonomy of local government in the exercise of its functions with appropriate accountability to their constituents; restraint in the exercise of controls over local government; and effective involvement of local government in collaborative exercises for which local government responsibilities and insights are relevant.

Solidarity, which might also be described in terms of mutual consideration, responds to the complexity with which each level of government must deal in a multi-level state. By definition, each level has responsibility to the people in its jurisdiction for the exercise of its particular powers. In addition, however, in exercising its powers each level of government must have regard to the interests of others in the context of the federation as a whole. From the standpoint of local government, this principle requires regard for the position of other local governments, of the relevant constituent unit, and of the centre. The requirement is, of course, reciprocal. The principle does not absolve each jurisdiction from acting in

38 See Arban, chapter 1 in this volume.

the interests of its people; rather, the interests of the people of each jurisdiction are understood in the context of the whole. The principle is subtle, but important. It should not be understood to mean that the interests of higher levels of government always prevail. On the contrary, it is designed to ensure that the perspectives that lower levels of government bring to the table are valued and internalized.

The relevance of subsidiarity in the context of local government is obvious. Subsidiarity protects the sphere of authority of local government, insofar as it encompasses matters that can effectively be handled at the local level.[39] In the case of small local government units, the modicum of primary legislative power is unlikely to be extensive. For the purposes of the application of this principle, however, public power should be understood to be exercisable by local government in other forms, including through the adaptation of more general norms to local conditions. The diversity of local government, in terms of size and capacity, suggests another application for subsidiarity as well, as support for asymmetry. Asymmetry already has some limited application in systems of multi-level government, for regions that, for one reason or another, need powers that are greater than the norm. In relation to local government, asymmetry might be a more regular tool. If the size and capability of particular categories of local government so warrant, the principle of subsidiarity would support a larger measure of authority than is exercisable by other local government groupings. As an obvious example, the role of major cities might be enhanced and explained in this way.[40]

The principle of equivalence recognises the need for a match between public responsibilities and resources. It is particularly significant at the local level, where own-source revenues are often limited. The principle applies both to the revenue arrangements that finance the general functions of local government and to the need for additional funding that is adequate to meet further functions that are transferred from time to time. Such funding arrangements should be transparent, to facilitate local accountability. Funds should be understood to flow as of right, from public funds held in the name of the federation as a whole, rather than as a result of grace and favour from the higher levels of government.

B. Processes

The principles identified in the earlier section assume that local governments have significant autonomy in the exercise of local powers, for which they are accountable to the people of the local area.

[39] See Cahill and O'Sullivan, chapter 3 in this volume.
[40] See also Hirschl (n 16) ch 5, 221–30.

In a functioning system of multi-level government, however, many occasions arise in which the actions of levels of government impinge on each other, raising questions about process. Such occasions arise also in relations between the federal level of government and constituent units. Typically, however, these are dealt with through bilateral or multilateral intergovernmental meetings or, sometimes, as in Germany, through the functions of a 'federal chamber'. The diversity and numbers of local government make such mechanisms impracticable, creating a need for new solutions. Effective solutions need to be developed to meet the contexts in which they need to operate. Two sets of circumstances that demand consideration for this purpose are briefly canvassed below.

The first is where another level of government is authorised to take action that affects one or more local government bodies. Such action might include, for example, conferral of new functions or the initiation of boundary changes.[41] The principles of comity and solidarity require a process that enables effective consultation and broad-based agreement. Transparency must be sufficient to ensure the accountability of all involved.

A second set of circumstances arises when a significant public policy challenge draws on the competencies and capabilities of multiple levels of government, including local government. Many examples could be given including, by way of illustration, reduction in the use of plastics and responses to climate change generally. In circumstances of this kind, processes are needed to ensure mutual exchange of knowledge and perspectives between levels of government and buy-in to the ultimate solution on all sides. How this might best be achieved is unclear and may vary between policy initiatives. The multilateral forums in which the centre and constituent units sometimes meet cannot accommodate the range and diversity of local government. It may be that, in some circumstances, selected representatives of local government can play a useful role in such forums, as a supplement to other processes. In some circumstances a two-stage process may be needed in which constituent units grasp and internalise the perspectives of their local governments and take these to meetings with the centre. In other circumstances it may be possible to contain the groups whose views are particularly useful by reference to type or geographical area. It may be desirable in any event to establish forums in which representatives of major cities meet with constituent unit governments regularly or with other cities and other levels of government across the federation as a whole. More consideration is needed to determine how such processes can be organised to ensure that the principles underpinning multi-level government are met.

[41] See, eg, Constitution of Netherlands (1814) art 123; Constitution of Portugal (1976) art 249; and Constitution of Greece (1975) art 102(1).

C. Constitutionalization

It follows from what has been said so far that the role that local government plays in multi-level government is likely to be enhanced by formal recognition in some way. It may be that formal recognition is appropriately achieved through entrenchment in some form in the federal constitution, in the constitution of a constituent unit, or both. The diversity of approaches currently on offer, canvassed earlier in section III of this chapter, provides a range of experiences on which to draw and suggests at least the following propositions.

First, constitutional recognition does not necessarily ensure that the roles of local government are protected and respected and the contribution of local government maximised. For this to occur, the principles and processes identified earlier in this section are needed as well, or even instead.

Secondly, the terms in which entrenchment occurs need careful attention. The characteristics of the local level of government differ from those of the level of constituent units. It is not practicable to place them on a par. Even Nepal, which goes furthest down the track in seeking to do so, fails to equate the two, at least in terms of shared rule. Rather, constitutionalization, if it occurs, needs to fit the characteristics of local government, reinforcing its strengths in multi-level government and recognising its limitations. It should not, for example, make local government boundaries unduly rigid in federations in which internal population shifts can be expected to occur, overburden local government, or undermine the position of the constituent units on which the federal principle also depends. It may be that the light touch constitutionalization, found in Germany and elsewhere, offers an appropriate model on which to build.

Third, the possibility of constitutionalization encourages further reflection on the position of cities. If local government is constitutionally recognised, it may be that the genre of cities should also be at least acknowledged by name and, perhaps, defined. It may be that some cities become constituent units, where that is feasible within the configuration of the federation. Whatever occurs, it once more is important not to rigidify either cities or processes relating to them in ways that might prove counterproductive.

V. Conclusion

One purpose of this chapter was to consider whether the entrenchment of local government in a federal constitution, with or without specific reference to cities, should be a normative aspiration in federations throughout the world. In pursuing this question, the chapter examined both the contribution that a local level of government makes to the goals of federalism and the challenges of incorporating it into a constitution as a third tier of government. The chapter also pointed to the diversity of local government bodies, both within particular federations and between federations more generally, including in the extent of constitutionalization. The issue of cities, as a particular manifestation of local government, is considered throughout in this context. The chapter shows that a normative expectation of constitutionalization would reach both too far and not far enough. It argued instead for substantive recognition of local government, of which federal constitutional recognition may or may not be part, in the form of a working partnership with other levels of government.

It is relatively easy to identify the principles on which such a partnership might be based. We defined these in terms of comity, solidarity, subsidiarity, and equivalence. Putting them into practice may be more difficult, however. There may be cultural obstacles, in federations where the contribution of local government has been consistently underestimated and downplayed. We hope that this chapter can assist to overcome difficulties of this kind by pointing to the gains of partnership with local government. A second difficulty is more practical: it concerns the processes that might be used to put such a partnership into effect, through the interactions between levels of government. This difficulty is attributable to the very characteristics of local government that make it an asset in a federation: size, diversity, and flexibility, across a very large number of units. This difficulty is raised, but not resolved, in this chapter. We think it likely that there already are informal practices in federations across the world that would throw light on how such processes might evolve. We hope that by opening debate here on the concept of partnership, the chapter will encourage further research, and further dialogue, on the detail of intergovernmental relations involving local government. We suspect that a generic answer to this challenge is also unlikely, in view of the differences in the contexts in which local government operates in federations throughout the world.

3

Subsidiarity and the City

The Case for Mutual Strengthening

*Maria Cahill and Garry O'Sullivan**

It seems to be a near universal feature of the intellectual project of justifying enhanced formal and material autonomy for cities that adherents invoke subsidiarity and believe that it offers a presumptive endorsement of the case for city autonomy. Subsidiarity's application to city autonomy is taken as 'seemingly obvious'.[1] When that initial instinct is made to marinate, however, the flavours become more complex. One part of that complexity is imbued by subsidiarity, which is a nuanced concept that extends beyond supporting the autonomy of smaller units. While it tends towards decentralisation, it also mandates intervention by central authorities in certain circumstances. Another part of that complexity is provided by scholarship on the city: it is noteworthy that even within the relatively small body of literature proposing increased autonomy for the city, a variety of justifications are given for that position.

This chapter does not seek to evaluate the merits of the case for city autonomy, but rather to explore the points of contact and synergy between the concept of subsidiarity and the project of justifying increased city autonomy. We believe that thoughtful exploration of the case for city autonomy in the light of subsidiarity raises important questions on both sides: questions about how the practical example of the city induces reconsideration of some theoretical assumptions within subsidiarity scholarship, and questions about the extent to which subsidiarity offers a conceptual paradigm within which the city can frame and sharpen its ambition for autonomy. We also believe that this exploration offers great potential

* We would like to thank participants at the 2019 workshop on this topic at Melbourne Law School for inspiring the inclusion of this chapter, as well as Erika Arban, David Thunder, and Sam Bruce for their critical constructive feedback on earlier drafts. The chapter also benefitted from Maria's participation in the RESPUBLICA project at the University of Navarra's Institute for Culture and Society, which receives financial support from Fundación Ciudadanía y Valores y Proeduca SL.

[1] Ran Hirschl, *City, State: Constitutionalism and the Megacity* (OUP 2020) 221. See also Daniel Weinstock, 'Cities and Federalism' in James E Fleming and Jacob T Levy (eds), *Federalism and Subsidiarity* (New York U P 2014) 266 (hereafter Weinstock, 'Cities and Federalism'); Loren King, 'Cities, Subsidiarity, and Federalism' in James E Fleming and Jacob T Levy (eds), *Federalism and Subsidiarity* (New York U P 2014) 299; Yishai Blank, 'Federalism, Subsidiarity and the Role of Local Governments in an Age of Global Multilevel Governance' (2010) 37 *Fordham Urban L J* 536; Benjamin Gussen, *Axial Shift: City Subsidiarity and the World System in 21st Century* (Palgrave Macmillan 2019).

Maria Cahill and Garry O'Sullivan, *Subsidiarity and the City* In: *Cities in Federal Constitutional Theory.* Edited by: Erika Arban, Oxford University Press. © Maria Cahill and Garry O'Sullivan 2022. DOI: 10.1093/oso/9780192843272.003.0004

for learning on both sides. For subsidiarity scholars, the case of the city presents a new lens through which to refresh perspectives because subsidiarity is being invoked in this instance to justify the granting of decision-making authority to an entity that has generally not enjoyed constitutional recognition. For city autonomy scholars, deeper exploration of the nuances of subsidiarity presents the prospect of understanding the extent to which subsidiarity can support the case for enhanced autonomy of cities and reveals explanatory and justificatory openings for further development of this new field of scholarship.

Happily, it will not be difficult to keep this focus on opportunities for mutual learning and strengthening throughout the chapter, because the justifications for city autonomy given by city scholars track well with the various models of subsidiarity articulated by the subsidiarity scholars. Four types of justifications for increasing city autonomy will be discussed in this chapter: the consistency argument, the expertise argument, the stake-holding argument, and the distinctiveness argument. That is not to say that these arguments are only alternatives and cannot be made congruently. Nor it is to say that these arguments could not be made on their own terms, without invoking subsidiarity, nor again that these arguments rely, for their value to the cause of city autonomy, on their ability to hang onto subsidiarity's coattails. However, since there is a general level claim made by city scholars that the cause of city autonomy is supported by subsidiarity, it seems fair to evaluate the arguments that they put forward in defence of city autonomy by reference to subsidiarity. And, at that point, some disaggregation is required, because, in reality, each of these arguments endorses a different theory or model of subsidiarity. These models, as we will deal with them, are referred to as the subsidiarity-as-federalism model, the subsidiarity-as-efficiency model, the subsidiarity-as-democracy model, and the subsidiarity-as-respect-for-distinctiveness model.

Section I will examine the consistency argument in light of the subsidiarity-as-federalism model, while section II will assess the expertise argument in light of the subsidiarity-as-efficiency model. In these two instances, although there are lessons to learn on both sides, it will be argued that the bulk of the learning to be done falls on the side of the subsidiarity scholars. Section III will investigate the stake-holding argument in light of the subsidiarity-as-democracy model, while section IV will study the distinctiveness argument in light of the subsidiarity-as-respect-for-distinctiveness model. In these two instances, although again there is potential for mutual strengthening, we believe that the greater opportunity exists on the side of the city scholars. Having evaluated the arguments for city autonomy in view of the various models of subsidiarity, section V will then focus on the two key pathways on which city autonomy scholarship can embark to further strengthen the intellectual defence of this position.

I. The Consistency Argument and Subsidiarity-as-Federalism

The most straightforward argument for increasing the autonomy of cities is the consistency argument, which simply contends that, to the extent to which states have accepted the existence of different levels of government within a federal structure, it is hypocritical for those states not to also recognise cities as autonomous sites of decision-making. Weinstock makes this point quite emphatically, when he states that: 'states that already recognize the rule of subsidiarity [within a federal arrangement] ... ought to extend the reach of that rule ... to encompass cities ... on pain of arbitrariness'.[2] Effectively, then, this is a competence-based defence of city autonomy, which argues that the city is capable of holding and exercising a suite of competences in the same way that regional or state or federal level authorities do.

The argument self-consciously adopts the subsidiarity-as-federalism model, assuming that subsidiarity is nothing more than a rule in a constitution which 'tells us how power should be organized within a federal arrangement'.[3] It is clear, thanks, in particular, to Arban's chapter in this volume, that subsidiarity and federalism share some intellectual history and constitute a response to similar overlapping concerns about centralisation of the state.[4] But there are some crucial differences, the implications of which need to be considered. Two of the distinguishing features of federalism, as Arban explains, are that it 'presents a constitutionally entrenched division of legislative powers between the central government of the state as a whole, typically for purposes of common interest, and a number of constituent units variously labelled ... for the purposes of local autonomy', and that, generally speaking, both levels 'are autonomous in their own spheres of powers'.[5] Typically, federal arrangements establish a system of exclusive competences: authority is held either at one level or at the other level, and there should be as little overlap as possible. There may be a relationship of supervision in which one level reviews the action of the other, which tends to be applied and interpreted in a competitive spirit, as a check by one level on the power of another. Admittedly, newer federal arrangements can be framed and/or interpreted in more cooperative ways. However, as Blank notes, such '[c]ontemporary attempts to read the federal principle [in this way] are either influenced by the subsidiarity principle or ... simply reflect the idea behind it', rather than being truly federal arrangements.[6] In any case, the point is that federalism is inherently aligned with constitutionalism, because it favours the establishment of powers endowed with specific competences which are free to exercise those competences subject to certain limits.

[2] Weinstock, 'Cities and Federalism' (n 1) 265.
[3] ibid, 261.
[4] Arban, chapter 1 in this volume.
[5] ibid, 17.
[6] Blank (n 1) 550.

Subsidiarity, on the other hand, is not so obviously compatible with constitutionalism, because subsidiarity fundamentally problematizes authority, rather than reifies it in the way that constitutions do.[7] As Paolo Carozza neatly explains:

> Subsidiarity by its very terms refers to the need for more contextual, fact-specific decisions, and it necessarily works, if at all, as much or more through rhetoric and politics as through formal doctrine. The detailed criteria by which subsidiarity operates are not suited to abstract reasoning *ex ante*, but instead need to be worked out over time, and the conclusions to which it leads will always be contextual and dynamic, containing the fluidity and flexibility of *phronesis* (practical judgment).[8]

Moreover, subsidiarity does not exclusively vest authority at any level, preferring instead to express a 'principled preference for proximity', which can be rebutted in certain circumstances, as determined by the logic of subsidiarity itself.[9] This being so, subsidiarity is not reducible to a federal rule without the amputation of its vital limbs. Understood as a principled preference for proximity, subsidiarity offers hope to city scholars. It provides a paradigm within which they could engage in an iterative, collaborative process of making a political case for greater autonomy in certain contexts.

In adopting the subsidiarity-as-federalism model, by contrast, proponents of city autonomy make life difficult for themselves, on three counts. First, because they immediately set themselves up as being in direct competition with the existing political communities within which they operate, and therefore a threat to those from whom they are seeking recognition. Not a promising beginning. Second, because by setting the terms of the debate such that they have to argue that cities are ready and capable of assuming exclusive competence for particular policy areas, they set a high empirical threshold which it is not immediately obvious that all cities are able to reach. Third, because when subsidiarity has been interpreted as the animating principle within federal arrangements, for example in Canada,[10] Germany,[11] and Italy,[12] it usually ends up having a disappointingly centralising

[7] Dominic Burbidge, 'The Inherently Political Nature of Subsidiarity' (2017) 62 *Amer J Juris* 143; Gráinne de Búrca, 'Re-appraising Subsidiarity's Significance after Amsterdam' (1999) Harvard Law School Jean Monnet Working Papers 1999/07; Maria Cahill, 'Subsidiarity as the Preference for Proximity' (2021) 66 *Amer J Juris* 129.

[8] Paolo G Carozza, 'Subsidiarity as a Structural Principle of International Human Rights Law' (2003) 97 *Amer J Intl L* 38, 79.

[9] Cahill (n 7).

[10] Eugénie Brouillet, 'Canadian Federalism and the Principle of Subsidiarity: Should We Open Pandora's Box?' (2011) 54 *Sup Ct L Rev* 601; Andreas Follesdal and Victor Muñiz Fraticelli, 'The Principle of Subsidiarity as a Constitutional Principle in the EU and Canada' (2015) 10 *Les Ateliers de l'Ethique* 89.

[11] Greg Taylor, 'Germany: A Slow Death for Subsidiarity?' (2009) 7(1) *Intl J Const L* 139.

[12] Erika Arban, 'Re-centralising Subsidiarity: Interpretations by the Italian Constitutional Court' (2015) 25 *Reg & Fed Stud* 129.

effect, which is perhaps explained by the fact that the constitutional arrangements establishing the federal structure are interpreted at the federal level. The writing on the wall suggests that the federal model will not bode well for the concrete realisation of the project of city autonomy.

For city scholars, the benefits of the subsidiarity-as-federalism model are largely confined to the initial appeal of the consistency argument and the need to avoid hypocrisy. On closer inspection, this model fails to offer significant support for the cause of city autonomy. For subsidiarity scholars, on the other hand, the example of the city is especially helpful in making manifest the practical implications of the theoretical distinctions between federalism and subsidiarity. For this reason, we believe that consideration of the consistency argument in defence of city autonomy based on the subsidiarity-as-federalism model offers a valuable moment of opportunity for the strengthening of scholarship on subsidiarity.

II. The Expertise Argument and Subsidiarity-as-Efficiency

A second argument for increasing the autonomy of cities is the engaged expertise argument, sometimes called the epistemic superiority argument,[13] which holds that decisions should be made at the level at which there are high levels of context-sensitive knowledge about the relevant issues and/or at the level which is most responsive to the views of local experts who are most likely to propose the effective policy solutions. It is an outcome-based defence of city autonomy because it focuses on the likely value of the policy decisions that are made. Essentially, the argument is simply that 'that local government is best situated to do the job'.[14] Weinstock elaborates the argument as follows:

> In virtue of the experience and knowledge obtained simply by inhabiting and negotiating the specific spatial characteristics of the cities in which they live, [inhabitants of cities] are better situated than outsiders to engage in fine-grained evaluation of the manner in which policy proposals will interact with the constraints and opportunities presented by these characteristics to generate normatively desirable results.[15]

This argument relies on the benefits of both knowledge-as-data and knowledge-as-experience. Not only do urban dwellers have 'more direct access to facts about how to realize desirable public policy ends in the particular spatial contexts',[16] but they

[13] King (n 1) 302.
[14] Hirschl (n 1) 222.
[15] Weinstock, 'Cities and Federalism' (n 1) 273.
[16] ibid.

also, as King notes, have expertise that comes 'by virtue of living in the city' because 'we are more familiar with what we experience directly'.[17] This is borne out in real-world examples of creative city-level solutions to seemingly intractable problems, from the introduction of an Ultra Low Emission Zone in London to tackle air pollution, to the work of the Mahila Housing SEWA Trust which trains women leaders to conduct climate vulnerability assessments in the slums of Ahmedabad to the successful housing policy of the Community Shelter Board in Columbus, Ohio. But the expertise argument is also contradicted by empirical findings. As King acknowledges, sociological research shows that the role of overarching authorities can be critical to the creation of 'expertise' at the local level, because the overarching authorities are more effective in collecting data, disseminating information, monitoring practices, and motivating citizens to participate in inclusive local deliberations.[18]

The expertise argument tracks well with the subsidiarity-as-efficiency model, which holds that decisions should be taken by the decision-making authority which is most capable of finding effective policy solutions. The European principle of subsidiarity, enshrined in the text of art 5(3) of the Treaty on European Union (Maastricht Treaty), for example, endorses a model of subsidiarity-as-efficiency, as follows:

> Under the principle of subsidiarity, in areas which do not fall within its exclusive competence, the Union shall act only if and in so far as the objectives of the proposed action cannot be *sufficiently achieved* by the Member States ... but can rather, by reason of the scale or effects of the proposed action, be *better achieved* at Union level.[19]

Given that it makes intuitive sense that whichever level is most capable of achieving good policy outcomes should exercise the relevant authority, and further that the European principle of subsidiarity is the most prominent legal articulation of the principle of subsidiarity, one might expect that city autonomy scholars would leap at the opportunity to associate their project with the model of subsidiarity-as-efficiency endorsed by the European Union.

Instead, however, city scholars not only refrain from endorsing this model but express open concerns both about the European principle of subsidiarity and about the subsidiarity-as-efficiency model. It may be that they are aware that the European principle of subsidiarity has had a demonstrably centralising, rather than decentralising, effect.[20] King expresses 'grave reservations' about the principle, not

[17] King (n 1) 304.
[18] ibid, 307–9.
[19] Emphasis added.
[20] Gareth Davies, 'Subsidiarity: the Wrong Idea, in the Wrong Place, at the Wrong Time' (2006) 43 *Common Market L Rev* 63, 77; Gabriël A Moens and John Trone 'Subsidiarity as Judicial and Legislative

least for its capacity to generate unnecessary administrative burdens.[21] Blank describes the European model of subsidiarity as 'confusing' and urges that one should not 'collapse [subsidiarity] theory into this particular practice of it'.[22] Moreover, Blank also goes on to articulate two very pragmatic reasons for abandoning the whole idea of subsidiarity-as-efficiency. The first is that, despite the illusion that it is an easy-to-use rule, subsidiarity-as-efficiency is very difficult to apply in a context where there are more than two levels of governance, because it becomes impossible to compare the relative efficiency of five or six levels of decision-making in respect of particular policy areas.[23] Weinstock underscores this point by noting that the expertise argument does not privilege the city as a site of decision-making: it can apply 'both beneath and beyond the level of the city'.[24] The multiplication of decision-making levels may, in reality, facilitate authorities to escape, rather than assume, their responsibility.

Blank's second reason for abandoning the subsidiarity-as-efficiency model is that what we mean by 'efficient' management of homelessness, violence, immigration, or climate change is precisely what needs to be discussed rather than assumed:

> [I]n the most important cases, subsidiarity does not provide the answer to the basic *political* dilemma: who should decide what? The presumptive answer: 'the one that can most efficiently do it' is only helpful when all other things are equal and when it is clear what efficiency means in a concrete situation.[25]

It is difficult to disagree with the principle that 'every decision or governmental function should be given to the "smallest" and "closest-to-the-citizen" jurisdiction, under the condition that such jurisdiction can perform it efficiently'.[26] However, on reflection, as Blank concludes, 'unless the matter at hand is highly technical (and technical questions can always turn into difficult political and ideological ones), the principle of efficiency only begs the question'.[27]

A third reason for rejecting the subsidiarity-as-efficiency model in the context of city autonomy—and perhaps an implicit explanation for the reluctance of city scholars to endorse this model—could be that there are temporal aspects to efficiency. If a city were recognised as a decision-making authority tomorrow, it might be quite inefficient and ineffective at making policy decisions tomorrow, especially

Review Principles in the European Union' in Michelle Evans and Augusto Zimmerman (eds), *Global Perspectives on Subsidiarity* (Springer 2014) 162.

21 King (n 1) 313.
22 Blank (n 1) 533–4.
23 ibid.
24 Weinstock, 'Cities and Federalism' (n 1) 274.
25 Blank (n 1) 537 (emphasis in original).
26 ibid, 540.
27 ibid, 538.

as compared with whatever decision-making authority is making policy in those areas today. But, a year from now, the city might be far more efficient and effective at policy-making in these areas than the current policy-maker is today.

For city scholars, the expertise argument holds an enduring appeal, but they are careful to refrain from endorsing the European principle of subsidiarity and they even criticise the subsidiarity-as-efficiency model on pragmatic grounds. For subsidiarity scholars, such reaction against the subsidiarity-as-efficiency model, in the context of general support for the expertise argument, is a valuable point of reference that invites further reflection and debate.

III. The Stake-holding Argument and Subsidiarity-as-Democracy

The stake-holding argument (sometimes expressed as the spheres of concern argument or the all-affected principle) argues that decision-making authority should be exercised at a level that allows maximum participation by and accountability to those who are most affected by the decisions made. It is a process-based defence of city autonomy. Hirschl presents the stake-holding argument in the following way:

> [C]ities stand at the front line of major public policy challenges ranging from managing multiculturalism, diversity, and social integration to handling widening socioeconomic gaps, crime prevention, poverty, and homelessness. The sheer scope and nature of these challenges warrant substantial representation in the policy-making venues that deal with them.[28]

Not only does the magnitude of the challenges mandate participation of those affected by them, but there is a sense that these issues need to be met as specific challenges faced by particular communities, rather than abstract problems without lived context. The attraction of this argument, as King frankly puts it, is that it promises them 'freedom from domination under, and inefficiencies resulting from, indifferent, ill-informed, or corrupted distant authorities'.[29] Weinstock envisages wide-ranging consequences of applying the all-affected principle as a process-based defence of autonomy of the city, arguing that, if we accept that 'people should have democratic say in policy decisions in the proportion that they are affected by them' then 'the lion's share of decision-making authority over the spatial dimensions of policy should be vested in cities'.[30]

[28] Hirschl (n 1) 224.

[29] King (n 1) 303.

[30] Weinstock, 'Cities and Federalism' (n 1) 272. Acknowledging that the edges of cities are not clearly delineated and cannot be, he relies on Brighouse and Fleurbaey to argue that the all-affected principle should be applied proportionally, rather than absolutely: at 285. See further Harry Brighouse and Marc Fleurbaey, 'Democracy and Proportionality' (2008) 18 *J Pol Phil* 137.

When subsidiarity is invoked alongside the stake-holding argument, the spheres of concern principle or the all-affected principle, it tends to be invoked only to assent to the normative commitments of these principles. The thought seems to be that subsidiarity either has no normativity of its own or else that its normativity is exactly co-extensive with these principles.[31] Thus, we have the subsidiarity-as-democracy model, a theory defended most comprehensively by Nick Barber.[32] Barber's theory of subsidiarity as democracy is rooted in his interpretation of the preambular invocation of subsidiarity in the Treaty on European Union, where it expresses a commitment to taking decisions 'as closely as possible to the citizen'.[33] Barber reads this as a commitment to democracy, where democracy is understood to be a principle of maximising participation:

> The principle of subsidiarity—subsidiarity as a principle of constitutionalism—should be understood as a development of one of the oldest and most basic maxims of democratic government: that what touches all should be approved by all.[34]

Theorising subsidiarity-as-democracy as a constitutional principle, Barber argues that it is best understood as a vertical separation of powers: 'the division of decisions between democratic units'.[35] A horizontal separation of powers balances majoritarian decision-making by some branches of government with non-majoritarian decision-making by other branches of government—a conscious design feature included to avoid over-privileging democratic majorities. But a vertical separation of powers commits to democracy all the way down: all of the possible decision-making units must be democratic.

Even though the subsidiarity-as-democracy model tracks well with the stake-holding argument, city autonomy scholars do not get a free pass by invoking this model, because it imposes more intellectual burdens on them than they may be aware of. For example, Barber makes the point that:

[31] For example, it seems that as far as Weinstock is concerned subsidiarity merely provides the possibility of a rule that would instantiate the value expressed by the all-affected principle: Weinstock, 'Cities and Federalism' (n 1) 270.

[32] Nicholas W Barber, 'The Limited Modesty of Subsidiarity' (2005) 11 *Eur L J* 308 (hereafter Barber, 'Limited Modesty'); Nicholas W Barber, *The Principles of Constitutionalism* (OUP 2018) (hereafter Barber, *Principles*).

[33] The preamble commits to the idea of 'creating an ever closer union among the peoples of Europe, in which decisions are taken as closely as possible to the citizen, in accordance with the principle of subsidiarity'.

[34] Barber, *Principles* (n 32) 191. See also Barber, 'Limited Modesty' (n 32) 316–17.

[35] Barber, *Principles* (n 32) 187.

> Before a power is allocated to a democratic unit, or a new democratic unit is created, subsidiarity requires us to ask whether that body will provide a vibrant democratic forum in which decisions can be made.[36]

The kind of democratic vibrancy that Barber has in mind is not only formal, in the sense of official decision-making processes and structures. It also includes a much thicker understanding of democracy, for which Barber relies on Sarah Song's argument that successful democratic units are those in which social solidarity exists: persons involved in the decision-making process are capable of and willing to listen to each other, to change their minds through deliberation, and to value each other's interests.[37] The model thus highlights an incompleteness in respect of existing arguments for city autonomy, and poses a threefold challenge to this literature.

A first challenge is that it cannot simply be assumed that cities already have (or have the capacity to create) decision-making structures within which all those affected will be facilitated to participate. Nor can it be assumed that such participation will be forthcoming. There is no detailed exposition within the city autonomy literature of the types of institutions or decision-making structures that might be developed at city level to realise the potential of this argument. Should cities have—or create—legislative and executive chambers? Should decisions be made by referendum of the city residents, who perhaps also have a right of initiative? Should city charters or constitutions be written and revised with popular input? A second challenge is that the democratic vibrancy of the city needs to be interrogated. If participatory decision-making structures were to exist at the city level alongside those at the national and supranational level, could we safely assume that citizens would still engage to the same level with all of those institutions, or is it possible that they might become democratically jaded? Will they engage in constructive ways, showing willingness to listen to each other, to change their minds through deliberation, and to value each other's interests? Given that cities are often characterised by anonymity and anomie, is it realistic to assume the requisite solidarity? Moreover, although Barber does not mention this, it seems possible that formal majoritarian democracy might impede the development of democratic vibrancy, if formal processes applied to controversial social problems such as how to tackle homelessness (eg, the building of social housing in a certain neighbourhood) or crime (eg, the provision of a rehabilitation centre for juvenile convicts in one part of the city) were to create faction and division rather than goodwill and solidarity.

[36] Barber, *Principles* (n 32) 196. Although Barber argues that the pre-existence of such conditions in a particular space could count as a democratic unit for the purposes of the vertical separation of powers, he notes that sometimes the requisite level of social solidarity will not always pre-exist such a unit as a site of democratic decision-making within the vertical separation of power: ibid, 196–7.

[37] ibid, 195, citing Sarah Song, 'The Boundary Problem in Democratic Theory: Why the Demos Should Be Bounded by the State' (2012) 4 *Intl Theory* 39.

A third challenge is that, as Barber envisages, units smaller than the city could also be viable democratic units for the purposes of subsidiarity-as-democracy: one can imagine that some villages and smaller towns might display higher levels of democratic vibrancy than some cities would.[38]

For subsidiarity scholars, the example of the city provides a useful point of reference for the articulation of the subsidiarity-as-democracy model. For city scholars, on the other hand, this model is revealed to be more demanding than city scholars might first have imagined. It does not confer a simple endorsement of the legitimacy of their claim, but rather articulates a set of hurdles to be cleared, inviting city autonomy scholars to clarify both the level of autonomy that should be vested in cities and the ways in which that autonomy should be exercised. The practical tensions that arise in this regard will be explored later in this chapter.

IV. The Distinctiveness Argument and Subsidiarity-as-Respect-for-Distinctiveness

When city autonomy scholars try to justify the autonomy of the city, they make conscious appeal, as noted above, to the consistency argument, the expertise argument, and the stake-holding argument. Yet, the overall thrust of their argument is simply that the city is special. This argument, the distinctiveness argument, seeks to defend the autonomy of the city not by reference to decision-making competence or decision-making outcomes, or decision-making processes, but simply by reference to what the city is. It can best be understood as an ontology-based defence of city autonomy. The length and strength of the arguments made by city autonomy scholars in defence of the distinctiveness of the city, far outweigh the length and strength of other arguments based on competence, outcome, and process. Correspondingly, much of the audacity of the intellectual project of advocating for city autonomy seems to draw life from the distinctiveness of the city.

The case for the distinctiveness of the city is a multivariate case which can be analysed from the perspective of three attributes: physical attributes; political attributes; and sociocultural attributes.[39] Firstly, the physical attributes of the city reference the fact that cities are generally places of especially *dense complex integration and proximity*.[40] In cities, it is claimed, residents must share spaces in ways others

[38] Interestingly, King (n 1) 309 notes that the spheres of concern argument does not privilege the city, but can be used by all smaller communities of concern who can show that they are immediately impacted by decisions made that are particularly relevant to them.

[39] Arban has similarly addressed the city as unique socioeconomic and political spaces: Erika Arban, 'Constitutional Law, Federalism and the City as a Unique Socio-economic and Political Space' in Ernst Hirsch Ballin and others (eds), *European Yearbook of Constitutional Law 2020: The City in Constitutional Law* (TMC Asser P 2021) (hereafter, Arban, 'Constitutional Law, Federalism').

[40] Many authors make reference to this city attribute of proximity: Hirschl (n 1) 197–206 (argument 4); King (n 1) 304; Weinstock, 'Cities and Federalism' (n 1) 270. Arban, 'Constitutional Law, Federalism' (n 39) 339, also refers to geographical homogeneity.

do not,[41] which may be described as an assumption of experienced[42] proximity.[43] Hirschl refers to this as 'extreme density' defined as a 'very high population-to-space ratio on a large scale without viable exit options'[44] (which is perhaps the defining characteristic of a megacity, as opposed to a global city, which we examine in section V of this chapter). For King, this gives rise to cities as 'imagined coherent things' which 'are characterized by dense patterns of *complex integration* and thus considerable *interdependence*'.[45] The physical attributes of the city create the conditions for the development of the expertise argument, because urban dwellers, by virtue of physical proximity, are likely to reason about policy in constructive ways.[46]

Secondly, the political attributes of the city reference the city's distinct *political community* and the issues unique to it. City dwellers, as a collective, are described as being the product of immense diversity, giving rise to multifaceted spheres of concern.[47] Hirschl focuses on three categories of concern: social factors give rise to concerns such as the right to housing and health not being adequately met; economic factors accentuate a structural dependence on big businesses and entrenched inequality in some districts; and political factors highlight the underrepresentation of voters due to the 'one person one vote' principle, as well as a universal application of certain norms to a value diverse community.[48] The argument is that the concerns originating from the city's 'super-diversity' are unique to the city.[49] 'No other parts of the polity', Hirschl believes, 'present integration or accommodation challenges and opportunities similar in their scope and nature to those facing large urban centers'.[50]

Thirdly, the sociocultural attributes of the city reference its capacity to create and sustain *identity*. Weinstock alludes to this with his 'folk conception' of the city, whilst King posits the existence of an 'imagined coherence' inspired by Benedict Anderson's theory of nation states as socially constructed 'imagined communities'.[51] The historic prominence of the city state in ancient Athens and Rome also suggests a separate city identity prior to the birth of the modern Westphalian state.[52] Allied with this is the ancient argument, taken from Aristotelian philosophy, that

[41] Daniel Weinstock, 'Self-determination For (Some) Cities?' in Alex Gosseries and Yannick Vanderborght (eds), *Arguing About Justice: Essays for Philippe Van Parijs* (U de Louvain P 2011) 379 (hereafter, Weinstock 'Self-determination').

[42] King (n 1) 299.

[43] Blank (n 1) 554 (unique traits 1, 2, 5). King (n 1) 305 also describes this as the proximity conjecture.

[44] Hirschl (n 1) 175.

[45] King (n 1) 300 (emphasis in original).

[46] Weinstock, 'Cities and Federalism' (n 1) 272. King (n 1) 302 refers to this as 'epistemic superiority'.

[47] King (n 1) 303.

[48] This is to categorise the six specific justifications that Hirschl (n 1) later develops.

[49] ibid, 226.

[50] ibid.

[51] Weinstock, 'Cities and Federalism' (n 1) 267–9; King (n 1) 299. See also section V of this chapter regarding defining the city.

[52] Arban 'Constitutional Law, Federalism' (n 39) 326–8.

cities are versions of the good life: living in solidarity by virtue of 'difference, plurality and experimentation'.[53]

In truth, none of these arguments, on its own, is enough to defend the distinctiveness of the city. The level of population density varies as much between a mega-city and a less populous global city as it does between an ordinary city and a village. A diverse political community might be more likely to exist within a city, but diverse groups may also live in towns and villages. As Arban notes, 'there is no single solution that would perfectly fit all contexts' and smaller countries with less pronounced urban/rural divides may experience the same challenges within and beyond the city.[54] Weinstock, for his part, does at least indirectly acknowledge that one of his arguments for city autonomy, the defence of group-differentiated rights for national minorities,[55] is applicable to groups that live outside a city as a form of localism. The most promising argument for city autonomy is the one based on its sociocultural attributes, but this is underdeveloped.

It matters enormously, of course, whether the advocates of city autonomy have made a convincing case for the distinctiveness of the city, and the success of the entire project of city autonomy may turn on their ability to do so. But, for our purposes, it is already interesting and instructive that the case for the city is being made in terms that rely on its distinctiveness. To a subsidiarity scholar, this kind of argument echoes a different model of subsidiarity, one that we can call the subsidiarity-as-respect-for-distinctiveness model. This model, as Blank neatly puts it, 'aims to recognize the singularity and uniqueness of every social sphere and its place in the total social structure',[56] focusing both on the particularity of the specific social sphere in question and on its potential contribution to the wider community. Within this model, as Blank explains:

> Each of these social entities (or human associations) has its own uniqueness, its own capacities, and its own abilities and potential. None is superior to the other, and together they form a whole, a totality (which is not necessarily the totality of the nation).[57]

The crucial feature of this model of subsidiarity is that it is irrepressibly cooperative: each association or social sphere must be allowed to make its own contribution without unnecessary intervention, but each must also be entitled to assistance from other social entities when such assistance is needed. Within this model, it is an advantage that the application of subsidiarity 'will be a messy affair, spanning

[53] Blank (n 1) 554. Weinstock, 'Self-determination' (n 41) 381 also makes reference to 'the good life', citing Will Kymlicka, *Multicultural Citizenship: A Liberal Theory of Minority Rights* (OUP 1996).
[54] Arban 'Constitutional Law, Federalism' (n 39) 332.
[55] Weinstock, 'Self-determination' (n 41) 383.
[56] Blank (n 1) 541.
[57] ibid, 542.

several spatial and institutional scales and fostering considerable interdependence across jurisdictional lines to foster and nurture the epistemic promise of city dwellers'.[58] All of the difficulties associated with the battle over exclusive competences that might appear inevitable using the subsidiarity-as-federalism model are hereby side-stepped. That is not to say that there will be no disagreement about where and by whom authority is exercised, but it is to say that the subsidiarity-as-respect-for-distinctiveness model frames such disagreement as what Michael Tomasello would call 'cooperative argumentation'.[59]

The appeal of the subsidiarity-as-respect-for-distinctiveness model for city scholars would seem to be that it acknowledges and relies on the arguments for the distinctiveness of the city, which seem to be the arguments that city autonomy scholars hold most dear. But should they put their trust in such this model? Blank argues that this model of subsidiarity is 'inherently socially conservative since it sanctifies and congeals the social institutions and associations that already exist', with the result that it entrenches the social *status quo*.[60] He also warns that another 'major risk' of this model of subsidiarity is that it depoliticises that which should remain political, namely, the decision 'regarding which level of government and which political community will control which resource and determine which issue'.[61] Other subsidiarity scholars hold the opposite view, reasoning that, by calling attention to the distinctiveness of particular associations, this model is precisely what creates space for associations to make fresh claims for political recognition and autonomy. De Búrca, for example, understands subsidiarity as offering a 'conceptual space in which [the right] balance can be negotiated' and 'a language though which the ongoing debate is channelled'.[62] Burbidge argues that this model of subsidiarity is inescapably and 'inherently political',[63] while, as noted above, Carozza understands this model to be one that is highly sensitive to context, working 'through rhetoric and politics' in a way that will always be fluid, flexible, and dynamic.[64] Building on these positions, Cahill has argued that this model of subsidiarity is characterised by a principled preference for proximity which is designed to initiate, rather than foreclose, conversations about the level at which decisions should appropriately be taken.[65]

City scholars consider that there is something that the city can do that no other political community can do as well as it can. For subsidiarity scholars, it is noteworthy and thought-provoking to see how valued the distinctiveness argument is in practice by those who wish to argue for greater autonomy for an entity which

58 King (n 1) 309.
59 Michael Tomasello, *A Natural History of Human Thinking* (Harvard U P 2014) 111.
60 Blank (n 1) 543.
61 ibid, 548.
62 See de Búrca (n 7).
63 Burbidge (n 7) 148–9.
64 Carozza (n 8).
65 Cahill (n 7).

has not yet been given (due) recognition. The example of the city provides a useful point of reference for the refinement of the subsidiarity-as-respect-for-distinctiveness model. For city scholars, this model may offer an opportunity to capitalise on the argument from distinctiveness, which seems to be their most cherished argument in favour of city autonomy. But, again, this model demands more from city scholars than they might have expected: it demands, as will be developed below, that they define the city with much greater specificity, disaggregating the different kinds of cities to definitively avoid a 'one size fits all' approach to city autonomy. Given that—according to this model—decisions about the allocation and exercise of authority are understood as reflexive prudential conversations that set up co-operative decision-making structures, honest and intelligent use of this model of subsidiarity will articulate solutions that are bespoke to the city and the policy issue in question. Consequently, the realisation of this model will seek to respect the potential of the city to make a meaningful contribution and to place that city in cooperative collaboration with the other political units with whom it can helpfully engage.

V. Strengthening the Project of City Autonomy

Putting city autonomy scholarship and subsidiarity scholarship into conversation with each other creates opportunities for mutual learning on both sides, but since this collection is focused on the place of the city, we draw this chapter to a close by focusing on two key pillars that are needed to strengthen the argument for city autonomy. Although the importance of these two pillars has been revealed to us through reflection on the subsidiarity models, we contend that these pillars are fundamental to the development of the project of city autonomy, whether or not that project seeks to ground itself by reference to subsidiarity. However, we submit that these pillars are fundamental to the development of the project of city autonomy, whether or not that project seeks to ground itself by reference to subsidiarity. The first pillar focuses on clarifying what is meant by 'the city', in order to make it possible to invoke the subsidiarity-as-respect-for-distinctiveness model. The second pillar seeks to make concrete what is meant by 'autonomy', in order to make it possible to invoke the subsidiarity-as-democracy model.

A. The onus to define the city

We need to know how the city is to be defined in order to put forward an intelligible theoretical case for the legal autonomy of the city.[66] Two elements deserve

[66] Arban has also emphasised the importance of defining the city. Remarking on the absence in Hirschl's book of any specific definition of the city, she contends that it 'proves ... the fact that the

consideration: the first is whether it is possible to define the city in a bounded way, the second is whether the case for city autonomy applies to all cities, or only those of a certain size or with a certain status.

In relation to the effort to define the boundaries of a city, Weinstock suggests that to insist on distilling down what is meant by the city is to fall into a trap of 'legal positivism'.[67] Instead, he argues for a 'folk conception' of the city 'that is unproblematically available both to the citizen who says of herself that she lives in Saint Louis, irrespective of the legal facts on the ground (which may make it the case that she lives in Clayton), and to the external observer who sees an almost seamless whole where the law has established boundaries'.[68] However, if the city is to be recognised by law, we contend that it should be capable of being defined in law. Perhaps intuiting this rebuttal, Weinstock goes on to list four conditions which he claims are present to a sufficient degree in a city: (1) a certain spatial integration; (2) a certain agglomeration threshold in terms of population and area; (3) a certain minimal degree of population density; and (4) its inhabitants live the major aspects of their lives within the confines of the city. Summing up this 'fuzzy bounded' description, 'a city', he explains, 'is an integrated and organized territory of a certain scale and density within which most residents lead the major aspects of their lives'.[69]

King agrees with the spatial integration criterion, adding that it is 'not merely dense but multifaceted and often characterized by subtle forms of interdependence'.[70] To King, cities should not be categorised in terms of metrics such as population, rather they are experienced 'as durable yet dynamic sites of dense integration—of people, practices, sites, traditions'.[71] This then, he says, establishes an 'imagined coherence' related to, as noted earlier, Anderson's description of the nation state as an imagined community.[72] In contrast to Anderson's theory—predicated on the fact that members will never know all of their fellow members—King argues that the imagined community of the city is grounded on the 'visceral experiences of elements of the city', thereby emphasising the importance of proximity.[73] Although it is surely true that the experiences of nationhood and patriotism are not fully susceptible to legal articulation, it is nonetheless the case that the boundaries of state territory and citizenship are defined in and by law. So although

city remains a rather elusive construct that is difficult to chart in absolute terms.' Erika Arban, 'City, State: Reflecting on Cities in (Comparative) Constitutional Law' (2021) 19 *Intl J Const L* 343, 349 (hereafter Arban, 'City, State').

67 Weinstock, 'Cities and Federalism' (n 1) 266.
68 ibid, 268.
69 ibid, 269.
70 King (n 1) 299.
71 ibid.
72 Benedict Anderson, *Imagined Communities: Reflections on the Origin and Spread of Nationalism* (Verso 1983).
73 King (n 1) 299.

the experience of community solidarity within the city which Weinstock and King rightly emphasise cannot be legally captured, this does not mean that the burden of defining the city is removed. It might be suggested that a legally robust definition will require a specific threshold of a certain population level and population density expressed as a percentage of the total population or a precise numerical limit. A consequence of such a definition would be that cities could lose their legal status due to declining population. As many reports are indicating, this may in fact be a pressing issue for large Western cities in the wake of the COVID-19 pandemic.[74] To circumvent this issue, Arban has suggested that, in addition to diversity and spatial factors such as density or size/population, reference could also be made to a city's 'historic, socioeconomic, and especially political relevance'.[75] Acknowledging the historic importance, economic importance, and political and cultural importance of cities appropriately honours their place as 'unique socioeconomic and political spaces'.[76]

In relation to the effort to disaggregate different kinds of cities, the literature uses three terms—'a megacity', 'a global city', and 'a city'—and the choice and definition of these terms have significant implications for the number of potential cities that can be thought to be deserving of autonomy. Megacities are generally distinguished by the quantity of the population, with the accepted level ranging from more than five, eight, or ten million people.[77] The most commonly cited figure—arising from the United Nations definition—is ten million people, which places the number of megacities at approximately thirty-three.[78] Under this definition, the term includes cities such as Bangalore, London, and Shanghai. Global cities, as discussed in the seminal work of Sassen,[79] have more nebulous characteristics. Sassen's original description was deliberately loose to accommodate change, but it was based around the flow of information and capital with seven specific hypotheses around the global city model.[80] From this label, different indexes have been created to determine a city's global ranking, which can place the number of global cities at anywhere from 151[81] to

[74] See Conor Dougherty and Ben Casselman, 'House Hunters Are Leaving the City, and Builders Can't Keep Up' (*New York Times*, 29 May 2021) <https://www.nytimes.com/2021/05/29/business/economy/new-home-building-suburbs.html> accessed 3 October 2021; Bethan Staton, 'London Exodus Leaves Schools Short of Pupils' (*Financial Times*, 30 May 2021) <https://www.ft.com/content/b557a784-e1e1-4625-a237-14d435723200> accessed 3 October 2021.

[75] Arban, 'City, State' (n 66) 350.

[76] Arban 'Constitutional Law, Federalism' (n 39) 332.

[77] Klaus Baier and others, 'Towards Integrated Intentional Agent Simulation and Semantic Geodata Management in Complex Urban Systems Modeling' (2015) 51 *Computers, Environment and Urban Systems* 47.

[78] United Nations, *The World's Cities in 2018: Data Booklet* (UN Department of Economic and Social Affairs 2018) 2.

[79] Saskia Sassen, *The Global City: New York, London, Tokyo* (2nd edn, Princeton U P 2001).

[80] Saskia Sassen, 'The Global City: Introducing a Concept' (2005) 11 *Brown J World Affairs* 28–30.

[81] 'Global Cities Index: New priorities for a new world' (Kearney, 2020) <https://www.kearney.com/global-cities/2020> accessed 3 October 2021.

707.[82] What is noticeable from a comparison of global cities and megacities is the difference in location. The former—a grouping dominated by economic power—are largely located in the Global North, whereas the latter are located largely in the Global South. All megacities are likely to be global cities, but the converse does not hold. The significance of this is that, if the project of city autonomy were to focus on megacities, prominent global cities, such as Brussels, Sydney, and Dubai, would not feature. This renders the choice of terminology an important one for the potential success of the project in a comparative context.

The broad term 'city' is the one most often employed in the literature but even this is subject to varying interpretations. The UN, for example, cites three methods of definition: (1) 'the city proper', which aligns with an administrative boundary; (2) the 'urban agglomeration', which accounts to a contiguous urban area to delineate the city's boundaries; and (3) the 'metropolitan area', which encompasses the degree of economic and social interconnectedness of nearby areas, such as interlinked commerce or commuting patterns.[83] On this account, it is possible the project could include both London and Leeds and New York City and Newark, despite these cities having dramatically different institutional capacities. Consequently, these different approaches have significant implications for territory and population. Finally, the literature does not currently distinguish between city autonomy for cities that are currently the capital cities of their nation states and those that are not. Capital cities can often represent something more than just population density due to their political and institutional significance. Some capital cities, for example Canberra or Washington DC, are not particularly large or commercially significant but they are crucial to their nation's governing infrastructure. In this sense, they are often bound up with the central government—indeed the city's name, such as Washington or Moscow, can become synonymous with the governing power of the nation—and it is unclear to what extent this has implications for the limits of a capital city's autonomy.

It seems to us that if cities are to be recognised by law in more formal ways, then city autonomy scholars cannot avoid the burden of definition. By way of analogy, it may be worth noting that the Montevideo Convention requires in order to achieve recognition at international level, a putative state should possess four characteristics as prerequisites: (1) a permanent population; (2) a defined territory; (3) a government; and (4) a capacity to enter relations with other states.[84] The political and administrative competence as well as the social and cultural consequence of cities varies very significantly from one to the next. For this reason, and because the arguments for the autonomy of the city are largely premised on political and

[82] Globalization and World Cities (GaWC) Research Network, 'The World According to GaWC 2020' (Loughborough University, 21 August 2020) <https://www.lboro.ac.uk/gawc/world2020t.html> accessed 3 October 2021.

[83] United Nations (n 78) 1.

[84] The Montevideo Convention on the Rights and Duties of States, art 1.

administrative competence and are sensitive to the extant levels of social solidarity, the justifications for recognition are more or less compelling depending on the kind of city. It seems to us that a cogent and thoughtful disaggregation of the various kinds of cities and a framing of justifications for city autonomy by reference to these definitional elements would help to make discussions on the viability of city autonomy sharper and more sensitive to complex realities.

B. The onus to clarify the scope of autonomy

Having addressed city autonomy through the lens of subsidiarity, we respectfully suggest that efforts to articulate city autonomy *in the abstract* will not properly respect city distinctiveness and will likely not build a compelling case for city autonomy. There are hints, in the scholarship, that the case for city autonomy is about achieving autonomy at a sub-constitutional level by improving the democratic credibility of cities as decision-making sites. There are stronger hints that the case for city autonomy ultimately targets the achievement of city autonomy through constitutional recognition. And there are weaker hints in the shadows that the case for city autonomy is ultimately targeting extra-constitutional recognition, perhaps in competition with state-to-state relations. But all of these arguments could only be fairly considered in the context of particular cities or, at the very least, through a nuanced disaggregation of regular cities, megacities, and global cities. Subsidiarity would demand that the viability of these options should be considered and defended not in the abstract but in relation to the specific distinctiveness of specific cities.

Nonetheless, what follows is a reflection on three possible options—differing considerably in ambition—that we think deserve further careful consideration in the literature.

The first possibility is to *democratise* the city at the sub-constitutional level. In essence, the objective here may be twofold: to improve the effectiveness of governance through localised decision-making or to improve the accountability of governance through increased physical proximity between the decision-making actors and those who are affected by their decisions.[85] The former objective would assume that policy-makers in a locality benefit from better information because of being nearest to the actual issues that city inhabitants face. The effect of this, it is thought, is that governance might more robustly incorporate the views of those who live in that area and thereby result in better outcomes for city living.[86] The latter objective,

[85] In essence, these incorporate the scholars discussed earlier relating to the expertise argument and the stake-holding argument.
[86] It might be said that both of these objectives are articulations hinted at in two arguments discussed earlier in this chapter, namely the expertise and stake-holding arguments respectively.

on the other hand, would aim to make a virtue of representative proximity. That is, the goal appears to be to encourage and foster citizen participation in the democratic process. The manner in which either form of democratisation is achieved might range from experimental participatory decision-making, administrative changes—in the form of amending voting laws and city governance structures—to more largescale power for those who govern cities, such as mayors, in key policy areas.[87] However, democratisation is likely to be unit agnostic: it is a preference for all forms of proximity, which—if respecting its democratic principles—would include towns and villages, as well as the city. By refraining from elevating any unit to the constitutional level, however, it neither poses drastic disruption to the pre-existing constitutional order nor embraces the distinctiveness of the city. A more concrete overall evaluation of the project of city autonomy might reveal that its core aims could be accommodated within this less disruptive option, however the democratic compromise required presents difficult questions for the practicality of the city's distinct status as claimed by city scholars.

The second possibility is to *institutionalise* the city at the constitutional level. The objective here would be recognition of the city's special status in a nation's constitutional order from a functionalist and normative standpoint.[88] For Hirschl, the appeal of this option can be understood through acknowledging that the 'byroad' of administrative law does not compare with the constitution's 'elevated legal and symbolic status in a given polity's legal hierarchy'.[89] Within this perspective, in order to fully express its status, the city must find its place on 'public law's main highway: constitutional law'.[90] In this regard, it would be a legally autonomous ascent from democratisation through to the constitutional entrenchment of the city. Albeit the degree to which this will hold is dependent upon the existing constitutional order's malleability—or lack thereof—to change, this option assumes that there is a greater degree of legal rigidity in constitutional law. Where a written text exists, implementing institutionalisation would likely take the form of constitutional amendment and incorporation via a special framework for the city itself.[91] On the weak end, it could involve symbolic recognition by merely referencing the special status of (particular) cities in the constitution.[92] On the strong end, it could

[87] Hirschl (n 1) also proposes a range of diverse measures that could empower the city, which is likely to be achievable without constitutional amendment or constitutionalising the city, such as intra-metropolis equalisation (at 207–18), proportional representation systems, and mixed urban–rural electoral districts (at 178–81).

[88] ibid, 16.

[89] ibid (emphasis omitted).

[90] ibid.

[91] Arban 'Constitutional Law, Federalism' (n 39) 339–40, alludes to the reality that 'constitutional rigidity might represent an almost insurmountable obstacle' in those countries with a very stringent amendment process, such as the United States.

[92] Of course, if the aim is one of constitutional signalling, those smaller units might reasonably ask why their locality is not also given special status, which poses practical conundrums for even the most amendable constitutions.

extend wide-ranging powers to a defined city that would establish a separate and parallel set of institutions (such as a parliament and judiciary) with specific areas of autonomy.[93] As Hirschl notes, constitutions 'define and signal who we are as a political community, what moral and political ideals we cherish and strive for, and how we wish for others to reflect upon our polity'.[94] Institutionalising a city in either manner would, therefore, signal the societal standing of a city in a legally more significant manner. Yet this approach—predicated on the capacity to legally define a city—is confined within, and owes its powers to, the state-centric constitutional order. Although the city would be elevated to the constitutional level through 'constitutional tinkering',[95] it would still be subservient to the state. In that respect, it might not be thought to truly respect the thriving *identity* of the city as articulated by Weinstock and King. If it is accepted that a city possesses a uniquely important cultural and political identity, it might follow that the identity of city is at least equal, if not superior, to that of the state. Weinstock, citing Bell and de Shalit's work on city identities and ethea,[96] concludes that city autonomy 'need not' undercut 'national solidarity in a morally unattractive way'.[97] For some, it would surely be the case that constitutional recognition would sufficiently honour the specialness of the city and provide a working, if imperfect, framework for city autonomy. Yet, for others, the degree of civilizational uniqueness achieved by the city might justify the contemplation of a third possibility.

The third possibility would be to *globalise* the city at the extra-constitutional level.[98] Radical and groundbreaking, this possibility would be rooted in the desire to free the city from the shackles of the existing Westphalian constitutional order, by elevating the city to the level of an autonomous entity equal to the state itself.[99] It could draw some inspiration from sovereign city-states, such as the Vatican City or Singapore,[100] but it could go much further than those models. One thread in the city autonomy literature is the idea that large cities face a set of challenges that set them apart them from towns and villages and at the same time creates common

[93] This may also include revenue raising powers, which Hirschl emphasises as a requirement: Hirschl (n 1) 181–91.

[94] ibid, 16.

[95] King (n 1) 297.

[96] Daniel A Bell and Avner de-Shalit, *The Spirit of Cities: Why the Identity of a City Matters in a Global Age* (Princeton U P 2011).

[97] Weinstock, 'Self-determination' (n 41) 384.

[98] Riegner has discussed the concept of 'global governance' for cities where 'local governments go global and international institutions go local', however this would appear to require the cooperation of the nation state to some extent, rather than the city itself being the sovereign actor. Michael Riegner, 'International Institutions and the City: Towards a Comparative Law of Glocal Governance' in Helmut Philipp Aust and Anél du Plessis (eds), *The Globalisation of Urban Governance* (Routledge 2018) 38.

[99] Hirschl (n 1) 11 notes that '[t]his state-centered [Westphalian] conceptualization of territorial sovereignty may regard large cities as potential competitors of state authority, or at the very least as sites of potential mass mobilization and popular political resistance'.

[100] Gussen has demonstrated an analytical framework of three types of city depending on political and economic independence, which includes a Territorial City, Charter City, and City-State in ascending order of both political and economic independence. Gussen (n 1) 446.

ground with other large cities irrespective of national borders. Could it be that cities might connect and engage directly with each other outside of the traditional state-centric model through a kind of extra-national or supranational (con)federation of cities with joint global governance?[101] The parameters of this suggestion are murky: it evades definitional clarity in terms of how it could be implemented and where authority would ultimately lie.[102] A collaborative effort by several cities would be necessary in order to establish such an arrangement, which would, in itself, present significant coordination challenges.[103] It is not clear that this is a possibility that is being seriously considered in the city autonomy literature, and it is certainly not at all clear that this kind of proposal could be justified by reference to subsidiarity. To the extent to which city scholars wish to advance and defend a new model of a globalised city, with or without shared governance arrangements with other global cities, we would suggest that a particularly compelling justificatory case would be needed, alongside a more detailed articulation of the practical considerations to be taken into account in the development of such a model.

VI. Conclusion

This chapter has focused on the ways in which subsidiarity scholarship and city autonomy scholarship can mutually inform and shape each other. We have argued that subsidiarity scholarship can be refined by close analysis of the concrete example of the case of city autonomy, which exposes the dangers of eliding the difference between subsidiarity and federalism and between subsidiarity and efficiency, and which showcases the surprising attraction of a model of subsidiarity that focuses on the distinctiveness of the (putative) decision-making level involved. We have also argued that city autonomy scholarship can be strengthened by deep reflection on the challenges that subsidiarity scholarship poses to it, principally by demanding greater clarity about how the city is to be defined and requiring greater specificity about what level of autonomy is being proposed. As scholars on both sides rise to the challenges that have emerged from this process of mutual learning, there are valuable opportunities for strengthening the intellectual defences provided both for the concept of subsidiarity and for the project of city autonomy.

[101] Blank (n 1) 517–20 uses this phrase within the context of cities coming together to come up with policy responses to global issues that are commonly faced by large cities, but it is not clear whether he is hinting at a similar model of such a radical nature.

[102] Gussen alludes to this twofold expression of globalising the city where he envisages an 'axial shift' (as a result of what he terms the Fourth Industrial Revolution) where an 'initial sovereign role for cities ... without the current mediation of nation-states' will give way to 'one civilization, where there are thousands of ... sovereign cities forming a network of loose (continental) confederation under a global constitutional framework': Gussen (n 1) 14–15.

[103] See ibid, 444–52, for Gussen's similar conception of an 'Olympic' Word System of cities, which draws upon the novel area of a 'polycentric' constitutional order.

4

Cities in Federal Systems

Comparative Perspectives

*Ran Hirschl**

I. Cities in Federal Constitutional Theory: A Glaring Omission

The 21st century has been hailed the 'century of the city'. The figures behind this label are mind boggling. Consider that a century ago only one in ten people lived in an urban area; today, 56 per cent of the world population lives in cities. Given the increase in total population from the early 1900s to present, that means the world's urban population has increased nearly thirtyfold within a century. This shift is an unprecedented transformation of the organization of society, both spatially and geopolitically. The ever-expanding urbanization trend, arguably the most significant demographic trend of our time, is set to continue. The forecasts for 2030 or 2050—let alone for 2100—range from the disturbing to the near-dystopian. Projections suggest that megacities of 50 million or even 100 million inhabitants will emerge by the end of the century, mostly in the Global South.[1] Yet our constitutional institutions and imagination have failed to keep pace with this new reality. Cities have remained, by and large, absent from constitutional law and constitutional thought, not to mention from comparative constitutional studies more generally.[2]

* Professor of Government and Earl E. Sheffield Regents Professor of Law, University of Texas at Austin. This chapter draws in part on materials included in Ran Hirschl, *City, State: Constitutionalism and the Megacity* (OUP 2020). I am grateful to Erika Arban, Zachary Rosen, Yiwei Jin, and to the participants in the *Cities in Federal Theory* workshop (20–21 June 2019) at the University of Melbourne, for their helpful comments and suggestions on an earlier draft of this chapter.

[1] United Nations Department of Economic and Social Affairs, Population Division, *World Urbanization Prospects: The 2018 Revision* (United Nations 2019) (hereafter *World Urbanization Prospects*); Daniel Hoornweg and Kevin Pope, 'Population Predictions for the World's Largest Cities in the 21st Century' (2017) 29 *Environment & Urbanization* 195. The figures indicate that more than approximately 88 per cent of worldwide urbanization from 1960 to present day has taken place in Asia, Africa, and Latin America, and that over 95 per cent of worldwide urbanization in the coming three decades will take place in those three continents.

[2] Ran Hirschl, *City, State: Constitutionalism and the Megacity* (OUP 2020) (hereafter Hirschl, *City, State: Constitutionalism and the Megacity*).

Ran Hirschl, *Cities in Federal Systems* In: *Cities in Federal Constitutional Theory*. Edited by: Erika Arban, Oxford University Press. © Ran Hirschl 2022. DOI: 10.1093/oso/9780192843272.003.0005

As I have shown elsewhere, the constitutional blind spot with respect to urbanization and the metropolis is baffling.[3] Pertinent legal discourse about cities occurs largely within the confines of administrative law or municipal law, with occasional excursions to so-called global law, but seldom in constitutional law.[4] Within legal academia, scholars of international and global law have identified the inter-connectivity of the urban with national and international governance levels.[5] And there has certainly been an increasing involvement of cities in international policy-making, particularly in environmental protection and global climate change regimes, but also in areas such as anti-poverty, international migration, and refugee policies.[6] While lacking formal standing in international law, international city and mayoral networks have formed around an array of common goals—from joining the UN-Habitat program, to vowing to implement the Paris Agreement, to demanding representation at global and pan-European policy-making forums concerning the refugee crisis. Meanwhile, progressive cities and city leaders have assumed important roles in advancing initiatives in key policy areas, such as public housing, education, undocumented migration, and climate change. Cities worldwide have declared themselves 'sanctuary cities' (often with respect to migrant and refugee-related policies) or 'human rights cities', promoting and implementing various human rights protections at the municipal level.[7] However, very little of this innovative energy has extended into constitutional thought or constitutional jurisprudence.

The same blind-spot exists in federal constitutional theory and practice.[8] Respect for subsidiary levels of government, for local autonomy, and for place-based difference in general is perhaps the key feature of federalism as a theoretical concept and

[3] ibid.

[4] A few examples of such global law accounts are: Yishai Blank, 'Localism in the New Global Legal Order' (2006) 47 *Harv Intl L J* 263; Gerald E Frug and David J Barron, 'International Local Government Law' (2006) 38 *Urb Lawyer* 1; Helmut P Aust, 'Shining Cities on the Hill? The Global City, Climate Change, and International Law' (2015) 26 *Eur J of Intl L* 255; Janne E Nijman, 'The Urban Pushback: Intl Law as an Instrument of Cities' (2019) 113 *Proceedings of the ASIL Annual Meeting* 119.

[5] See, eg, Nijman (n 4); Yishai Blank, 'The City and the World' (2005) 44 *Columbia J of Transnational L* 875.

[6] See, eg, Helmut P Aust, 'The Shifting Role of Cities in the Global Climate Change Regime: From Paris to Pittsburgh and Back?' (2019) 28 *Rev of EC & Intl Enviro L* 57.

[7] See, eg, Barbara M Oomen, Martha F Davis, and Michele Grigolo (eds), *Global Urban Justice: The Rise of Human Rights Cities* (CUP 2016).

[8] As with any generalization of this kind, there are notable exceptions. A few examples, in addition to the chapters in this timely volume, include Erika Arban, 'Constitutional Law, Federalism, and the City as a Unique Socio-Economic and Political Space' in Hirsch Ballin and others (eds), *European Yearbook of Constitutional Law 2020* (Asser P 2021) 323; Richard C Schragger, *City Power: Urban Governance in a Global Age* (OUP 2016) (hereafter Schragger, *City Power*); Daniel Weinstock, 'Cities and Federalism' in James E Fleming and Jacob T Levy (eds), *Federalism & Subsidiarity: NOMOS LV* (NYUP 2014) 259; Loren King, 'Cities, Subsidiarity and Federalism,' in Fleming and Jacob T Levy (eds), *Federalism & Subsidiarity: NOMOS LV* (NYUP 2014) 291; Yishai Blank, 'Federalism, Subsidiarity, and the Role of Local Governments in an Age of Global Multilevel Governance' (2010) 37 *Fordham Urb L J* 509; Jacob T Levy, 'Federalism, Liberalism and the Separation of Loyalties' (2007) 101 *Amer Pol Sci Rev* 459; Gerald Frug, 'The City as a Legal Concept' (1980) 93 *Harv L Rev* 1057.

as a practical mode of political and constitutional government. As Stephen Tierney observes, one of the key elements differentiating federalist arrangements from unitary states is that:

> rather than seek to assimilate or overcome territorial difference as has been the constitutional experience of most unitary states, the federal state explicitly accepts the political and sociological salience of this difference, offering a constitutional form of government that is constructed in response to, and respect for, this difference.[9]

The federal state is comprised of multiple territorial polities, 'each of which retains its own constitutional personality and carries its particular constitutional subjecthood from constituent moment into constitutional form and hence into lived constitutional practice'.[10] Federalism's embedded predisposition towards subsidiarity and regionalism[11] has been supported in recent years by what has been termed 'neo localism'—essentially, strategic devolution of power to the local level in an attempt to better implement national goals—and by a backlash against political convergence, globalism, and supra-nationalism, spawning an array of localist counter-movements that claim to represent the 'genuine identity' of a particular polity, region, or community.[12]

Yet despite these theoretical predispositions and political realities, cities are often excluded from the purview of contemporary federalism, both in theory and in practice. As Heather Gerken writes of the American context: 'Federalism scholars have typically confined themselves to states, the only subnational institutions that possess sovereignty.'[13] With few exceptions, the same is true in other federalist settings around the world. Worldwide, the Westphalian, state-centred framework continues to dominate the theory and practice of federalism, with its notion of sovereign territorial states divided along ethnic, religious, and linguistic cleavages and reflecting conventional notions of nationhood, peoplehood, and/or historical patterns of conquest and settlement. In this universe, cities, home to the majority of mankind, ubiquitous and crucial to every aspect of 21st-century society, culture, economics, and politics, are virtually absent, 'the forgotten stepchildren of both federal politics and scholarship'.[14]

It is telling how little attention has been devoted in political theory, let alone in constitutional theory, to federalism's unit question. As Jacob Levy observes, this

[9] Stephen Tierney, 'Federalism and Constitutional Theory' in Gary J Jacobsohn and Miguel Schor (eds), *Comparative Constitutional Theory* (Edward Elgar P 2018) 57.

[10] ibid. See also Arban, chapter 1 in this volume.

[11] See Cahill and O'Sullivan, chapter 3 in this volume.

[12] Ran Hirschl, 'Opting Out of "Global Constitutionalism"' (2018) 12 *L & Ethics of Human Rights* 1.

[13] Heather Gerken, 'Foreword: Federalism All the Way Down' (2010) 124 *Harv L Rev* 6, 21.

[14] King (n 8) 295.

gap is particularly troubling when one considers the prevalence of federalism and the dominant status of state-sized, subnational units in contemporary federalism. For Levy, one of the few authors to have addressed the unit size issue:

> federations are made up of provinces that are too few, too large, too rigid, too constitutionally entrenched, and too tied to ethnocultural identity to match theories based on competitive federalism, Tiebout sorting [supposed optimization of public service provision based on competition across local jurisdictions], democratic self-government, or subsidiarity.[15]

If the leading theories of federalism are to be taken seriously, Levy argues, they warrant a much more flexible, decentralized model of federalism, composed of smaller constituent units than the typical state- or province-sized ones.[16] Similarly, Weinstock notes that if we are to take ideals of subsidiarity and stakeholding seriously, it is unclear why 'both theoretical discussions about, and ... the practice of, real-world federal arrangements [should stop] at the level of provinces, länder, US states and the like' and continue to exclude cities.[17]

As I have suggested elsewhere, the silence concerning cities in federal theory, and in constitutional theory more generally, may have a number of causes. One is simple historical inertia—the modern state completed its conquest of the city in early modern times. Another is 'spatial statism', the notion that public law, through its spatial ordering, helps to sustain a state-oriented locus and focus of sovereign control of its territory in the face of competing forces, real or perceived.[18] A third reason is intellectual path dependence; for well over a century now, federal constitutional theory has been predicated upon traditional subnational units such as states, provinces, Länder, cantons, and regions, and a well-established, hard-to-change matrix of institutional hierarchies and political incentives reflects this disposition. Then there is constitutional rigidity—a combination of dated constitutional arrangements and impossibly burdensome amendment procedures—which makes city empowerment through constitutional reclassification very difficult to achieve and often politically costly.

There may well be other reasons too. As Richard Schragger and others point out, the stalemate may also reflect the fact that cities, unlike capital, are fixed in place. This 'anchored-ness' means that cities have no credible 'exit' or 'capital flight' options and are therefore limited in their bargaining power.[19] Fierce competition among cities may ensue, often to the detriment of conceptualizing cities as a unified order of government. What is more, as Schragger suggests, the city as a unit

15 Levy (n 8) 459.
16 ibid, 460–3.
17 Weinstock (n 8) 269–70.
18 Ran Hirschl and Ayelet Shachar, 'Spatial Statism' (2019) 17 *Intl J Const L* 387.
19 Schragger (n 8).

is caught between constitutional theory's traditional attention to the state and liberalism's attention to individual rights and liberties. The city—neither a state, nor an individual or a private entity—does not enjoy a prime position under either of these emphases. Furthermore, the modern city's super-diversity may play a role here too. Large cities tend to be culturally diverse, cosmopolitan, and socially progressive—these facts often put cities and their residents at odds with the worldviews and policy preferences of central governments or of voters in semi-urban and rural areas. Relatedly, a combination of constitutionally entrenched malapportionment, political tampering with electoral districts, and a systemic bias against city voters in first-past-the-post electoral systems (common in federal systems, eg US, Canada, Australia, India, Pakistan, and Nigeria) has systematically weakened the political representation of cities and their residents and negatively impacted predominantly urban policy issues such as transit, density, and affordable housing.[20] The aggregative result of these trends is that cities—by far the most common form of modern life and home to the vast majority of humanity—are underrepresented and undertheorized in federal constitutional thought.

In this chapter, I consider two questions concerning the constitutional status of cities in federal systems. First, what is the significance of the federal/unitary distinction in determining the constitutional status of cities? I suggest, in a nutshell, that the evidence is mixed and inconclusive, and that ultimately the Global North/Global South distinction—and in particular the tendency towards stagnation in the former versus a tendency towards innovation in the latter—appears more significant than the federal/unitary dimension in assessing the constitutional status of cities. Second, what do national constitutions say about the urban/rural divide—one of the most significant factors in contemporary politics—and how significant is the federal/unitary dimension in addressing that challenge? Here too, the data suggest that despite the central place of subsidiarity and local autonomy in federalism theory, the constitutions of federal countries are no more likely than the constitutions of unitary states to commit to addressing the urban/rural divide. This in turn raises the possibility that federal constitutional theory's preoccupation with traditional subnational unit boundaries may in fact lead to conceptual rigidity and institutional path dependence when it comes to addressing new spatial challenges such as urban agglomeration, the rise of megacities, or the increasing salience of the urban/rural divide. It also suggests that one of the questions at the centre of this volume—whether federalism is favourable or unfavourable to cities—may be viewed as auxiliary to other, more pertinent factors such as the North/South distinction, constitutional 'newness', or malleability that facilitate constitutional innovation in this area, as well as concerted political will to constitutionally empower

[20] See, eg, Jonathan A Rodden, *Why Cities Lose: The Deep Roots of the Urban-Rural Divide* (Basic Books 2019); Catherine Boone and Michael Wahman, 'Rural Bias in African Electoral Systems: Legacies of Unequal Representation in African Democracies' (2015) 40 *Electoral Studies* 335–46.

cities, and to overhaul the spatial dimensions of constitutional governance more generally.

II. The City in Federal Constitutions: Northern Stagnation, Southern Innovation

A close look at the status of cities in some of the world's leading federal constitutional orders reveals a mixed picture. In most federal constitutional orders of the so-called Global North, hard-wired constitutional arrangements continue to subjugate cities to higher orders of government. By contrast, several federal constitutional orders in the Global South have been experimenting with city empowerment, with various models and with various degrees of success. This suggests that the North/South distinction, possibly restructured as old vs new constitutional orders, may have more purchase than the traditional federal/unitary distinction in explaining city status in national constitutions.

Prime examples of the stagnation concerning city status in Global North federal systems include the United States, Canada, and Australia. Cities in the United States, some of which are among the world's largest, lack constitutional personality, and are principally at the mercy of state governments, constitutionally speaking. Doctrines such as 'Dillon's Rule' and home rule (the 'Cooley Doctrine'), formulated in the mid-19th century and endorsed by the US Supreme Court in the early 20th century, continue to govern the constitutional status of American megacities today.[21] American constitutional jurisprudence on city power therefore represents a very small fraction of the country's federalism case law. Meanwhile, America's dated yet rigid constitutional structure equips states with the powers to draw electoral district boundaries in a way that frustrates urban representation, and, most importantly, allows state legislatures to 'pre-empt' city legislation. Leading experts on American cities' constitutional status note that states often frustrate cities' efforts to address the welfare of urban residents by implementing redistricting and rezoning to dilute local power to the suburbs.[22] Instances of pre-emption have increased considerably in the last decade: states have pre-empted or overridden city ordinances on issues as diverse as gun control, tobacco regulations, living wage regulations, sanctuary city policies, municipal civil rights law, LGBTQ anti-discrimination rights, posting nutritional information in restaurants, and anti-plastic and environmental protection legislation. Several states have also enacted laws that prohibit cities from joining international city networks.

[21] See, eg, *Atkin v Kansas*, 191 US 207 (1903), *Hunter v Pittsburgh*, 207 US 161 (1907).

[22] Richard Briffault, 'The Challenge of the New Preemption' (2018) 70 *Stanford L Rev* 70 1995; Richard C Schragger, 'The Attack on American Cities' (2018) 96 *Texas L Rev* 1163. See also Briffault, chapter 5 in this volume.

Canadian cities may well be even weaker than their America counterparts. Lacking any direct constitutional powers, cities and municipalities in Canada exist only as bodies of delegated provincial authority, entirely dependent on provincial legislation for their power and sources of revenue. Large Canadian cities, the front-line delivery agents of Canadian multiculturalism and social integration, are governed by a constitutional order that dates back to 1867—at which time metro Toronto's population was less than 50,000; today it is 7.5 million. Under this system, 'municipal institutions' are creatures of provincial governments, controlled exclusively by provincial authority (through s 92 of the *Constitution Act 1867*) alongside 'charities', 'eleemosynary institutions' (non-profits), 'shops' and 'saloons and taverns'. Since 85 per cent of Canada's population lives in cities, with more than 50 per cent of the nation's population concentrated in six metropolitan areas, it would be something of an understatement to say that the constitutional non-status of cities in 21st-century Canada reflects serious constitutional datedness. And Canada is purportedly one of the world's leading constitutional democracies, featuring abundant scholarly awareness for and legal recognition of diversity and differentiated citizenship. This democracy deficit may violate some of the country's constitutional pillars, as defined by the Supreme Court of Canada.[23]

Similarly, Australia's constitutional order allows for near-complete state domination of cities and metropolitan governance more generally.[24] Despite some ambivalence in High Court jurisprudence on the Commonwealth's (federal) power to invest in massive urban renewal projects, Australia's major cities remain patently underrepresented within the existing constitutional order. Unlike in Canada, Australia's Constitution does not specify the states' enumerated powers. Instead, it identifies only the Commonwealth (federal) Parliament's powers (primarily in ss 51 and 52). Any legislative area not granted to the Commonwealth remains exclusively with the states. Since local government was a subject of colonial legislation prior to confederation, it is not one of the powers given to the Commonwealth. Consequently, Australia's large cities—Sydney (metro population 5.2 million; approximately two-thirds of New South Wales's population); Melbourne (metro population 5 million; approximately three-quarters of Victoria's population); and Brisbane (metro population 2.5 million; approximately half of Queensland's population)—are largely at the mercy of state governments. The states effectively control key policy areas ranging from education, health, and policing to planning, land

[23] In its decision in *Reference Re Secession of Quebec* [1998] 2 SCR 217, the Supreme Court of Canada stated that the Canadian Constitution is based on four equally significant underlying principles: (1) federalism, (2) democracy, (3) constitutionalism and the rule of law, and (4) the protection of minorities. None of these principles trumps any of the others. See also Hoi Kong, chapter 6 in this volume.

[24] Graham Sansom and Jeremy Dawkins, 'Australia: Perth and South East Queensland' in Enid Slack and Rupak Chattopadhyhay (eds), *Governance and Finance of Large Metropolitan Areas in Federal Systems* (OUP 2013) 10–48; Cheryl Saunders, 'Constitutional Recognition of Local Government in Australia' in Nico Steytler (ed), *The Place and Role of Local Government in Federal Systems* (Konrad-Adenauer-Stiftung 2005) 47–63.

use, infrastructure, and major utilities. Three prominent and unsuccessful attempts to amend Australia's Constitution to empower cities have either failed in referenda (1974 and 1988) or were withdrawn due to lack of support (2013).

In Europe, although practices vary considerably, there is in general slightly greater constitutional attention to local government, whether rural or urban. The European Charter of Local Self Government, which came into force in 1988, suggests that European cities may be better off than their counterparts in the United States, Canada, or Australia. It protects the basic prerogatives of local government (without distinguishing between small townships and large cities) exercised by directly elected councils, and affirms the capacity of local authorities, within the limits of the law, 'to regulate and manage a substantial share of public affairs under their responsibility and in the interests of the local population'. Article 2 states that the principle of local self-government must be recognized in domestic legislation and, where practicable, in the constitution. However, in reality, the Charter's net effect on enhanced city constitutional power in Europe has been modest at best, as the constitutional status of cities continues to reflect established national constitutional traditions.[25]

The German Basic Law, to pick one example, protects the regulatory competences of municipalities in local affairs 'within the limits prescribed by law' (art 28.2). The German Federal Court has held that this competence includes local affairs that have not been explicitly assigned by law to other levels of government, and that it may be overridden only in the name of public interest (the definition of which remains vague).[26] In practice, however, the residual power German municipalities enjoy with respect to regulating local affairs not addressed by other laws has been limited considerably by a large number of federal and Länd statutes. What is more, the German constitutional structure does not differentiate between villages, small towns, and large urban centres. Consequently, the Rhine-Ruhr metropolitan region (Germany's largest urban agglomeration, with more than 11 million people) lacks any autonomous constitutional standing or personality; it is not even mentioned in the state constitution of North Rhine-Westphalia within which it lies. The same is true of Frankfurt, described in Saskia Sassen's seminal work as a 'global city' alongside New York, London, and Tokyo[27]—yet the Hessian state constitution contains not so much as a whisper about Frankfurt.

Italy's constitutional order, established in the aftermath of the Second World War, is known for its highly decentralized character. But it was not until 2015 that Italy's major cities, hitherto subsumed by Italy's 107 provinces, were granted

[25] Giovanni Boggero, *Constitutional Principles of Local Self-Government in Europe* (Brill 2017); Chris M G Himsworth, *The European Charter of Local Self-Government: A Treaty for Local Democracy* (Edinburgh U P 2015).

[26] Christian Bumke and Andreas Voßkuhle, *German Constitutional Law: Introduction, Cases, Principles* (OUP 2019) 418–20.

[27] Saskia Sassen, *The Global City: New York, London, Tokyo* (Princeton U P 2001).

enhanced status through art 114 of the Constitution. Accompanying legislation created an elected metropolitan mayoral position in each of these cities and granted extended autonomy to the designated cities with respect to matters such as local planning and zoning, provision of local police service, and local transportation. However, the new legal framework did not grant these cities any transformative fiscal autonomy beyond what was needed to assume authority over the devolved governance functions. What is more, a package of constitutional changes, which would have enhanced the central government's power vis-à-vis the regions while removing the entire 'provincial' status from the constitution, was defeated by a 59 per cent to 41 per cent margin in a national referendum held in December 2016. The outcome has been a somewhat convoluted 'half-baked' system of city autonomy that may have non-trivial long-term effects on city autonomy but which, for the time being, 'has not yielded the promised territorial simplification and has quickly led to a very unbalanced and inefficient system, while exponentially expanding administrative costs without a corresponding increase in the quality of essential services'.[28]

Even in Spain, where regional and territorial identities are deeply rooted in history and are reflected in the constitution, cities do not possess much power. Section 2 of the Spanish Constitution 1978 recognizes the right to autonomy of Spain's 'regions and nationalities', and at the same time declares 'the indissoluble unity of the Spanish nation.' Since 1983, the country has been divided into 17 autonomous communities (*comunidades autónomas*). Each autonomous community is granted a core set of legislative competences, and has its own elected Parliament whose members elect a regional government. There are two further levels of government below the national and regional. These are provinces and municipalities, whose powers and responsibilities are set out in the *Basic Law on Local Government 1985*. Additionally, the *Local Government Modernization Act 2003* establishes governance guidelines for municipalities with populations larger than a pre-determined threshold. The metropolitan area of Madrid (population 6.5 million) is one of the 17 autonomous communities, with a governing body called the Autonomous Community of Madrid. A special law for Madrid as a capital city reinforces the existing competences and devolves some functions from the central government and the Community of Madrid to the city level. However, observers of Spanish federalism have noted that since 1980 both the Autonomous Community of Madrid and the government of Catalonia (with respect to Barcelona) have avoided the creation of strong metropolitan councils that might become rivals to the autonomous communities themselves.[29] Consequently, the self-governance capacities of Madrid

[28] Erik Longo, 'Local Governments and Metropolitan Cities: The Italian Experience and its Comparative Relevance' in Erika Arban, Giuseppe Martinico, and Francesco Palermo (eds), *Federalism and Constitutional Law: The Italian Contribution to Comparative Regionalism* (Routledge 2021) 163.

[29] See, eg, Francisco Velasco Caballero, 'Kingdom of Spain' in Nico Steytler (ed), *Local Government and Metropolitan Regions in Federal Systems* (McGill-Queen's U P 2009) 311.

and Barcelona are not substantively greater than that of any other Spanish municipality. The result is that in Spain too, neo-secessionist regionalism has been largely limited to traditional subnational units.

When we turn our gaze to federal constitutional orders in the Global South, a different picture emerges. Major attempts to bolster the constitutional status of cities have taken place in federal or quasi-federal countries as diverse as India, Brazil, and South Africa. At the same time, we have seen the constitutional empowerment of large cities in both federal countries (typically by designating them as autonomous states, as with Mexico City, Buenos Aires, and Addis Ababa) and formally unitary countries such as South Korea, Vietnam, and Taiwan.[30] While not all the attempts in the Global South to constitutionally bolster city status have proven equally successful, the fact remains that constitutional innovation in this area occurs almost exclusively outside of North America or Europe.

Let us consider a few prime examples of this trend. India's federal system has traditionally left most urban governance responsibilities to state governments, with little attention paid at the national level to addressing urban agglomeration. However, in 1993, two constitutional amendments were adopted that aimed to address local government. The 73rd Amendment deals primarily with governance of rural settlements and townships, while the 74th Amendment addresses cities. The latter defines a metropolitan area as 'an area having a population of one million or more comprised of one or more districts and consisting of two or more Municipalities or Panchayats or other contiguous areas'. Article 243W(a) of the Constitution allows state legislatures to 'endow the Municipalities with such powers and authority as may be necessary to enable them to function as institutions of self-government …' These laws 'may contain provisions for the devolution of powers and responsibilities upon Municipalities at the appropriate level'. Note that it does not *require* states to devolve power to cities, but instead suggests that state legislatures *may* do so if they are so inclined, and also that state legislatures preserve discretion over the scope and nature of devolved powers. The 12th schedule attached to the 74th Amendment lists 18 concrete policy areas, including urban planning and urban poverty alleviation, wherein state legislatures may devolve power to city authorities. In addition, art 243ZE provides for the establishment of metropolitan planning committees for each designated metropolitan area. On paper, then, the 74th Amendment represents a serious exercise in constitutional empowerment of cities and local government more generally.

In practice, however, the impact of this constitutional change on urban self-government has been varied at best, with most observers assessing its real effect as limited. Because of the traditional strength of the states in Indian politics, and the

[30] The Constitution of South Korea, for example, establishes 17 subnational units, of which eight are designated 'first-level' cities (including Busan, Daegu, Gwangju, Incheon, and Seoul), with Sejong as a special self-governing city.

significance of state governors' support for national parties and their leaders, the 74th Amendment left the actual designation of 'metropolitan areas' in the hands of state governors, provided the designations met the criteria in the amendment as well as 'such other factors as they deem fit'. Essentially, state governors are free to determine their own criteria for classifying urban centres within their respective states.[31] Consequently, state governments maintain legislative, administrative, and financial control over cities. State-controlled agencies continue to dominate key city-related policy areas, from transportation and housing to land use and low-income neighbourhood improvement. The result is that 'despite the promise offered by 74th Amendment, urban local governments in India are rendered largely powerless since the Amendment does not ensure autonomy from the state government and also because states have refused to implement its core vision'.[32]

The federally driven constitutionalization of the urban development agenda in Brazil has been more active and more successful, although it, too, is tamed by vast socio-economic inequalities and by the vagaries of national and intergovernmental politics in a large federal country. Nonetheless, Brazil's example provides a positive counterpart to India's amendments 73 and 74. In 1986, a national constituent assembly was established to write a new constitution for Brazil. Extensive popular input was sought through public hearings and public submissions of proposed provisions and amendments. Following a charged debate, the new federal constitution was adopted in 1988. It included art 182, warranting that 'urban development policy, carried out by the municipal public authority, according to the general guidelines fixed by law, is intended to order the full development of the social functions of cities and to guarantee the well-being of their inhabitants'. According to art 182.1, each city with at least 20,000 inhabitants—more than 85 per cent of Brazil's population live in cities that meet this criterion—must have a master plan approved by the city council as its basic tool for urban development and expansion policy. Article 183 further states that 'an individual who possesses as his own an urban area of up to two hundred and fifty square metres, for five years without interruption or opposition, using it as his or as his family's residence,

[31] See Michael Castle-Miller, 'The Urban Situation: Cities' Place in Decentralized Government Frameworks' (2014) 1 *Indonesian J of Intl & Comparative L* 1047.

[32] Mathew Idiculla, 'Unpacking Local Self-Government: The Uncertain Power of Cities in the Indian Constitution' (2020) 53 *VRÜ Verfassung und Recht in Übersee* 30. In neighbouring Nepal, the 2015 Constitution includes an extensive list of local government powers: see, eg, pt 17 'Local Executive', pt 18 'Local Legislature' sch 8 'List of Powers/Jurisdiction for Local level', and sch 9 'List of Concurrent Powers/Jurisdiction for Federation, State and Local Level'. However, recent studies suggest that the actual devolution of power in Nepal has been protracted and inefficient: see, eg, Keshav Kumar Acharya and Habib Zafarullah, 'Institutionalising Federalism in Nepal: Operationalising Obstacles, Procrastinated Progress' (2020) 23 *Pub Admin & Policy* 125. Other studies analyse the inclusion of extensive local government powers in the Nepalese Constitution in the context of the participatory constitution-drafting process in that country and its quest to accommodate ethnic and racial tensions in the Nepalese society. See, eg, Michael G Breen, *The Road to Federalism in Nepal, Myanmar and Sri Lanka: Finding the Middle Ground* (Routledge 2018) 121–7.

shall acquire title over it, provided he does not own another property'. In other words, 'adverse possession' principles, aimed at preventing forced evacuations of long-term dwellers by land developers, were constitutionally recognized. Perhaps even more importantly, the inclusion of these two provisions in the new constitution signalled a transition to a new era in which elements of urban governance and reform are federally protected against encroachment by subnational governments, local authorities, or private-sector actors.

The federal entry into the urban governance scene was complemented by the adoption of the City Statute in 2001 as well as the establishment of the Ministry of Cities and the National Cities Council in 2003. The City Statute—the first of its kind in Latin America—regulates the implementation of arts 182 and 183, and explicitly acknowledges the right to a sustainable city in Brazil's large urban centres.[33] It prioritizes the collective good and 'social function' of urban life and urban land (essentially placing emphasis on improving the living conditions of Brazil's urban poor and the notion that urban land should not remain vacant when it can serve a useful public purpose). The City Statute further defines guidelines that must be observed by federal, state, and local governments to ensure a democratic civil society voice in city management. Created by President Luiz Inácio Lula da Silva upon his election in 2002, the federal Ministry of Cities (shut down by President Jair Bolsonaro in 2019) was aimed at expanding the federal stake in urban affairs while offering solutions to unsuitable housing and infrastructure in Brazil's ever-expanding cities. Its portfolio included responsibility for urban development policy and sectoral policies for housing, sanitation, and urban transportation. However, as well intended as these initiatives were, the political reality in Brazil at both the federal and the intergovernmental levels is such that the actual, on-the-ground effects of these reforms have depended largely on the political alignment of federal, state, and megacity leaders. When this alignment exists, federal and state support for megacity projects is likely; conversely, when there is a change of power, there is a tendency to discontinue funding for urban development projects.[34]

The post-Apartheid Constitution of South Africa, enacted in 1996, features what is arguably the most comprehensive and successful endeavour to date to grant cities constitutional status and standing. As part of its distinct democratizing break with the country's political and constitutional past, the new South African Constitution explicitly aimed to curb provincial power and empower local government. To that end, art 40(1) holds that 'government is constituted as national, provincial, and local spheres of government which are distinctive, interdependent

[33] José Roberto Bassul, 'City Statute: Building a Law' in Celso Santos Carvalho and Anaclaudia Rossbach (eds), *The City Statute of Brazil: A Commentary* (Cities Alliance and Ministry of Cities, Brazil 2010) 71–91; Edesio Fernandes, 'The City Statute and the Legal-Urban Order' in Celso Santos Carvalho and Anaclaudia Rossbach (eds), *The City Statute of Brazil: A Commentary* (Cities Alliance and Ministry of Cities, Brazil 2010) 55–70.

[34] Greg Clark and Tim Moonen, *World Cities and Nation States* (John Wiley & Sons 2016) 126.

and interrelated'. Chapter 7 (ss 151–164) of the Constitution marks a further fundamental shift away from the pre-1996 order.[35] It builds upon and operationalizes art 40(1) by giving municipalities the ability to legislate and administer regulations in a number of areas (eg municipal planning, health services, public transport, and trade) and, most important, the ability to raise funds in these areas, subject to some oversight by provincial and national governments.

As the Constitutional Court noted shortly after the new Constitution came into effect:

> The constitutional status of a local government is thus materially different to what it was when Parliament was supreme, when not only the powers but the very existence of local government depended entirely on superior legislatures. The institution of elected local government could then have been terminated at any time and its functions entrusted to administrators appointed by the central or provincial governments. That is no longer the position. Local governments have a place in the constitutional order, have to be established by the competent authority, and are entitled to certain powers, including the power to make by-laws and impose rates.[36]

Chapter 7 of the Constitution sets out three categories of municipalities. A 'category A municipality' refers to major urban centres, currently the metropolitan areas of Johannesburg (metropolitan population 10 million), Cape Town (4.5 million), and Durban (3.5 million), as well as the smaller urban areas of Bloemfontein and East London. The creation of these unified metropolitan governments and, by extension, integrated urban space, was a direct response to the Apartheid policy of excluding certain neighbourhoods (notably Soweto in Johannesburg) from city boundaries and administration, thereby depriving these neighbourhoods from representation, services, or subsidies.

Chapter 7 further provides that a municipality has the 'right to govern, on its own initiative': s 151(3). Section 156 provides three avenues for municipalities to exercise their power: executive authority, the right to administer, and the authority to make and administer bylaws. In addition, s 156(5) enables municipalities to exercise any power incidental to the effective performance of their functions. Municipalities' significant revenue-raising functions are entrenched in s 229 of the Constitution, which confers the ability to impose rates on property and surcharges on fees for services as well as other taxes if authorized by national legislation. The Constitutional Court has referred to the municipal revenue-raising power as an

[35] Robert Cameron, 'The Upliftment of South African Local Government?' (2001) 27 *Local Govt Stud* 97, 102.

[36] *Fedsure Life Assurance Ltd v Greater Johannesburg Transitional Metropolitan Council* 1999 (1) SA 374 (CC) [38].

'original power', clarifying that the imposition of rates and surcharges does not require enabling federal legislation.[37] Additionally, municipal governments are entitled to an equitable share of the revenue raised by the national government, to enable them to provide basic services and perform the functions allocated to them.[38]

To be sure, the success of constitutional reforms depends on many political, social, and economic factors beyond the constitutional text's immediate reach. That said, most observers of municipal affairs in South Africa agree that the constitutional recognition of local government has been quite effective in allowing cities to provide improved services to their residents. This seems to hold true even when a major city (such as Cape Town) is governed by an opposition party (the Democratic Alliance).[39] This is not to say that the relations between major South African cities and the other orders of governments do not occasionally sour. However, unlike in India or Brazil, the constitutional order and the constitutional jurisprudence stemming from it successfully shield cities from the exclusive grip of federal or provincial governments.

The constitutional protection provided to South African cities has been reinforced by several landmark rulings of the South African Constitutional Court pertaining to intergovernmental disputes under the 1996 constitution. In its 2010 decision in *City of Johannesburg Metropolitan Municipality v Gauteng Development Tribunal*, to pick one example, the Constitutional Court ruled that cities have exclusive authority over municipal planning, including zoning and land use management, and that national or provincial powers may not be used in ways that usurp or subvert municipal planning powers.[40] In another important decision two years later, the Constitutional Court ruled that while intergovernmental cooperation is to be favoured, a national competence may be limited by the exercise of a municipal competence.[41] Specifically, the Court held that the granting of mineral mining rights by the national government cannot circumvent municipal zoning decisions. In a 2020 decision involving a state-owned communication service provider whose built structure contravened Cape Town's zoning laws, the Court sided with the city authorities and affirmed the constitutional objective of establishing 'wall-to-wall municipalities with powers to control and regulate land use within their areas of jurisdiction', separate and distinct from provincial and national planning.[42]

[37] *City of Cape Town v Robertson* 2005 (2) SA 323 (CC) [56] (Moseneke J).

[38] A municipality's claim to an equitable share of national revenue was found to be justiciable in *Uthukela District Municipality v President of the Republic of South Africa* 2003 (1) SA 678.

[39] See, eg, Robert Cameron, 'Vertical Decentralisation and Urban Service Delivery in South Africa: Does Politics Matter?' (2014) 32 *Development Pol'y Rev* 81.

[40] See *City of Johannesburg Metropolitan Municipality v Gauteng Development Tribunal* 2010 (2) SA 554 (SCA); confirmed by the Constitutional Court in *City of Johannesburg Metropolitan Municipality v Gauteng Development Tribunal* 2010 (6) SA 182 (CC).

[41] *Maccsand (Pty) Ltd v City of Cape Town* 2012 (4) SA 181 (CC).

[42] *Telkom SA SOC Ltd v City of Cape Town* 2021 (1) SA 1 (CC).

In summary, despite federalism's favourable predisposition toward principles of subsidiarity, local government,[43] and accommodation of place-based difference—certainly when compared to the centralized, single polity ethos at the core of unitary states—federalism *per se* does not seem to entail an improved constitutional status for cities. Whereas in some federal systems, notably the United States, Canada, and Australia, the city is virtually non-existent constitutionally, in other federal countries, virtually all of which are in the so-called Global South, constitutional reform backed by political will has brought about constitutional empowerment for cities. In other words, the North/South division appears more consequential in this area than the federal/unitary one. This may reflect necessity factors—the bulk of urban growth over the last few decades has taken place in Asia, Africa, and Latin America.[44] It may also reflect the fact that most Global South constitutions are newer and oftentimes more malleable to transformation and renewal, and therefore tend to be more attuned to the urban challenge than rigid constitutional orders adopted well before the current 'urban age'.

III. Federalism and the Urban/Rural Divide

The urban/rural divide has proven to be of critical significance in contemporary politics. In some countries, urban voters tend to subscribe to a moderate neo-liberal political and economic agenda while rural voters are largely more supportive of agrarian reform, land redistribution, peasant and indigenous rights, and so on. In other countries, the spatial dimension of political ideologies or considerations of space and place—while often correlated with other factors such education, occupation, age, or mobility—have proven a key factor associated with support for, on the one hand, traditional, nationalist, and socially conservative ideological platforms (often enjoying larger support in rural areas) and, on the other hand, liberal, cosmopolitan, and socially progressive worldviews (often enjoying larger support in urban areas). In these polities, that pattern translates into greater support for nationalist-populist parties, leaders, and policies in rural areas, and greater support for universal values and social inclusiveness in urban areas.

In the 2016 US presidential election, for example, the percentage of vote for the Democrats in large metro areas was 67 per cent, while it was 52 per cent in small metro areas and 43 per cent in rural areas. In the South and interior West, the percentages were 54 per cent, 44 per cent, and 32 per cent, respectively. The urban/rural divide was even greater in the 2020 presidential elections. The Democrats' margin of victory in large metro areas increased compared to 2016; the margin of support

[43] See Saunders and Arban, chapter 2 in this volume.

[44] See *World Urbanization Prospects* (n 1); Hirschl, *City, State: Constitutionalism and the Megacity* (n 2) 1–9.

for the Republicans was the largest in rural areas, with mid-size metro areas or suburbs of big cities, small metro areas and deep suburbs, and mostly rural areas with small towns aligned accordingly. The data show that in nearly half of counties with less than 100 people per square mile, Joe Biden averaged about 30 per cent of the vote. In the 170 counties with more than 2,000 people per square mile, he averaged about 55 per cent of the vote. The divide was clearly evident within single states, including in Georgia, Pennsylvania, and Michigan. Similar patterns are evident in many other settings worldwide, whether federal[45] or unitary.[46] Even in Hungary, Poland, and Turkey—three of the most exhaustively studied examples of democratic backsliding in contemporary comparative constitutional accounts—the rural/urban divide is glaringly evident. In Hungary, an explicitly anti-Orbàn candidate representing the opposition Democratic Coalition Party won the October 2019 Budapest mayoral elections. Similarly, most support for the six-party opposition alliance unsuccessfully aiming to topple Orbàn in the 2022 general elections came from the urban intelligentsia in Budapest and in other major cities. Residents of Istanbul elected an anti-Erdoğan mayor in two separate elections, in defiant response to Erdoğan's warnings to his supporters that losing Istanbul would mean losing Turkey. And in Poland, Rafal Trzaskowski, the liberal mayor of Warsaw, made it to the second, winner-take-all round of the country's presidential election before narrowly losing to incumbent president Andrzej Duda—a leading figure associated with the populist right-wing Law and Justice party (PiS)—in what Polish media described as a 'cities against countryside' election.

However, despite the conclusive evidence of the significance of place in explaining levels of support for traditional, nationalist, or even authoritarian political platforms, federal constitutional theory has remained largely mum on the matter. To be sure, occasional exceptions exist. In addressing the rural/urban divide in the US, for example, a handful of legal scholars have suggested that a more decentralized, region-based notion of federalism may be required to diffuse the concentration of power in Washington.[47] Some political scientists who engage closely with constitutional design have proposed compulsory voting in an attempt to better reflect the median voter position,[48] while others advocate for proportional representation for both Congress and Senate elections as remedy for the systemic

[45] See, eg, Austria or Switzerland, where residents of Vienna or Zürich, respectively, consistently prefer parties, platforms, leaders, and worldviews to the left of the national or cantonal median voter. For a recent account of the political significance of the urban/rural divide in Canada, see David A. Armstrong II, Jack Lucas, and Zack Taylor, 'The Urban-Rural Divide in Canadian Federal Elections, 1896–2019' (2022) 55 *Canadian J Pol Sci* 84–106.

[46] See, eg, Israel, where Tel-Aviv is often referred to as '*Medinat Tel Aviv*' (Hebrew: 'the state of Tel Aviv'), referring to the city's cosmopolitan, liberal, and socially progressive character, in contrast with the rest of the country.

[47] See, eg, Yishai Blank and Issi Rosen-Zvi, 'Reviving Federal Regions' (2018) 70 *Stanford L Rev* 1895–993; David Fontana, 'Federal Decentralization' (2017) 104 *Virginia L Rev* 727–95.

[48] Jonathan Rodden, 'Geography and Gridlock in the United States' in Nathaniel Persily (ed), *Solutions to Political Polarization in America* (CUP 2015) 104–20.

anti-urban representation biases.[49] These exceptions notwithstanding, federal constitutional theory continues to be fixated with a traditional national/subnational unit matrix that blocks fresh thinking about emerging spatial challenges such as urban agglomeration and the urban/rural divide. Given the resurgence of place as socio-political cleavage, the common assumption that the state (or province, Länder, and the like) must be the constituent unit in federalism, and consequently in the design of electoral systems in federal polities, deserves to be revisited.[50]

Formal constitutional recognition of the urban/rural divide in national constitutions is an intuitive response to spatially anchored 'left behind' sentiments. Here too, the federal/unitary conceptual matrix proves less significant than the Global North/Global South division in explaining formal constitutional commitment to addressing the urban/rural divide. Some of the countries whose national constitution addresses that divide are federal while others are quasi-federal or unitary. However, the vast majority of them are in the Global South.

In several Global South constitutional orders, direct reference is made to the need to balance urban and rural interests. The 2015 Constitution of Ecuador, for example, establishes that '[p]ersons have the right to fully enjoy the city and its public spaces, on the basis of principles of sustainability, social justice, respect for different urban cultures and a balance between the urban and rural sectors': art 31. In establishing institutions of local government, it further states that '[t]he urban and rural population of the canton shall be proportionately represented on the council': art 253. It goes on to state that strengthening the development of organizations and networks of producers and consumers, along with those for the marketing and distribution of food stuffs, will be pursued 'so as to promote equity between rural and urban spaces': art 281.20. In neighbouring Bolivia, art 19.12 of the 2009 Constitution states:

> [T]he State, at all levels of the government, is responsible for promoting the development of housing for social benefit, using adequate financing systems, based on principles of solidarity and equity. These plans shall be directed preferentially to families with scarce resources, to disadvantaged groups and to rural areas.

In some Global South settings, most notably in Latin America, the 'rural' intersects with other constitutionally recognized categories, notably peasant and indigenous populations. For example, art 147.2 of the Bolivian Constitution further commits the state to 'proportional participation of the nations and rural native indigenous peoples shall be guaranteed in the election of members of the assembly'. Article

[49] Arend Lijphart, 'Polarization and Democratization' in Nathaniel Persily (ed), *Solutions to Political Polarization in America* (CUP 2015) 73–82.

[50] Yann Allard-Tremblay, 'Divide and Rule Better: On Subsidiarity, Legitimacy and the Epistemic Aim of Political Decision-Making' (2017) 34 *J Applied Philos* 696.

147.3 states that the law 'shall define the special districts of the rural native indigenous peoples, in which population density and geographical continuity shall not be considered as conditional criteria'. Article 126 of the Constitution of Panama[51] states that the law shall 'establish means of communication and transportation to link rural and indigenous communities with centres of storage, distribution and consumption'. Article 119 of the Constitution of Guatemala,[52] entitled 'Obligations of the State', commits the state to:

> actively promote programs of rural development which tend to increase and diversify the national production based on the principle of private property and of the protection of family patrimony. The peasant [campesino] and the artisan must be provided with technical and economic assistance.

Key international declarations such as the UN Declaration on the Rights of Indigenous Peoples[53] and the Declaration on the Rights of Peasants[54] further illustrate the frequent overlap in the formal recognition of the 'rural' with categories such as peasant and indigenous populations living in remote geographic and economic hinterlands.

Meanwhile, the Constitution of The Gambia[55] lists 'improvement in the quality of life in rural communities and redressing economic imbalances between rural and urban communities' among the country's economic objectives: art 215.3. Article 236 of the Constitution of Egypt 2014 expressly commits the state to 'develop and implement a plan for the comprehensive economic and urban development of border and underprivileged areas ... '. Article 36.2 of the Constitution of Ghana[56] commits the government to:

> undertaking even and balanced development of all regions and every part of each region of Ghana, and, in particular, improving the conditions of life in the rural areas, and generally, redressing any imbalance in development between the rural and the urban areas.

Likewise, Uganda's Constitution[57] states that '[t]he State shall take necessary measures to bring about balanced development of the different areas of Uganda and between the rural and urban areas': ch 12.

[51] Constitution of Panama 1972; rev 2004.
[52] Constitution of Guatemala 1985, rev 1993
[53] UNGA Res 61/295 (2 October 2007) UN Doc A/RES/61/295.
[54] United Nations Declaration on the Rights of Peasants and Other People Working in Rural Areas, UN Human Rights Council Res 39/12 (28 September 2018) UN DOC A/HRC/RES/39/12.
[55] Constitution of The Gambia 1996, rev 2018.
[56] Constitution of Ghana 1992, rev 1996.
[57] Constitution of Uganda 1972, rev 2017.

Several Asian countries make similarly ambitious constitutional commitments to address the urban/rural divide. Article 16 of the Constitution of Bangladesh,[58] for example, states that:

> the State shall adopt effective measures to bring about a radical transformation in the rural areas through the promotion of an agricultural revolution, the provision of rural electrification, the development of cottage and other industries, and the improvement of education, communications and public health, in those areas, so as progressively to remove the disparity in the standards of living between the urban and the rules areas.

Article 21 of the Constitution of the Philippines establishes that 'the State shall promote comprehensive rural development and agrarian reform'. Section 73 of the revised Constitution of Thailand 2017 states that:

> the State should provide measures or mechanisms to enable farmers to efficiently carry out agriculture which yields produce of high quantity and quality that is safe, low cost and competitive in the market, and should assist indigent farmers to have land for making a living through land reform or any other means.

According to the Constitution of Cambodia[59] 'the State shall promote economic development in all sectors and particularly in remote areas, especially in agriculture, handicrafts and industry, with attention to policies on water, electricity, roads and means of transportation, modem technology and credit systems': art 61. It also expressly commits the country to providing adequate conditions to women living in rural areas: for example arts 46 and 72. Similarly, art 61.3 of the Constitution of Vietnam[60] confirms that 'the State shall prioritize the educational development in mountainous and island areas, regions inhabited by ethnic minority people and regions encountering exceptional difficulties'. The Constitution of Turkey[61] commits to 'economic, social and cultural development, in particular the rapid, balanced and harmonious development of industry and agriculture throughout the country': art 166. And the Constitution of South Korea 1987 states that '[t]he State shall have the duty to foster regional economies to ensure the balanced development of all regions': art. 123.2.

In other instances, constitutional treatment of local government has taken into account the urban/rural divide. Constitutional reforms in India and Brazil, described above, are examples of this trend. In India, the 73rd and 74th constitutional

[58] Constitution of Bangladesh 1972, rev 2014.
[59] Constitution of Cambodia 1993, rev 2008.
[60] Constitution of Vietnam 1992, rev 2013.
[61] Constitution of Turkey 1982, rev 2017.

amendments were aimed at enhancing the constitutional autonomy of local government and articulated a vision of decentralized power and responsibility through the provision of constitutional status to urban centres. Interestingly, the Indian model distinguishes between rural settlements (addressed in the 73rd Amendment) and cities (addressed in the 74th Amendment), thereby formally recognizing the difference between, yet equality of, rural and urban areas. In practice, however, the long-standing reality of subnational control over cities and politically driven intergovernmental affairs have brought about mixed results.[62] Brazil's City Statute 2001, alongside arts 182 and 183 of the Constitution of Brazil 1988, address matters of urban development and self-governance. An array of additional constitutional provisions (eg arts 5, 43, 153, 184, and 187) further protect rural land, rural property and the rights of rural area dwellers, with art 194.2 establishing 'uniformity and equivalence of benefits and services for urban and rural populations'.

In short, as with the constitutional emancipation of cities, the federal/unitary distinction does not appear to be highly consequential when it comes to constitutional recognition of the urban/rural divide. Some national constitutions that address the urban/rural divide are federal while many others are quasi-federal or unitary. By contrast, as with the constitutional status of cities discussed earlier in this chapter, the North/South distinction appears quite significant in accounting for the constitutional attention devoted to the urban/rural divide.

IV. Conclusion

As extensive urbanization marches on, an ever-widening gap emerges between what is expected of a modern metropolis and what cities can actually deliver in the absence of adequate constitutional standing, representation, taxation powers, or robust policy-making authority. The coronavirus pandemic has accentuated the disparity between the tremendous challenges that ever more populous urban centres face and cities' limited independent capacity to provide services and support for their residents. Federal constitutional theory has thus far failed to address, or even acknowledge, the mounting urban challenge. With few exceptions, federal constitutional theory's spatial imagination continues to be limited to states, subnational units, and occasionally regions. In that conceptual universe, cities—home of the majority of humankind—seldom exist.

This omission may appear counter-intuitive, given federalism's favourable predisposition toward principles of subsidiarity, local government, and accommodation of place-based difference. However, historical inertia and established patterns of state dominance, constitutional rigidity, and lack of political incentives to

[62] Hirschl, *City, State: Constitutionalism and the Megacity* (n 2) 119–28.

empower cities converge to maintain the status quo. Furthermore, it may well be that because federal constitutional theory focuses almost exclusively on traditional territorial units, its ability to deal with new challenges such as urban agglomeration, the rise of megacities, and the re-emergence of the urban/rural divide will be hindered.

In this chapter, I have provided a comparative overview of city status in national constitutions worldwide, federal and otherwise. The exploration focused on two main dimensions: the constitutional (non)status of cities as a distinct and autonomous order of government, and the constitutional commitment to addressing the urban/rural divide. As this two-pronged comparative inquiry suggests, the North/South division appears much more consequential than the federal/unitary one in explaining constitutional renewal concerning city status. In stark contrast to most other areas of constitutional law, much of the innovative constitutional thinking concerning city governance and autonomy emanates from Asia, Latin America, and parts of Africa. The same holds true with respect to constitutional attention to the urban/rural divide. While most leading political theory and social science accounts of cities and urbanization have been written by scholars from the Global North, when it comes to actual constitutional innovation in those areas—whether related to the constitutional status of cities or to the urban/rural divide—the world beyond Europe and North America has taken the lead. To remain relevant in an ever more urbanized world, federal constitutional theory will not only have to take the urban challenge more seriously—it will have to set its global gaze southward.

PART II

CITIES AS NEGLECTED CONSTITUTIONAL UNITS OF ANALYSIS IN FEDERAL THEORY

5

The New Preemption

Placing Cities in American Federalism

*Richard Briffault**

I. Introduction

The last dozen years have witnessed heightened conflict between American states and cities. Cities depend on their states for their legal authority, and states have delegated considerable regulatory autonomy to their cities to deal with local public health, safety, and land use matters. But states and cities often have divergent priorities and concerns, and their governments are accountable to different constituencies. When there is disagreement between a state and a city, states typically have the authority to displace—or 'preempt'—city decisions.[1] As will be discussed further below, this is a matter of state jurisprudence, undisturbed by federal constitutional law. State preemption has long been a feature of state–local relations but preemption has sharpened in nature and broadened in scope since around 2010, due to the increasingly intensive partisan and ideological divide between many state governments and their cities.[2]

Many cities are actively pursuing progressive policy agendas in areas like workplace equity, environmental regulation, anti-discrimination, public health, and the treatment of immigrants. They have adopted local laws or policies that, *inter alia*, raise the minimum wage and require paid sick leave and family leave; limit single-use plastic bags; regulate hydraulic fracking; extend civil rights protections to LGBTQ people; regulate firearms; and minimize cooperation with federal immigration law enforcement.[3] However, while these cities have moved left, many of their states have veered right. Since the 2010 elections, more than half the states have had so-called 'Republican trifecta' governments, that is, state houses in which

* Joseph P Chamberlain Professor of Legislation, Columbia University School of Law.

[1] Richard Briffault and others *Cases and Materials on State and Local Government Law* (9th edn, West Academic P 2022) 482–553.

[2] Richard Briffault, Nestor M Davidson, and Laurie Reynolds, *The New Preemption Reader: Legislation, Cases and Commentary on the Leading Challenge in Today's State and Local Government Law* (West Academic P 2019) 11–14 (hereafter Briffault, Davidson, and Reynolds, *New Preemption Reader*).

[3] Richard Briffault, 'The Challenge of the New Preemption' (2018) 70 *Stan L Rev* 1995, 1999–2002 (hereafter Briffault, 'Challenge').

Richard Briffault, *The New Preemption* In: *Cities in Federal Constitutional Theory.* Edited by: Erika Arban, Oxford University Press. DOI: 10.1093/oso/9780192843272.003.0006

Republicans control the governorship and both houses of the legislature.[4] These states have pursued conservative political, economic, and social goals.[5] In so doing, they have not only rejected progressive policies at the state level but have moved aggressively to preempt city action.

This 'new preemption'[6] is less about replacing the often-criticized 'patchwork' of local laws on a subject with uniform statewide standards—a longstanding justification for preemption—and more about preventing any regulation, state or local, on that subject. Some preemptive measures are economic in focus, designed to prevent the imposition of employment, environmental, or consumer protection requirements on business. Many are ideological, blocking local regulation of firearms, expansion of anti-discrimination laws, protection of undocumented immigrants, or removal of monuments commemorating the Confederacy.[7] The COVID-19 pandemic prompted state measures curtailing local mask mandates or stay-at-home orders more restrictive than those of their states.[8]

In a particularly striking departure from traditional preemption laws, which simply nullified local measures, several states have enacted punitive preemption statutes that threaten local officials or local governments[9] with fines, civil liability, or the cut-off of state aid for adopting local laws subject to preemption.[10]

To be sure, not all contemporary state–local conflicts involve conservative states and progressive cities. Liberal states adopt measures that constrain conservative communities, or impose costs on the local fisc without regard to party or ideology. But the most salient form of this new preemption has consisted of Republican-dominated state governments pursuing a conservative economic, social, and cultural agenda by blocking progressive urban initiatives and curtailing city powers.[11]

The emergence of this new preemption brings out in bold relief several significant features of American federalism. First, it highlights the failure of federalism to recognize cities apart from their states. Although the Supreme Court often includes cities in the protection federalism affords against the federal government, it has provided little protection for cities from their states.

[4] ibid, 1997–98.

[5] Alexander Hertel-Fernandez, *State Capture: How Conservative Activists, Big Businesses and Wealthy Donors Reshaped the American States—and the Nation* (OUP 2019) 238–42 (hereafter Hertel-Fernandez, *State Capture*).

[6] Briffault, 'Challenge' (n 3); Briffault, Davidson, and Reynolds, *New Preemption Reader* (n 2).

[7] Briffault, Davidson, and Reynolds, *New Preemption Reader* (n 2) 11–13, 17–43.

[8] Kim Haddow and others, 'Preemption, Public Health, and Equity in the Time of COVID-19' (*ChangeLab Solutions*, 11 February 2021) <https://www.changelabsolutions.org/preemption-public-health-equity-time-covid-19> accessed 18 May 2021> (hereafter Haddow, 'COVID-19').

[9] For a further discussion of local government, see Saunders and Arban, chapter 2 in this volume.

[10] Briffault, Davidson, and Reynolds, *New Preemption Reader* (n 2) 13–14, 43–48.

[11] Katherine Levine Einstein and David M Glick, 'Cities in American Federalism: Evidence on State-Local Government Conflict from a Survey of Mayors (2017) 47 *Publius: J of Federalism* 599.

Second, this latest round of state–local conflicts provides new insight into a basic tension within the theory of federalism.[12] Federalism is a means of bringing together distinct self-governing political communities within a larger community to provide the component communities with greater security, broader markets, and effective governance of common problems while still preserving a significant measure of sovereignty for the member communities.[13] Federalism also advances the subsidiarity principle[14] by providing autonomy for units of government closer to the people.[15] These two theories of federalism are not necessarily at odds; indeed, American federalism's treatment of the states is consistent with both. But the new preemption shows how these theories can come into conflict and underscores how American federalism is ultimately rooted in community self-determination, with the states as the only relevant communities.

Third, the new preemption provides an opportunity to consider the role of subnational constitutions in recognizing and protecting cities. In the United States, all the states have constitutions of their own, and nearly all give some formal recognition to local governments. Through their 'home rule' provisions, most authorize some city law-making. To be sure, state constitutions typically are far more effective in delegating authority than in providing protection, but they do establish a constitutional foundation for city autonomy. State constitutional law also casts light on the place of cities in federalism theory. To the extent that state constitutions provide for a degree of 'intrastate federalism',[16] it is based more on the subsidiarity rather than the community self-determination model. If cities are to be recognized in federalism more generally, that is likely to follow the template of enhanced state constitutional home rule rather than the state-based federalism of American constitutional law.

Although this chapter focuses on cities in American federalism, it may be applicable to cities in federalism theory more broadly. To the extent that other federal systems, like the American, treat cities as something other than fundamental components of the federal union, this chapter suggests that cities are unlikely to obtain the hard federalism protections accorded to American states or their counterparts in other federal systems. But cities may be able to obtain softer but still significant subsidiarity-type protections by focusing on building up their place in the constitutions (or comparable foundational rules) of the subnational units that are hardwired into the federal structure.

[12] For a further discussion of the theory of federalism and especially its relation to cities, see Arban, chapter 1 in this volume.

[13] Daniel Weinstock, 'Cities and Federalism' in James E Fleming and Jacob T Levy (eds) *Federalism and Subsidiarity* (New York U P 2014) 260–66 (hereafter Weinstock, 'Cities and Federalism').

[14] For a more comprehensive treatment of the subsidiarity principle, see Cahill and O'Sullivan, chapter 3 in this volume.

[15] ibid.

[16] Rick Su, 'Intrastate Federalism' (2016) 19 *U Pa J Const L* 191.

This chapter proceeds as follows. Section II sketches the basic features of the new preemption and the challenge it poses to local autonomy. Section III turns to the place—or lack thereof—of cities in American constitutional law. Section IV analyses what the status of cities in constitutional law indicates about the theory of American federalism. Section V pivots to state constitutions, and suggests how state constitutional law could be the way to find a place for cities in American federalism. Section VI concludes.

II. The New Preemption: A Brief Overview

The new preemption has swept across a wide range of areas of local law-making. More than thirty states now restrict the authority of cities to regulate employment relations. They bar, *inter alia*, local minimum wage laws, paid family or sick leave requirements, local fair (or predictive) scheduling laws, and so-called 'ban-the-box' laws that restrict the ability of employers to inquire into the criminal records of prospective employees. Michigan's Local Government Labor Regulatory Limitation Act of 2015—known colloquially as the 'Death Star'—comprehensively bars local governments from adopting, enforcing, or administering local laws or policies concerning employee background checks, minimum wage, fringe benefits, paid or unpaid leave, work stoppages, fair scheduling, apprenticeships, or remedies for workplace disputes.[17]

States have barred local regulation of firearms, tobacco products, and pesticides; restricted local environmental measures, such as bans on non-reusable plastic bags and on hydraulic fracturing ('fracking'); prevented local nutrition and food policy actions, such as calorie counts and other menu labelling rules; and blocked municipal broadband and local regulation of aspects of the sharing economy, such as ride-sharing and home-sharing platforms. Although in some areas, like the minimum wage, there are state laws in place and preemption just prevents cities and counties from going further, in most others, the thrust of preemption is largely deregulatory, displacing local initiatives without adopting statewide rules.[18] Frequently, the state preemption measures simply track templates developed by the American Legislative Exchange Council ('ALEC'), an ideological non-profit organization consisting of business representatives and conservative state legislators, and funded largely by corporations and corporate foundations. Business and trade groups have also actively promoted state restrictions of local regulation. The rhetoric often justifies preemption as promoting uniform statewide labour, economic, or environmental rules and so reducing the costs of interlocal variation.[19] But in

[17] Briffault, Davidson, and Reynolds, *New Preemption Reader* (n 2) 18–20, 35–38.
[18] ibid, 27–35.
[19] Hertel-Fernandez, *State Capture* (n 5).

practice the new preemption's version of uniform regulation is often no regulation at all.

Some state preemption measures grow out of the cultural, demographic, or ideological divide between states and their cities. This can be seen in the ongoing conflicts over firearms regulation, the extension of anti-discrimination protections to LGBTQ people, and 'sanctuary' for undocumented aliens. Residents of urban areas often view these issues and react to the underlying concerns differently than rural or suburban voters and their legislative representatives. Rather than let local policies reflect these varying local preferences and values—so some have more extensive gun regulations and extend the scope of anti-discrimination law and others do not—preemption imposes the values of the state legislative majority on the cities that disagree with them. A particularly striking flash point has been the status of memorials honouring the Confederacy. As local protests prompted cities—often with Black or politically liberal populations—to take down the Confederate monuments on their streets or in their parks, several states responded with laws protecting the monuments and denying their cities the authority to move them—or even to cover them up.[20]

The COVID-19 pandemic sparked another round of ideological preemption. As stay-at-home orders, business closures, and masking got caught up in the intense partisan, ideological, and cultural crossfires of 2020, several states blocked local public health initiatives. Arizona's Governor prohibited local governments 'restricting persons from leaving home due to the COVID-19 public health emergency', and the Texas Attorney General sued local governments from imposing shutdowns and masking orders more restrictive than the state's. At least, those states adopted some COVID restrictions. The Governor of Iowa did not impose a statewide stay-at-home order but still told local officials they lacked authority to do so. Georgia's Governor sued the mayor of Atlanta when she adopted a mandatory masking rule. In Florida, the Governor ultimately permitted local masking orders but barred local governments from enforcing them or collecting fines for other COVID-related violations. The Governor of Nebraska announced he would bar any city that imposed a masking rule from receiving federal COVID-19 funds.[21]

Perhaps the most distinctive feature of the new preemption are its punitive measures. Instead of just nullifying inconsistent local acts—the traditional purpose of preemption—some states now punish local officials or local governments for supporting or seeking to enforce measures that are subject to preemption. This can include civil and sometimes criminal penalties and removal from office for local officials who implement or even simply propose or endorse certain preempted local laws. So, too, some states now penalize cities and counties that adopt preempted laws by cutting off state aid or exposing these localities to civil liability from hostile

[20] Briffault, Davidson, and Reynolds, *New Preemption Reader* (n 2) 12–13, 40–43.
[21] Haddow, 'COVID-19' (n 8).

interest groups. The most common areas for punitive preemption have been firearms and undocumented aliens ('sanctuary').[22] Florida provides that officials who commit 'knowing and willful violations' of the state's firearms preemption statute are subject to removal from office and are liable for civil fines of up to $5,000; moreover, those officials may not use public funds for their legal defence or to cover their fines.[23] Arizona subjects officials who violate firearms preemption to removal from office, and targets noncompliant local governments with liability for fines up to $50,000 for knowing and wilful violations.[24] Mississippi makes any 'elected county or municipal official under whose jurisdiction' a violation of firearms preemption has occurred civilly liable for up to $1,000, plus attorneys' fees and costs.[25] Oklahoma makes municipal officials civilly liable to any person whose rights protected by the state's firearms preemption law are violated by a local action.[26] Florida and Oklahoma also expose their cities to lawsuits from individuals and groups that claim their rights were violated by local firearms laws; damages in Florida can run up to $100,000 plus attorneys' fees.[27]

Texas has played a leading role in extending punitive preemption to sanctuary cities. The Lone Star state provides for the removal from office of any local official who 'adopt[s], enforce[s], or endorse[s] a [local] policy' that 'prohibits or materially limits the enforcement of immigration laws' and makes local governments liable for fines of up to $1,500 for a first violation and $25,500 for subsequent violations, with each day of a continuing violation treated as a separate violation.[28] Iowa provides for the cut-off of *all* state funds to any local government that 'intentionally' violates the state's requirement that local law enforcement agencies cooperate with federal immigration enforcement and prohibits local governments from adopting or enforcing policies that 'prohibit[] or discourage[] the enforcement of immigration laws'.[29] Tennessee provides that a local government entity that adopts or enacts 'a sanctuary policy' is ineligible for grants from the state department of economic and community development.[30]

The most aggressive punitive measure is surely Arizona's SB 1487,[31] which provides for the cut-off of state aid to localities for *any* local law the state Attorney General determines is preempted and which the local government then fails to promptly repeal. If the Attorney General concludes merely that the local measure '[m]ay violate' state law, the Attorney General must bring a special action in the

22 Briffault, Davidson, and Reynolds, *New Preemption Reader* (n 2) 43–51.
23 Fla Stat § 790.33(3)(c)(d),(e).
24 Ariz Rev Stat § 13-3108(I),(j).
25 Miss Code Ann § 45-9-53(5).
26 Okla Stat tit 21, § 1289.24(D).
27 Fla Stat § 790.33(f); Okla Stat tit 21, § 1289.24(D).
28 Texas Gov't Code Ann §§ 752.053,056(a)(b).
29 Iowa Code §§ 825.1–825.13.
30 Tenn Code § 7-68-103.
31 Ariz Rev Stat Ann § 41-194-01(A).

state Supreme Court to determine the issue. To contest the action and defend its law, the local government must 'post a bond equal to the amount of state shared revenue' it received in the preceding six months. As 'state shared revenue' constitutes roughly one-quarter of local revenues in Arizona, it will be virtually impossible for any local government to post the necessary bond. And no local government is likely to be able to withstand the coercive force of a complete cut-off of this shared revenue. The state Attorney General used SB 1487 to force Tucson to stop destroying firearms it had obtained through forfeitures or as unclaimed property, and to compel the town of Bisbee to drop its ban on single-use plastic bags. The Bisbee ruling demonstrates how punitive preemption laws can bludgeon a town into submission as Bisbee was forced to treat its law as preempted because it could not afford to litigate the issue and so didn't even receive a judicial hearing.[32]

III. The Place of Cities in the United States Constitutional Law

A. The *Hunter* doctrine and its limits

The United States Constitution does not recognize cities or any other local governments, and the United States Supreme Court has long treated all local governments, including cities, as essentially administrative arms of their states, no more protected from state regulation or displacement than the state's department of motor vehicles. The canonical statement of this vision of plenary state power over local governments came in the 1907 case of *Hunter v City of Pittsburgh*, which dealt with the merger of two Pennsylvania cities over the opposition of the residents of one of them:

> Municipal corporations are political subdivisions of the state, created as convenient agencies for exercising such of the governmental powers of the state as may be entrusted to them ... The number, nature, and duration of the powers conferred upon these corporations and the territory over which they shall be exercised rests in the absolute discretion of the state ... The state, therefore, at its pleasure, may modify and withdraw all such powers, may take without compensation such property ... expand or contract the territorial area, unite the whole or a part of it with another municipality, repeal the charter and destroy the corporation.[33]

In *Hunter*, the Court specifically rejected the argument that city residents have rights under the Contracts Clause or the Due Process Clause to have a specific city

[32] Briffault, Davidson, and Reynolds, *New Preemption Reader* (n 2) 86–93.
[33] 207 US 161, 178–79 (1907) (hereafter *Hunter*).

as their local government. Subsequently, the Court determined that local governments have no Equal Protection or Due Process rights against their states.[34]

The Supreme Court has not read cities entirely out of the constitution. First, *Hunter* itself draws a distinction between property a city holds in its governmental capacity and property it 'hold[s] … for the same purposes that property is held by private corporations or individuals'.[35] As to the latter, so-called 'proprietary' property, a city may assert federal constitutional arguments against its state. Although courts rarely find that municipal property is proprietary rather than governmental, *Hunter*'s caveat provides some support for scholarly arguments that a municipality's corporate status may offer a foundation for constitutional rights.[36]

Second, and more significantly, state laws changing city boundaries or stripping cities can be challenged as violating the constitutional rights of the individuals affected by these changes, not because the individual has a general right to a local government with certain boundaries and powers but because the state's action violates some other constitutional constraint. Thus, in *Gomillion v Lightfoot*,[37] the Supreme Court held that an Alabama law that redrew the boundaries of the city of Tuskegee to exclude most of its Black residents violated the equal protection and voting rights of the residents so excluded. *Gomillion* underscored that *Hunter* did not give states a constitutional blank check 'to manipulate in every conceivable way, for every conceivable purpose, the affairs of its municipal corporations'.[38]

Similarly, in a case involving a Washington state law that denied local school boards the authority to require the busing of children to promote desegregation but otherwise left intact the school boards' preexisting powers with respect to pupil transportation, the Court concluded that this unusual treatment of local power evinced unconstitutional racial discrimination.[39] Again, in *Romer v Evans*,[40] the Court found that Colorado's sweeping displacement of municipal gay rights' protections was an unconstitutional treatment of the people who would have benefited from the local ordinances.

In both *Washington* and *Romer*, the Court assumed that the state had broad authority as a matter of federal constitutional law to constrain or veto local decisions. The constitutional infirmity of the laws in those cases resulted from the particular mix of state actions: The state's delegation of some powers to localities combined with the targeted withdrawal of others unconstitutionally burdened individual (not local government) rights. Local governments may not enjoy any

[34] *Trenton v New Jersey*, 262 US 182 (1923); *Williams v Mayor & City Council of Baltimore*, 289 US 36 (1933).

[35] *Hunter* (n 33) 179.

[36] Yishai Blank, 'City Speech' (2019) 54 *Harv CR-CL L Rev* 365, 434–45 (hereafter Blank, 'City Speech').

[37] 364 US 339 (1960) (hereafter *Gomillion*).

[38] ibid, 344.

[39] *Washington v Seattle Sch Dist No 1*, 458 US 457 (1982) (hereafter *Washington*).

[40] *Romer v Evans*, 517 US 620 (1996) (hereafter *Romer*).

federal constitutional protection for their law-making authority but a state may not alter or abolish a local power in a manner that supports an inference that it intends to violate constitutionally protected individual rights.

Third, the Court has occasionally recognized the authority of Congress to expand the power of local governments relative to their states. In *Lawrence County v Lead-Deadwood School District,* the Court held that the federal Payment in Lieu of Taxes ('PILOT') Act—which provides for federal payments to local governments to offset the property tax loss resulting from the presence of tax-exempt federal properties in their jurisdiction, and gives those localities broad discretion in the use of the PILOTs—supersedes state laws that more tightly restrict local use of the PILOTs.[41] So, too, the Supreme Court effectively concluded that the Federal Power Commission's license of a municipal power project enabled the municipality to use eminent domain to take state land for the project notwithstanding a state law that denied municipalities the power to condemn state land without a specific state grant of authority.[42] Like the individual rights cases, these decisions are more about the power of the federal government under the Supremacy Clause rather than a foundation for any constitutional rights for cities.

Although the Supreme Court has not directly applied *Hunter* to a state–local conflict since the 1930s, two 21st-century cases illustrate the doctrine's continuing power. In 2004, in *Nixon v Missouri Municipal League*,[43] the Supreme Court considered whether a federal law preempting state laws 'prohibiting the ability of any entity' to provide telecommunication services barred a state from prohibiting its local governments from offering such services. Relying on the *Hunter* principle that as a matter of federalism local governments are simply 'convenient agencies for exercising such of the governmental powers of the State as may be entrusted to them in its absolute discretion'[44] the Court concluded 'any entity' should be read narrowly to exclude local governments. *Ysursa v Pocatello Education Association*,[45] decided in 2009, addressed a First Amendment suit against an Idaho law that permitted public employees to elect to have a portion of their wages deducted by their employer to pay union dues but prohibited the use of payroll deductions for use by unions for political activities. The unions accepted the rule for state employees but challenged the state's imposition of the ban on local governments. Although such state interference in the inner workings of a private corporation would raise a serious First Amendment question, the Court, in an opinion by Chief Justice Roberts, found the analogy to private corporations 'misguided'. 'A private corporation enjoys constitutional protections' but a locality, in classic *Hunter* language, is 'a subordinate unit of government created by the State to carry out delegated governmental

41 *Lawrence County v Lead-Deadwood Sch Dist No 40-1*, 469 US 256 (1985).
42 *City of Tacoma v Taxpayers of Tacoma*, 357 US 320 (1958).
43 541 US 125 (2004) (hereafter *Nixon*).
44 ibid, 140.
45 555 US 353 (2009) (hereafter *Ysursa*).

functions.... "It has no privileges or immunities under the federal constitution which it may invoke in opposition to the will of its creator".[46]

B. The federal constitution and the new preemption

Litigation arising out of the new preemption confirms the very limited role the federal constitution plays in state–local disputes. Four brief examples should suffice.

In *Lewis v Governor of Alabama*,[47] the Eleventh Circuit Court of Appeals rejected the argument that Alabama's preemption of local minimum wage increases, which nullified an ordinance that had just been adopted by the City of Birmingham, violated the Equal Protection Clause. Tracking *Gomillion* and especially the Washington school board case, the city emphasized that the state law transferred control over the minimum wage from a Black-majority city council to the white-majority state legislature and that undoing the minimum wage increase disproportionately burdened Birmingham's Black workers. The Court, however, determined that minimum wage laws 'were neutral economic regulations'[48] that affected both white and Black workers, and so fell within the state's traditional powers to set the boundaries of local regulation.

In a second Alabama versus Birmingham dispute, the Supreme Court of Alabama also relied on *Hunter* and distinguished *Gomillion*. The Alabama Memorial Preservation Act provides that certain monuments located on public property may not be 'altered' or 'disturbed'. The City of Birmingham placed a plywood screen around the Confederate Soldiers and Sailors Monument located in a city park. It defended its action by contending that the monument was 'forcing the City to speak' a message it did not wish to convey in violation of the city's First Amendment right to free speech. The state Supreme Court dismissed that claim out of hand. Repeatedly citing and quoting *Hunter* and *Ysursa*, the Court 'rejected any notion that a subdivision of the state has any "privileges or immunities under the federal constitution which it may invoke in opposition to the will of its creator"'.[49]

Tennessee v Federal Communications Commission[50] involved the latest round in the state–local struggle over telecommunications. North Carolina and Tennessee had authorized their municipalities to provide broadband services to their residents but barred them from extending their services to underserved nearby areas. The Federal Communications Commission found that federal law preempted the states, distinguishing *Nixon* in part because the states had actually authorized the municipalities to provide telecommunication services. The Court of Appeals

46 ibid, 363–64 (quoting Williams v Mayor of Baltimore, 289 US 36, 409 (1933)).
47 896 F.3d 1282 (11th Cir 2018).
48 ibid, 1298.
49 *Alabama v City of Birmingham*, 299 So.3d 220 (Ala 2019).
50 832 F.3d 597 (6th Cir 2016).

rejected that distinction. In so doing, the Court explicitly invoked the *Hunter* model of municipalities as 'nothing more than th[e] state's "convenient agencies"'. The Court also dismissed as 'hardly relevant' to the issue of federal power to affect the state–local relationship the fact that one of the restricted communities, Chattanooga, Tennessee, was a home rule municipality.[51]

One new preemption case did give local interests a partial victory. Texas's sanctuary city preemption law provided for the removal from office of local officials who 'endorse' sanctuary policies. A federal district court held that the endorsement ban violated the First Amendment rights of local officials; the Court of Appeals in *City of El Cenizo v Texas* affirmed the decision, but narrowed its holding to protect only elected officials, leaving open the question of whether the state could sanction other local public employees for pro-sanctuary speech.[52] Moreover, the Court rejected arguments that federal immigration law preempted the state law or that federal constitutional doctrine barring the federal government from 'commandeering' states and local governments to carry out federal programs applied to bar a state from commandeering a local government to serve that federal program.[53]

Taken together the new preemption cases confirm the lack of federal constitutional status for local governments. Even arguments premised on two of the theories for limiting state power that have been recognized by the Supreme Court—anti-discrimination and federal supremacy—fell short given the high standards set for them by the courts. The First Amendment provides some protection for local officials but—so far—not for local governments.

IV. The City and Theories of Federalism

A. Two theories of federalism

Daniel Weinstock has proposed that there are 'two ways in which federal arrangements can be justified'—'self-determination' and 'subsidiarity'.[54] By 'self-determination' he means that distinct political entities ought to be able to 'exercise some meaningful control over their affairs while also enjoying the benefits that come from being part of a larger political entity'.[55] 'Subsidiarity' is a principle that 'regulates authority within a political order, directing that powers or tasks should rest within the lower-level sub-units of that order unless allocating them to a higher level central unit would ensure comparative efficiency or effectiveness in achieving them'.[56]

51 ibid, 611–14.
52 890 F.3d 164, 182–85 (5th Cir 2018).
53 ibid, 176–81, 191–92.
54 Weinstock, 'Cities and Federalism' (n 13).
55 ibid, 262.
56 ibid, 261.

Both self-determination and subsidiarity play a role in American federalism. The United States is a union of self-determining states within the larger United States. The United States came together as a union of separate states to obtain the benefits of greater security, an internal common market, and more effective governance, while also preserving meaningful autonomy for the states. The United States government is constructed out of the states,[57] and the states enjoy constitutional guarantees of their existence and law-making authority. The Constitution repeatedly refers to the states and assumes that they will have a central role in governance. A commitment to the continuing existence and governing role of the states was part of the intent of the Framers and the original public meaning of the Constitution. In the words of Justice Anthony Kennedy:

> the Framers split the atom of sovereignty. It was the genius of their idea that our citizens would have two political capacities, one state and one federal, each protected from incursion by the other. The resulting Constitution created a legal system unprecedented in form and design, establishing two orders of government, each with its own direct relationship, its own privity, its own set of mutual rights and obligations to the people who sustain it and are governed by it.[58]

But there is another strand to the modern jurisprudence of 'our federalism'[59]—an emphasis on the role of federalism in enhancing participation, accountability, efficiency, and protection from tyranny that is captured by the concept of subsidiarity. As put most crisply and canonically by Justice Sandra Day O'Connor in *Gregory v Ashcroft*, federalism 'assures a decentralized government that will be more sensitive to the diverse needs of a heterogeneous society; it increases opportunity for citizen involvement in democratic processes; it allows for more innovation and experimentation in government; and it makes government more responsive by putting the States in competition for a mobile citizenry'. And, she added, '[p]erhaps the principal benefit of the federalist system is a check on abuses of government power'.[60]

The theories of federalism as a means of holding distinct self-governing communities together in a larger political entity and as a design for a decentralized, participatory, and more accountable government are not at odds. Far from it. The

[57] However, significant parts of the United States are not in any state. Daniel Immerwahr, *How to Hide an Empire: A History of the Greater United States* (Farrar, Straus & Giroux 2019). Puerto Rico, the US Virgin Islands, Guam, and American Samoa are part of the United States but are not states or part of any state. The only non-state jurisdiction that plays any role in the governance of the United States is the District of Columbia, which is also the only one that is part of the continental United States. The District has three Electoral College votes to cast during the election of a President. However, like the other non-state jurisdictions, the District has no voting representation in Congress.

[58] *US Term Limits, Inc v Thornton*, 514 US 779, 838 (1995) (Kennedy J, concurring).

[59] *Younger v Harris*, 401 US 37, 44 (1971).

[60] *Gregory v Ashcroft*, 501 US 452, 458 (1991).

Court often couples the two together. Justice O'Connor's paean to federalism's subsidiarity values followed immediately on her statement that 'our Constitution establishes a system of dual sovereignty between the States and the Federal Government'.[61] The Court repeatedly invokes subsidiarity when it determines that federalism requires narrowing or invalidating an act of Congress. In *Gregory*, the Court urged that '[t]his federalist structure of joint sovereigns preserves to the people numerous advantages',[62] which Justice O'Connor went on to list. In *Shelby County v Holder*, in invalidating a key provision of the federal Voting Rights Act, the Court explained that the 'allocation of powers' between the federal government and the states and the resulting 'federal balance "is not just an end in itself: Rather, federalism secures to citizens the liberties that derive from the diffusion of sovereign power"'.[63] In *Murphy v National Collegiate Athletic Association*, which applied the 'anti-commandeering' doctrine, which bars Congress from commanding the states to enact a law or enforce a federal regulation, the Court moved quickly from asserting that the doctrine 'is simply the expression of a fundamental structural decision incorporated into the Constitution' to create a federal system to invoking the normative reasons for anti-commandeering and federalism more generally as part of:

> the Constitution's structural protections of liberty ... The Constitution does not protect the sovereignty of States for the benefit of the States or state governments as abstract political entities ... To the contrary, the Constitution divides authority between federal and state governments for the protection of individuals ... [A] healthy balance of power between the States and the Federal Government [reduces] the risk of tyranny and abuse from either front.[64]

In short, federalism is not simply a matter of combining political communities; it advances decentralized, participatory, and responsive governance.

B. Placing cities in the theories of American federalism

1. Cities and states compared

Self-determination and subsidiarity theories are mutually reinforcing and two sides of the same coin when the issue is the scope of powers of the national government vis-à-vis the states, but the theories diverge when it comes to local governments and state–local conflicts. Local governments are not communities that

[61] ibid, 457.
[62] ibid, 458.
[63] *Shelby County v Holder*, 570 US 529, 543 (2013) (quoting and citing earlier cases).
[64] *Murphy v National Collegiate Athletic Association*, 138 S.Ct 1461, 1475, 1477 (2018) (citations omitted).

compose the union. They are not used to structure Congress. They have no role in selecting the Electoral College that elects the president, or in the constitutional amendment process. The Constitution does not guarantee their existence or territorial integrity, nor are any powers reserved to them. Local governments are not even mentioned in the Constitution at all.

Yet, the subsidiarity values called on to justify federalism—sensitivity to the diverse needs of a heterogeneous society; increased opportunity for citizen involvement in democratic processes, and for governmental innovation and experimentation; governmental responsiveness that results from competition for a mobile citizenry—are at least as strongly advanced by local governments as they are by the states. Cities are smaller than their states and there many more of them. It is easier for people to participate in city government, to get new city programs enacted that respond to distinct local preferences and concerns, and to vote with their feet by moving from one locality to another when dissatisfied with local policies or actions. From a subsidiarity perspective, if you like states you should love cities.

2. Decisions including cities in federalism

The Court's federalism decisions do reflect an awareness of the important role local governments play in advancing the subsidiarity theory of federalism. Many of the Court's leading federalism cases involve local governments. *Printz v United States*,[65] which extended the anti-commandeering doctrine from legislative to enforcement actions, was a case brought by county officials. The Court narrowed the scope of Congress's power to enforce the Fourteenth Amendment against the states in *City of Boerne v Flores*, which involved a Texas city's zoning.[66] Although the rationale of *Shelby County v Holder*'s invalidation of s 4 of the Voting Rights Act derived from the 'equal sovereignty' of the states, the case was about—as the caption indicates—the voting laws of an Alabama county.

The Court also frequently equates federalism with local self-governance and accountability to local electorates. Thus, the Court conflated state and local when in *Bond v United States* it invoked, but slightly modified, Justice O'Connor's *Gregory v Ashcroft* opinion, observing:

> The federal structure allows *local policies* more 'sensitive to the diverse needs of a heterogeneous society,' permits 'innovation and experimentation,' enables greater citizen 'involvement in democratic processes,' and makes government 'more responsive by putting States in competition for a mobile citizenry.[67]

65 521 US 898 (1997).
66 521 US 507 (1997).
67 564 US 211, 221 (2011) (emphasis added).

Outside the context of federalism disputes, the Court has acknowledged the value of local self-government and its vital place in the American political setting, albeit as a recognition of state decisions to empower local governments not as basis for granting local governments federal constitutional protection. In *Avery v Midland County*, the Court extended the one person, one vote doctrine from state legislatures to city councils and county commissions. It invalidated a state law that had provided for a different representative scheme because 'institutions of local government have always been a major aspect of our system, and their responsible and responsive operation is today of increasing importance to the quality of life of more and more of our citizens'.[68] As a result, the rule of population equality for the election of state representatives also applies to those local governments. The Court's major public education decisions—*San Antonio Independent School District v Rodriguez*[69] and *Milliken v Bradley*[70]—also relied heavily on the value of local autonomy in rebuffing Equal Protection arguments that would have, respectively, required a state to increase its share of the funding of public schools or led to a more regional governance structure for schools in the Detroit metropolitan area. *Rodriguez* stressed that significant local financial responsibility—notwithstanding the great disparities in local fiscal capacities and concomitant interlocal differences in spending—'permits and encourages a large measure of local participation and control of each district's schools at the local level'. Critical to local control 'is the opportunity it offers for participation in the local [decision-making] process ... Each locality is free to tailor programs to local needs. Pluralism also affords some opportunity for experimentation, innovation and a healthy competition for educational excellence.'[71] In other words, local control advances the subsidiarity value of federalism.

So, too, in *Milliken*, the Court overturned a local court order calling for the creation of a regional busing program, notwithstanding the lower court's finding that no other alternative would achieve school desegregation. The Court determined that the regional remedy threatened 'local control over the operation of schools; local autonomy has long been thought essential both to the maintenance of community concern and support for public schools and to the quality of the educational process'. Although school district boundaries were the product of state government decisions, the Court rejected the lower court's finding that 'school district lines are no more than arbitrary lines on a map drawn "for political convenience" ... [T]he notion that school district lines may be casually ignored or treated as a mere administrative convenience is contrary to the history of public education in our country.'[72] These celebrations of local autonomy were, however,

68 390 US 474, 481 (1968) (hereafter *Avery*).
69 411 US 1 (1973) (hereafter *Rodriguez*).
70 418 US 717 (1974) (hereafter *Milliken*).
71 *Rodriguez* (n 69) 49–50.
72 *Milliken* (n 70) 741.

entirely consistent with state-focused federalism. They occurred in settings in which the local government was exercising state-granted powers, and there was no state–local conflict. Localism was used to justify the state's decision and as a basis for rejecting an individual rights claim for a different arrangement. So, too, in the federalism cases in which the Court blurred the state and the local, there was no disagreement between state law and local interests. Only in *Avery* did the Court look to the practice of local self-government to invalidate a state law, and that was at the behest of an individual rights claim and not a claim by the local government itself. *Avery* is important because it recognizes local government as a distinct and significant level of government within the American constitutional order. Yet *Avery* rooted local autonomy not just in longstanding practice and contemporary policy-making significance but also in the decisions of the 'States [which] universally leave much policy and [decision-making] to their governmental subdivisions'. Local governments are elected, and thus subject to one person, one vote, because 'in providing for the governments of their cities, counties, towns, and districts, the States characteristically provide for representative government'.[73] Although *Avery* accorded cities and counties some of the dignity of governments, they enjoy that status because of the decisions of the states, and so still remain subordinate governmental *subdivisions* of their states.

3. Decisions excluding cities from federalism

In only a handful of doctrinal settings has the Court addressed the separation of cities and other local governments from their states, and it has consistently done so to the disadvantage of local governments. Thus, the Court has held that the Eleventh Amendment's sovereign immunity principle, which precludes Congress from authorizing suits against a state for money damages without the state's consent, generally does not protect cities, counties, and other local governments.[74] Similarly, although states are immune from suit under the federal civil rights law, 42 USC § 1983, cities and other local governments can be sued.[75] As a matter of federalism-influenced statutory interpretation, the Sherman Antitrust Act does not apply to actions taken by a state,[76] but the 'state action' exemption protects a local government only if it can show its regulation was adopted pursuant to 'a clearly articulated and affirmatively expressed … state policy'.[77] The more the local policy reflects an autonomous local decision, the more the locality opens itself up to potential antitrust liability. These cases recognize the de facto fiscal and

[73] *Avery* (n 68) 481.
[74] *Northern Ins Co of NY v Chatham Co*, 547 US 189 (2006); *Mt Healthy City School Dist v Doyle*, 429 US 274 (1977); *Lincoln Co v Luning*, 133 US 529 (1890).
[75] Compare *Will v Michigan Dept of State Police*, 491 US 58 (1989) (state not a person under § 1983) and *Monell v New York City Dept of Social Services*, 436 US 658 (1978) (city a person under § 1983).
[76] *Parker v Brown*, 317 US 341 (1943).
[77] *Community Communications Co v City of Boulder*, 455 US 40, 52 (1982).

decision-making independence of local governments from their states, but that operational separateness from the states is the rationale for denying, not granting, local governments the protections of federalism.

The Court's view of the constitutional status of local governments is perhaps best seen in *Reynolds v Sims*,[78] the case in which the Court applied the one person, one vote doctrine to state legislatures, and considered but emphatically rejected the argument that one house of a state legislature could be based on the equal representation of counties, much as each state gets equal representation in one house of the United States Congress:

> The system of representation in the two Houses of the Federal Congress is one ingrained in our Constitution, as part of the law of the land. It is one conceived out of compromise and concession indispensable to the establishment of our federal republic. Arising from unique historical circumstances, it is based on the consideration that in establishing our type of federalism a group of formerly independent States bound themselves together under one national government ... at the heart of our constitutional system remains the concept of separate and distinct governmental entities which have delegated some, but not all, of their formerly held powers to the single national government ...
>
> Political subdivisions of States—counties, cities, or whatever—never were and never have been considered as sovereign entities. Rather, they have been traditionally regarded as subordinate governmental instrumentalities created by the State to assist in the carrying out of state governmental functions ... The relationship of the States to the Federal Government could hardly be less analogous.[79]

In short, although the Supreme Court has frequently recognized the distinct position of local governments and their quasi-independence-in-fact from their states, and has turned to localist values in justifying many of its federalism decisions, federalism still remains a doctrine about the states as distinct self-governing components of the federal union. When the community self-determination and subsidiarity theories of federalism diverge, self-determination prevails and cities lose.

C. Making a new place for cities in federal constitutional law

The *Hunter* doctrine has been criticized by scholars as failing to account for the crucial importance cities and other local governments today provide as key service providers, public policy innovators, centres of public political engagement, and advocates for and representatives of diverse populations of minorities and new

[78] 377 US 533 (1964).
[79] ibid, 574–75.

Americans.[80] That criticism has grown sharper as the state–local tensions reflected in and reinforced by the new preemption have grown.

Some scholars have argued that after *Gomillion*, *Hunter* is not an absolute bar to cities' constitutional claims and may be cabined to the specific Contracts, Due Process, and Equal Protection arguments raised in the early 20th-century *Hunter* cases. They have urged that cities may have constitutionally protected free speech rights against their states.[81] *Ysursa* would appear to be a barrier to city First Amendment rights,[82] but even if cities could make a speech claim that would do little to limit the ability of states to preempt local policy-making. It could be argued that the Ninth and Tenth Amendments' protections of unenumerated rights that are 'retained by the people' or 'reserved . . . to the people' include a right to local self-government, or that the First Amendment's protection of 'the right of the people peaceably to assemble' was intended to protect local governments.[83] Although the original Bill of Rights might have only protected these rights against the federal government, arguably the Fourteenth Amendment incorporates them against the states. That would require a finding that there is a right to local self-government protected by the Due Process Clause, which would be in tension with *Hunter*. This position was advanced by scholars and jurists more than a century ago[84] and is consistent with evidence that some colonial-era American local governments exercised broad powers and were relatively independent from colonial governments,[85] but it has long been far outside the mainstream of American jurisprudence.[86] Even if a right to local self-government were recognized as a matter of federal constitutional law, that would still leave open the questions of the boundaries and powers of any specific local government, which has long been a matter of state law, subject to *Gomillion*-type evidence of racial discrimination. Absent a claim that the state's action violates individual rights, federal courts would likely be thrown back on state law. Indeed, as the next part of this chapter suggests, state law—specifically state constitutional law—may be the better place for grounding local constitutional rights.

80 Kathleen S Morris, 'The Case for Local Constitutional Enforcement' (2012) 47 *Harv CR-CL L Rev* 1; Blank, 'City Speech' (n 36).

81 Blank, 'City Speech' (n 36); Matthew A De Stasio, 'A Municipal Speech Claim Against Body Camera Video Restrictions' (2018) 166 *U Pa L Rev* 961; Josh Bendor, 'Municipal Constitutional Rights: A New Approach' (2013) 31 *Yale L & Pol'y Rev* 389, 425–26

82 *Ysursa* (n 45).

83 See Nikolas Bowie, The Constitutional Right of Self-Government (2021) 130 *Yale LJ* 1652.

84 *People ex rel Le Roy v Hurlbut*, 24 Mich. 44, 65–66 (1871); Amasa M Eaton, 'The Right to Local Self-Government' (1900) 13 *Harv L Rev* 638.

85 Hendrik Hartog, *Public Property and Private Power: The Corporation of the City of New York in American Law, 1730–1870* (Cornell U P 1983); James E Herget, 'The Missing Power of Local Governments: A Divergence Between Text and Practice in Our Early State Constitutions' (1976) 62 *Va L Rev* 999.

86 Howard Lee McBain, 'The Doctrine of an Inherent Right of Local Self-Government' (1916) 16 *Colum L Rev* 190.

V. Home Rule as State Constitutional Federalism

The vast majority of states have embedded a commitment to local home rule for at least some of their cities in their constitutions.[87] State constitutional home rule was first adopted in the late 19th century when cities were taking on new responsibilities in response to the multiple challenges resulting from industrialization, urbanization, and large-scale immigration but were limited by doctrines emphasizing local legal incapacity. The primary purpose and principal effect of home rule was to permit cities to adopt local laws to address local problems and conditions without having to wait for specific or express state authority.[88] '[H]ome rule made concrete, and legally salient, the notion that many basic police power functions—including the protection of health, safety, and general welfare—were well within the competence of, and even perhaps best effectuated by, municipal governments.'[89]

State constitutions contain other provisions that provide cities and other local governments with a measure of protection from their states. Special act bans limit the ability of state legislatures to target individual localities for the denial or grant of powers.[90] Special commission bans in a few states place some constraints on the ability of the legislature to transfer municipal functions out of local control.[91] Some state constitutions regulate the ability of the legislature to impose unfunded mandates on local governments.[92] Like home rule itself, these measures often fall short of providing effective protection for cities from state interference. But they are a starting point that can be a basis for further strengthening local government. More importantly, they reflect a determination by the vast majority of states that cities are entitled to constitutional recognition and the effects of past political efforts to make that recognition a reality.

Efforts to strengthen the constitutional status of cities within the states are ongoing. The National League of Cities ('NLC') just adopted a new set of Principles of Home Rule for the Twenty-first Century, which presents concrete proposals for limiting preemption and providing courts with standards for reviewing the constitutionality of preemptive actions.[93] It is too soon to tell what the effect of the NLC Principles will be. However, as some of the specifics were derived from rules or doctrines that have already been adopted by some state courts there is some hope that other state courts may be influenced by the NLC Principles.[94]

87 Briffault and others (n 1) 408–13.
88 ibid
89 Lynn A Baker and Daniel A Rodriguez, 'Constitutional Home Rule and Judicial Scrutiny' (2009) 86 *Denv U L Rev* 1337, 1354.
90 Briffault and others (n 1) 365–82.
91 ibid, 358–65.
92 ibid, 382–90.
93 National League of Cities, *Principles of Home Rule for the 21st Century* (National League of Cities, 2020).
94 ibid, 53–61

If home rule protections advance within state constitutional law, that will be an achievement of the subsidiarity rather than the community self-determination theory of federalism. Unlike the states within the United States, cities are not the structural building blocks of their states, and although some cities predated their states, states were not created by the coming together of their cities. States create their cities and determine their boundaries, either by specific legislative acts or pursuant to general enabling legislation. Indeed, new cities continue to be incorporated, some annex new territory, others lose territory or dissolve.[95] Although some cities are distinct communities with distinct characteristics, others are components of larger urban conurbations. Cities are not formally represented in the structure of state governments, and not formally involved in the state constitutional amendment process. Home rule and allied protections for cities and other local governments are based not so much on a commitment to self-determination for pre-existing political communities as on a determination that governance would be improved and democratic values of participation, responsiveness, and accountability enhanced if certain government functions are handled at the local level.

Moreover, it is appropriate that intrastate federalism be rooted in the subsidiarity rather than the community self-determination theory. Subsidiarity provides for the devolution of power to the lowest level of government capable of wielding it effectively and efficiently. But that level may change with new forms of economic activity, evolving housing patterns, transportation and energy needs, and environmental and equity concerns. Some services might be best performed at the neighbourhood level, others at the regional level, and that could change over time. New governmental structures might be needed such as the two-tier city-county structure in Miami-Dade County, Florida[96] or the tax-base sharing arrangement in the Twin Cities area of Minnesota,[97] and these, in turn, may be need to be revised over time. A community self-determination theory of federalism requires entities that are determinate, distinctive, and relatively longstanding—like our 'indestructible states'. It is unclear whether given their more fluid, evolving, and shape-shifting nature urban governance arrangements constitute the kinds of political entities that are consistent with the community self-determination model of federalism. But they fit easily within a subsidiarity-based theory of federalism.

VI. Conclusion

The state–local conflicts exemplified by the new preemption provide an opportunity for a deeper understanding of American federalism as well as an occasion to

[95] Briffault and others (n 1) 285–350.
[96] ibid, 700–704.
[97] ibid, 636–42.

reflect on the kind of federalism that could support cities. Although the Supreme Court's federalism cases often sound in the language of subsidiarity, the Court's treatment of cities in cases of city-state conflict indicate that American federalism is fundamentally rooted in a commitment to the fifty states as unique communities guaranteed a significant degree of self-government and a distinctive place in the American constitutional order. As a matter of American federalism, cities are units of their states and nothing more.

If cities are to find a more secure place in American federalism, it will most likely be through state home rule jurisprudence. State constitutions address local governments in their constitutional texts and through their constitutional histories, and their provisions instantiate at least a partial commitment to the subsidiarity principle. State law also has the potential for flexibility in the state–local relationship that subsidiarity requires.

This analysis may be relevant for other federal systems, particularly those, like the American, that provide relatively strong constitutional protection for the constituent units that are hard-wired into the federal structure because of the unique legal status of those units, but do little or nothing for other communities. These systems may deploy the rhetoric of subsidiarity, but that principle may extend only to the component states or state-like entities. Given the difficulties of adding cities to national constitutions, cities might be better off looking for alternative legal fora—such as subnational constitutions—and the admittedly softer subsidiarity-type protections of something like American-style home rule.

To be sure, the American experience also indicates the possible limits of that strategy. The new preemption demonstrates how home rule can be overborne by the ideological, cultural, and partisan politics of the moment. The challenge for cities is to persuade state decision-makers that local autonomy is itself a substantive value the states ought to respect. This will require a political commitment to a value not predictably tied to a specific substantive policy, party, or interest group. In this era of intense political and ideological polarization, that may be a lot to ask.

6
Constitutional Theory, Federalism, and Cities

*Hoi L Kong**

Around the world, populations, wealth, and work are concentrated in cities. Because city governments exercise their powers within constitutional frameworks, one would think that constitutional theorists would focus significant attention on cities. Yet as Ran Hirschl has noted, this is not the case.[1] The present collection fills this gap in the constitutional theory literature, but it does so in a specific way. Its focus is on cities in *federal* constitutional theory.

The qualifier is significant. Constitutional theorists can examine cities through lenses other than federalism. For instance, in jurisdictions where cities exercise authority that is delegated to them by other orders of government, constitutional theorists could apply to city powers constitutional theories relating to the scope and limits of public authority.[2] One could also adopt a rights-based framing and ask whether theories of specific constitutional rights need to be adjusted to the particular context of urban life. For instance, constitutional theorists could query whether city streets, as traditional loci of protest and debate, should be accorded special status within freedom of expression theory and doctrine.[3] And for cities that are independent states, one could examine how constitutional theories of sovereignty and interpretation—developed in the context of nation-states—apply to city-states.[4]

* The Rt. Hon. Beverley McLachlin, P.C., UBC Professor in Constitutional Law. I thank Alex Parkinson and Adrian Pel for excellent research assistance and Austin Horn for his careful work on the footnotes. I am grateful to participants of the Cities in Federal Theory Workshop, held at the Melbourne Law School's Centre for Comparative Constitutional Studies on 20–21 June 2019, and in particular Michael Crommelin, Alex Flynn, and Ran Hirschl, for perceptive comments and questions. Finally, I acknowledge with gratitude the Social Sciences and Humanities Research Council of Canada for funding aspects of this project.

[1] Ran Hirschl, *City, State: Constitutionalism and the Megacity* (OUP 2020).

[2] See, eg, Hoi L Kong, 'Something to Talk About: Regulation and Justification in Canadian Municipal Law' (2010) 48 *Osgoode Hall L J* 499 (hereafter Kong, 'Something to Talk About').

[3] See, eg, *Montréal (City) v 2952-1366 Québec Inc* [2005] 3 SCR 141. There is a distinct but related question of whether cities themselves should be granted rights to freedom of expression. See Yishai Blank, 'City Speech' (2019) 54 *Harv CR-CL L Rev* 365.

[4] See, eg, Andrew J Harding, 'Does the 'Basic Structure Doctrine' Apply in Singapore's Constitution: An Inquiry into Some Fundamental Constitutional Premises' in Jaclyn L Neo (ed), *Constitutional Interpretation in Singapore: Theory and Practice* (Routledge 2012) 32.

Hoi L Kong, *Constitutional Theory, Federalism, and Cities* In: *Cities in Federal Constitutional Theory*. Edited by: Erika Arban, Oxford University Press. © Hoi L Kong 2022. DOI: 10.1093/oso/9780192843272.003.0007

What, then, does it mean to develop a federal constitutional theory of cities? To begin, we should note that we can have theories of federalism that are not constitutional in nature.[5] Rod Macdonald, for example, defined federalism broadly as being 'about the deduction, division and allocation of power, about multiple and competing sources of authority, and about the complex and overlapping identities of agents'.[6] Understood in this way, federalism—as a set of institutions and an idea—can be manifest in a wide range of contexts, including the family and other non-state settings.[7] There is, therefore, no necessary connection between this broad conception of federalism and theories of constitutionalism, which apply to the nation-state. And as a consequence, one can use federalism, understood in this open-ended way, as a theoretical lens through which to analyse the governance structure of cities, without making any claims about federalism as a *constitutional* phenomenon.[8]

This chapter will argue that cities should be understood in light of a specific constitutional theory of federalism. In section I, I will argue for a particular version of republican theory that justifies constitutionally entrenching a division of powers between territorially defined jurisdictions.[9] We shall see that entrenchment in this context protects a set of interests that are properly characterized as constitutional in nature. In section II, I will argue that cities and their residents have interests and characteristics that can be described and understood in the terms of this republican theory. In section III, I will argue that according to a general theory of constitutional change, the Canadian Constitution should be amended to entrench the status of cities. I will conclude by showing how entrenchment in the Canadian context serves republican ends and by offering policy prescriptions for achieving entrenchment.

This chapter contributes to an emerging theoretical debate about whether federations should constitutionally entrench the jurisdictional status of their cities. In the context of this debate, I advance conceptual and normative arguments. Some

5 For a general discussion of theories of federalism, see Arban, chapter 1 in this volume.

6 Roderick A Macdonald, 'Kaleidoscopic Federalism' in Jean-François Gaudreault-Des-Biens and Fabian Gélinas (eds), *The States and Moods of Federalism: Governance, Identity and Methodology* (Éditions Yvon Blais Inc 2005) 263. On how a normative theory of federalism can be developed from features of the human condition, see Nicholas Aroney, 'The Federal Condition: Towards a Normative Theory' (2016) 61 *Am J Juris* 13.

7 Macdonald himself made this connection in 'Kaleidoscopic Federalism' (n 6). For commentary on the legal pluralist significance of this understanding of federalism, see Hoi L Kong, 'The Unbounded Imagination of Roderick A. Macdonald' in Richard Janda, Rosalie Jukier, and Daniel Jutras (eds), Unbounded Level of the Mind: Rod Macdonald's Legal Imagination (McGill-Queen's U P 2015) 73.

8 See, eg, Hoi L Kong, 'Toward a Federal Theory of the City' (2012) 57 *McGill L J* 475 (hereafter Kong, 'Federal Legal Theory').

9 I do not have space here to consider the alternatives to the republican theory I advance. I have argued elsewhere for republican theories of federalism and against liberal alternatives. Hoi L Kong, 'Republicanism and the Division of Powers in Canada' (2014) 64 *U Toronto L J* 359 (hereafter, Kong 'Division of Powers'). And I have made similar arguments in the municipal law context: see Kong, 'Something to Talk About' (n 2). I refer interested readers to those texts. In the conclusion of this chapter, I do argue briefly against market-based theories of federalism and cities.

arguments are conceptual, in that they aim to show how the reasons supporting entrenchment in this context are consistent with the reasons supporting entrenchment in federations, generally. Other arguments are normative, in that they respond to republican claims that are available to individual city dwellers, as well as to cities that have distinct cultural identities. To my knowledge, the specific conceptual and normative arguments I advance have not been made before. I hope, therefore, to move the theoretical debate in new directions.

I. Constitutional Theory, Federalism, and Republicanism

One goal of constitutional theory is to explain how the materials of a constitution are marshalled in order to justify the exercise of state power within a constitutional order.[10] This is an interpretive exercise that, according to Neil MacCormick, involves 'understanding how the rules [of a constitution] interact and cross-refer, and how they make sense in the light of the principles of political association that they are properly understood to express'.[11] This exercise is motivated by a concern for a particular vision of the rule of law or legality. Ronald Dworkin famously argued that legality requires that 'government must govern under a set of principles in principle applicable to all'.[12] According to Dworkin, when constitutions are interpreted in order to give effect to this value, they contribute to the formation of a 'genuine political community' in which 'people ... are governed by common principles, not just by rules hammered out in political compromise'.[13] And under this account of constitutional interpretation, citizens are participants in a society-wide process of responsive reason-giving. As a consequence, they form a community characterized by the mutual regard of its members.[14]

A. Federal constitutional theory

Federal constitutional theory should aim to identify the relevant principles of constitutions in federations in order to deliver on the above rule of law values. We should begin by noting that because constitutions in federations entrench the division of powers in a written document and through a discrete act of political will, they are, in the parlance of constitutional theory, 'modern'. According to Simone

[10] David Dyzenhaus, 'The Idea of a Constitution: A Plea for *Staatsrechtslehre*' in David Dyzenhaus and Malcolm Thorburn (eds), *Philosophical Foundations of Constitutional Law* (OUP 2016) 9, 27.

[11] Neil MacCormick, *Questioning Sovereignty: Law, State and Nation in the European Commonwealth* (OUP 1999) 93.

[12] Ronald Dworkin, *Justice in Robes* (Belknap P 2006) 176.

[13] Ronald Dworkin, *Law's Empire* (Belknap P 1986) 211.

[14] ibid, 211–15.

Chambers, a modern constitution is written and represents 'a conscious and deliberate formulation of the fundamental law that defines and limits government'.[15] And, as Dicey remarked, a federation—almost by definition—requires a constitution that is formulated in this way and for these purposes. Dicey wrote that the constitution of a federation is a complicated contract that 'contains a variety of terms which have been agreed to, and generally after mature deliberation, by the States which make up the confederacy'.[16] According to Dicey, the written constitution of a federation defines the legal authority of each legislature and limits that authority, insofar as the laws of a legislature are 'valid whilst within the authority conferred upon it by the constitution, but invalid or unconstitutional if they go beyond the limits of such authority'.[17]

Yet distinctive features of federations require that core assumptions about modern constitutions be qualified. A modern constitution is typically assumed to express 'political sovereignty', which according to Martin Loughlin and Stephen Tierney, 'connotes power that is created as a result of the symbolic drawing together of a multitude into a "people" or "nation"'.[18] Tierney qualifies this claim about the nature of constitutions, in the context of federal constitutions. Although a federal constitution strives for unity insofar as it creates a single state, it 'is a unity that both emerges from, and which in its foundational moment gives constitutional recognition and constitutional protection to the diversity from which it springs'.[19] In other words, a federal state is a single territorial polity that contains within itself multiple territorial polities. Each of these has a distinct 'constitutional personality' and a government that is separate from the central government.[20]

The central task of federal constitutional theory is to identify the principles that underlie the above features of federal constitutions. Federal constitutional theory will account for the fact that a federation's constitution is written, expresses a distinct act of political will, and enshrines a divided conception of the polity. Furthermore, the relevant principles will facilitate a process of constitutional interpretation that can deliver the rule of law benefits identified above. We shall soon see that the core relevant principle—non-domination—is republican in nature and in what follows, I will define it and then demonstrate how it applies to the interpretation of federal constitutions.

15 Simone Chambers, 'Contract or Conversation? Theoretical Lessons from the Canadian Constitutional Crisis' (1998) 26 *Pol & Soc* 143, 145.

16 AV Dicey, *Introduction to the Study of the Law of the Constitution* (Liberty Fund 2012) 79.

17 ibid, 81.

18 Martin Loughlin and Stephen Tierney, 'The Shibboleth of Sovereignty' (2018) 81 *MLR* 989, 1000.

19 Stephen Tierney, 'Federalism and Constitutional Theory' in Gary Jacobsohn and Miguel Schor (eds), *Comparative Constitutional Theory* (Edward Elgar P 2018) 45, 57.

20 Ibid.

B. The republican norm of non-domination

Philip Pettit has articulated perhaps the most influential republican theory of domination. According to Pettit, one in general has dominating power over another if one has '(1) ... the capacity to interfere (2) on an arbitrary basis (3) in certain choices that the other is in a position to make'.[21] In the context of the state, action is undertaken on an arbitrary basis when it is 'sectional or factional in character'.[22] How, then, are we to determine whether state action bears these characteristics or when the state stands in a relationship of domination vis-à-vis its citizens?

Pettit provides us with two kinds of indicia. The first relates to a given polity's perception of an instance of domination. He argues that it will be 'common knowledge' when the conditions of domination are met in a particular set of circumstances.[23] In a constitutional polity, the constitution itself sets out the polity's commitments to the common good, as well as the criteria for determining when state action does not accord with it. The constitution therefore provides a substantial part of a polity's common knowledge about when state action is arbitrary, in the sense that it does not comport with the common good. And because arbitrary action does not aim at the common good, as defined by the constitution, it is, in Pettit's terms, sectional or factional in nature.

The second kind of indicia relates to the costs of being dominated by another. One who is subject to the arbitrary will of another individual or the state suffers in three ways: (1) from uncertainty about when her interests will be interfered with, (2) from having to constantly act with strategic deference towards the dominating party, and (3) from not being able to engage with the dominating party as an equal.[24] In a constitutional order, these conditions can arise when the state acts in ways that do not serve the rule of law ends identified above. For instance, a state actor creates uncertainty when it disregards the interest that citizens have in laws that can be justified according to established constitutional principles. When the state has the power to act in this way and with these consequences, it dominates those who are subject to its authority.

Imagine, for instance, a state that could violate at will a constitutionally entrenched norm of equality. Imagine further that it chose to do so by enacting discriminatory legislation that gave voice to a majority of the population's racial animus towards a minority group. Given the irrational nature of these impulses, it would be difficult to predict when they will arise and when the state will respond to them. The members of the targeted group would, as a result, be in a constant state of uncertainty. Moreover, they would constantly be motivated to defer to the

[21] Philip Pettit, *Republicanism: A Theory of Freedom and Government* (OUP 1997) 52 (hereafter Pettit, *Republicanism*).
[22] ibid, 56.
[23] ibid, 59.
[24] ibid, 83–7.

majority and, by virtue of this deferential stance, would be unable to engage in political life on equal terms with their fellow citizens.

One challenge for theorists in the republican tradition is to conceive of how to control state action so that it does not give rise to this kind of domination. According to Pettit, state action can be non-dominating if it tracks 'politically avowable, perceived interests'.[25] Pettit defines the relevant interests as those 'that are consistent with the desire to live under a shared scheme that treats no one as special. They are interests that those who are expected to give a system of government their allegiance may reasonably expect a government to track.'[26] As we have seen, a constitution provides criteria for determining what these interests are. When state action tracks these kinds of interests it accords with reasons related to the public good. It is therefore, by definition, not motivated by factional interests and is, on the terms of Pettit's theory, non-dominating.[27]

Consider, for example, a legislature that respected, and courts that enforced, a constitutionalized principle of equality. The state actors in this instance would not be responding to factional interests. They would rather respect the interest that the entire polity has in the value of equality. As a consequence, those citizens belonging to minority groups would be protected from domination, and free from pressures to constantly defer to the will of the majority. These citizens could instead interact with others as equals, secure in the knowledge that state action will be controlled by the norms entrenched in the constitution.

C. Republicanism, non-domination, and the division of powers

Let us turn now to assess how this general theory of a constitution applies in the context of federations. As we have seen above, the act of entrenching the division of powers in a constitution is typically a political *compromise*: at the founding, political actors with sufficient bargaining power constitutionalize their desire to control territory.[28] Yet because a constitution is an important source of a polity's common understanding of what the public good entails, the division of powers, once entrenched, becomes a Dworkinian constitutional *principle*.[29] When a state actor

[25] Philip Pettit, 'Republican Freedom and Contestatory Democratization' in Ian Shapiro and Casiano Hacker-Cordón (eds), *Democracy's Value* (CUP 1999) 163, 178 (hereafter Pettit, 'Contestatory Democratization'). See generally James Bohman, 'Cosmopolitan Republicanism and the Rule of Law' in Samantha Besson and José Luis Martí (eds), *Legal Republicanism: National and International Perspectives* (OUP 2009) 60, 61.

[26] Pettit, 'Contestatory Democratization' (n 25) 176.

[27] Pettit, *Republicanism* (n 21).

[28] Vicki C Jackson, 'Comparative Federalism: Its Strengths and Limits' in Gaudreault-Des-Biens and Gélinas, *The States and Moods of Federalism* (n 6) 146.

[29] ibid. It is possible that a constitution itself can be dominating, and in that case, a violation of it will not violate the common good. For the purposes of this chapter, I will assume that a constitution is legitimate only if it is non-dominating and thus a constitution that does enshrine and enforce domination is illegitimate and thus a constitution in name only.

contravenes the division of powers, therefore, it behaves in a way that is factional, sectoral, or arbitrary. We have seen that in the constitutional law context, these terms connote state action that diverges from the common good, as that idea is expressed by the constitution itself. Any violation of the division of powers would amount, therefore, to an affront to the value of legality. Yet in order to flesh out why a violation of the division of powers creates the concrete effects of domination—uncertainty, inequality, and undue deference—we will need to specify the interests that citizens have in the division of powers.

I label the kinds of arguments that explain the relevant interests the *general* and *multinational* cases. Because the United States is not a multinational federation, I call the republican argument made in the American context 'the general case'.[30] According to this republican conception, the political identity of citizens in a federation is bifurcated. For matters that are of federation-wide significance, citizens are members of the federal polity and exercise their democratic agency through the federal government. By contrast, for matters that are of subnational significance, citizens are members of their subnational political communities and exercise their agency through their subnational governments.[31] In this republican view, the governments of each level of government are the institutions through which citizens express their political agency on matters of the relevant scale. According to the *general* case, a constitution's division of powers provisions aim to safeguard this fundamental interest. For example, in most federations, a citizen voting on, or engaged in, political action in respect of foreign policy would be exercising democratic agency at the federal level. That same citizen, when she seeks to shape policy around local education issues, would typically be exercising her democratic agency at a subnational level. The division of powers protects her agency in both cases, by safeguarding the relevant governmental forums from being influenced by actors who do not belong to the relevant polity.

The *multinational* case for federalism adds to the general case an interest in minority group protection. Pettit has argued that in societies where divisions between a majority and a minority group are profound, members of the minority group may come to persistently doubt that decisions made over their opposition by the majority will take into consideration their interests.[32] In such circumstances, argues Pettit, constitutional designers concerned to give effect to the norm of non-domination may 'think about a federal structure in which each gets its own territory'.[33] A federation designed along these kinds of fault lines will aim to ensure

[30] See, eg, Cass R Sunstein, 'Interest Groups in American Public Law' (1985) 38 *Stan L Rev* 29, 44; S Candice Hoke, 'Preemption Pathologies and Civic Republican Values' (1991) 71 *Boston U L Rev* 685; Cass R Sunstein, 'Beyond the Republican Revival' (1988) 97 *Yale L J* 1539, 1561–2, 1578. For this distinction between general and multinational theories of federalism, and its implications for republican theory, see Hoi L Kong, 'Subsidiarity, Republicanism and the Division of Powers in Canada' (2015) 45 *RDUS* 13, pt I.

[31] Hoke (n 30) 713.

[32] Pettit, 'Contestatory Democratization' (n 25) 195.

[33] ibid.

that members of the minority group will, through subnational institutions of representative government, have decision-making power over issues that affect the minority's interests.[34] A constitutionally entrenched division of powers can aim to safeguard the autonomy of these institutions and to protect the relevant minority interests. A federation created by this kind of constitution is typically described as multinational.[35]

With the general and multinational case in view, we can now specify how domination arises in federations. Imagine a federal legislature that could violate the constitutional division of powers and legislate at will in areas of provincial legislation. The citizens of any province in that federation would be subject to the arbitrary will of the federal legislature, as that body would not be controlled by the constitution. Moreover, if this hypothetical federal legislature were to make and enforce laws beyond its constitutional competence and within the competence of a given province, the citizens of the affected province would be subject to the will of a legislature over which they would not exercise effective democratic control. This deficit of control would amount to a form of inequality as the citizens of the federation would exercise more than the share of democratic agency that the constitution allocated to them, while the citizens of the province would have their agency compromised. Finally, a provincial legislature in this kind of federation would have incentives to curry favour with the federal government in order to persuade it not to legislate beyond its constitutional competence.[36] In this hypothetical case, the province and its citizens—whether in the general or multinational case—would be in the condition of subservience that republicans describe as domination.

II. Republican Federal Constitutional Theory and the City

There are two ways that the republican federal constitutional theory developed above could apply to cities. In the first, relatively straightforward case, a city's powers would be entrenched in the constitution of a federation and the above analysis would apply directly. In respect of matters within the city's jurisdiction, city residents would exercise their democratic will through the city government. Any higher order of government that legislated outside of its constitutional jurisdiction

[34] Philip Pettit, 'Minority Claims under Two Conceptions of Democracy' in Duncan Ivison, Paul Patton, and Will Sanders (eds), *Political Theory and the Rights of Indigenous Peoples* (CUP 2000) 199, 214.

[35] See Kong, 'Division of Powers' (n 9).

[36] Authors writing on the federal spending power argue that because federal governments are not subject to the constitution's division of powers when they exercise this power, they place subnational governments in this position of subservience. For a description of these effects in Canada, see Robin Boadway, 'Recent Developments in the Economics of Federalism' in Harvey Lazar (ed), *Canada: The State of the Federation 1999/2000—Toward a New Mission Statement for Canadian Fiscal Federalism* (McGill-Queen's U P 2000) 69.

and within the city's jurisdiction would be acting arbitrarily, as it would violate the constitution. And if no institution, such as a constitutional court, could control that higher order of government, the city's government and residents would be subject to the constitutionally unconstrained will of that government. The city's residents would, therefore, be subject to domination, as their capacity to exercise their democratic agency through city government would be compromised.

The second, more difficult case arises when a city does not have its status entrenched in the constitution. In what follows, I will use Canada as a case study for the republican argument in respect of this more difficult case. Before I discuss the specifics of Canadian cities, I will argue that certain characteristics of cities argue in favour of their enjoying significant regulatory authority. With that argument in place, we will see that Canadian cities are subject to *consequences* of domination that are similar to the ones we canvassed above in our discussion of the republican theory of federalism.

A. A theoretical case for allocating significant powers to cities

A city can be described in terms of features that Daniel Weinstock has set out.[37] According to Weinstock, a city (1) is spatially integrated; (2) is of a certain scale; (3) has a minimal density; (4) and its inhabitants 'are capable of leading—and in large proportion do—the major aspects of their lives (work, leisure, education, residence)' there.[38] Loren King similarly argues that cities, by their nature, have a degree of 'dense integration' and create multifaceted relationships of interdependence that justify cities' possessing significant regulatory authority over matters that affect them.[39]

King further claims that there are two specific kinds of arguments in favour of allocating to cities this measure of regulatory power. First, he notes that according to general liberal-democratic arguments, state power—which ultimately is backed by coercion—'can only be legitimately authorized by reasons that are responsive to each citizen's equal moral standing as at once both the subject and the final author of that coercion. Decisions made closest to those most affected are more likely to satisfy this criterion of legitimacy.'[40] King labels this argument the 'liberal autonomy' rationale. Second, King argues that it is within associations, including families, communities, churches, and neighbourhoods that 'our broader

[37] For a similar description of cities, see Cahill and O'Sullivan, chapter 3 in this volume.
[38] Daniel Weinstock, 'Cities and Federalism' (2014) 55 *Nomos* 259, 269 (hereafter Weinstock, 'Cities and Federalism'). Weinstock labels this collection of criteria the 'folk conception' of the city. Political scientists have used various measures to define the community of interest that constitutes a city, including a census metropolitan area. See, eg, Andrew Sancton, *The Limits of Boundaries: Why City-Regions Cannot be Self-Governing* (McGill-Queen's U P 2008) ch 3, 25.
[39] Loren King, 'Cities, Subsidiarity and Federalism' (2014) 55 *Nomos* 291, 299.
[40] ibid, 301.

conceptions of justice and the good life are formulated and affirmed . . . and if government must interfere with civic or non-public associations, best that it do so in ways that are least intrusive and most carefully tailored to achieve whatever public purposes necessitated interference in the first place'.[41] If decision-making power is kept closest to those affected by its exercise, argues King, there is a greater likelihood that it will be exercised in ways that are solicitous and attentive to these association-related interests. King labels this argument the 'moderately communitarian' rationale.

Both the liberal autonomy and moderately communitarian arguments favour vesting significant regulatory power in cities. And the republican overtones of King's position emerge when he claims that his arguments reflect 'attention to freedom from domination under, and inefficiencies resulting from, indifferent, ill-informed, or corrupted distant authorities; but also recognition of the social conditions necessary for the meaningful exercise of such freedom'.[42]

B. The legal consequences of not constitutionally entrenching the jurisdiction of cities

These political theoretical arguments in favour of allocating significant regulatory authority to cities can be tied to a legal analysis of the place of cities within the Canadian federation. In Canada, a city is defined legally as a 'municipality' that has been delegated powers by the province in which it is located. In this sense, the City of Vancouver is the legal entity to which the Province of British Columbia has given specific municipal powers.[43] For the purposes of this chapter let us stipulate that Canadian cities possess all the features identified by Weinstock and King and use the terms city and municipality interchangeably. Let us further assume that King's arguments in favour of allocating cities regulatory authority apply to Canadian cities.

With these stipulations and assumptions in place, I turn now to describe the place of cities in the Canadian constitutional order. The Canadian Constitution does not recognize municipalities as an independent third level of government below the national and the provincial levels. Section 92(8) of the Constitution Act 1867 places municipalities under the exclusive control of provincial legislatures.[44] Judicial interpretation of this section has consistently affirmed provincial control over municipal governments, and traditionally, courts construed municipal

[41] ibid, 302.
[42] ibid.
[43] See Kong, 'Federal Legal Theory' (n 8).
[44] Although municipalities were not given a place in the Constitution as an independent level of government, they were given extensive powers in the legislation that was the basis of modern municipal law in Canada. See Municipal Act, 22 Vict, 1st sess c 99 (UK).

jurisdiction narrowly.[45] In recent decades, provincial legislation has granted cities general powers and courts have come to interpret municipal powers in a broad and purposive way.[46] Yet despite these developments, cities remain creatures of their provinces. As such, they are subject to any legislative changes that a province might choose to enact, including measures that would remove all regulatory authority from a given city or fundamentally reconstitute it.[47] There is, therefore, a significant gap between the regulatory authority that political theorists claim a city should enjoy and the position of cities within the Canadian constitution. We shall soon see the significance of this gap for a republican theory of city powers.

C. Republican domination and cities

If we take the Canadian case to stand for any federation in which a city's status is not constitutionally entrenched, we can see how the republican arguments for federalism do and do not apply. Consider first the ways in which the status of cities in these kinds of federations diverge from the position of provinces whose status is protected by the constitution. Because the interests of cities and their residents are not entrenched, they do not form part of a polity's constitutionally expressed 'common knowledge' of what the public good entails. As a consequence, if a province were to legislate in a way that did not track the interests of a city or its residents, it would not violate the constitution and the province would not therefore engage in a form of domination that is constitutionally recognized by the polity.

Yet cities in a federation of this kind are subject to *consequences* of domination that are similar to those that provinces subject to the uncontrolled authority of a federal government are exposed to. We saw above that provinces subject to the arbitrary authority of a federal government would suffer from uncertainty and would likely be unduly deferential to the federal order of government; provincial residents in this situation would also be less equal than their federal counterparts. We shall soon see that cities that are subject to the power of a province to legislate without considering their interests will also suffer from uncertainty and will also have incentives to act in a deferential way towards the province; city residents will also suffer from a form of inequality. In order to understand how these consequences

45 See, eg, *Merritt v Toronto (City)* (1895) 22 OAR 205; *Verdun (City) v Sun Oil Co* [1952] 1 SCR 222; and *Ottawa Electric Light Co v Ottawa (City)* (1906) 12 OLR 290, 299.

46 See Community Charter SBC 2003 c 26 (BC); Municipal Act SO 2001 c 25 (Ont); Municipalities Act SNL 1999 c M-24 (Nfld); and Municipal Powers Act RSQ c C-47.1 (Que). For the broad and purposive approach to interpreting statutes governing municipalities, see *Nanaimo (City) v Rascal Trucking Ltd* [2000] 1 SCR 342; and *114957 Canada Ltée (Spraytech, Société d'arrosage) v Hudson (Town)* [2001] 2 SCR 241.

47 See *Baie d'Urfé (Ville) v Québec (Procureur général)* [2001] JQ no 2954 (Que CS); *Baie d'Urfé (Ville) v Québec (Procureur général)* [2001] JQ no 4821 (Que CA).

arise, we will need to first specify the sense in which a city is subject to the arbitrary authority of its province.

Provincial power to interfere with the regulatory authority of cities is arbitrary in the sense that it can be exercised without considering the interests of cities and their residents and indeed without any supporting rationale at all. This meaning of arbitrariness aligns with the one contained in Pettit's general republican description of domination.[48] Provinces are able to act in this way *as a matter of law* because the constitution does not constrain their ability to do so. They are able to act arbitrarily *as a matter of politics* because city residents are typically unequal to residents in other parts of the province.

We should be precise about the nature of this political form of inequality. Provinces can typically disregard the interests of cities because city residents do not have *political power* equal to their rural or non-urban counterparts.[49] For example, the City of Toronto and its electoral districts are significantly under-represented in the Ontario provincial legislature.[50] As a consequence, a political party can command a legislative majority by promising to govern in a way that gives disproportionate weight to the interests of voters outside of the City of Toronto. And once this kind of party forms government, it can legislate without due regard for the City's interests.[51]

A city government faced with this kind of provincial legislature will have reasons to behave in ways that are unduly deferential. We have seen above that cities are, as a matter of political theory, due a significant measure of authority: cities have features that warrant regulatory authority commensurate with their interests. It is the gap between the claim that cities can make as a matter of political principle, on the one hand, and their political and legal position, on the other, that makes a given city's deference to its province undue. We have seen that a city government cannot engage with its province as a *legal equal*, because the Constitution empowers the province to legislate in ways that disregard city's interests. And a city government cannot engage with the province as a *political equal* because, in our example, the provincial government does not have electoral reasons to take seriously the interests of city residents. As a result, city officials in Canada need constantly to adopt a deferential stance towards provincial authorities in order to garner powers and resources that are commensurate with what they are due as a matter of normative

48 Pettit, 'Contestatory Democratization' (n 25) 176.

49 For a similar argument, see Hirschl (n 1) 70–1.

50 Michael Pal and Sujit Choudhry, 'Is Every Ballot Equal? Visible Minority Vote Dilution in Canada' (2007) 13 *IRPP Choices* 5, 7. For a description of how significantly under-represented elected officials from Montréal are in Québec's current government, and an assessment of the gap between the legislative initiatives of the government and the policy preferences of Montrealers, see 'Réconcilier Montréal et Québec' (*l'Actualité* 6 October 2021) <https://lactualite.com/societe/reconcilier-montreal-et-le-quebec/> accessed 18 October, 2021.

51 Timothy L Thomas, 'An Emerging Party Cleavage: Metropolis vs The Rest' in Hugh G Thorburn and Alan Whitehorn (eds), *Party Politics in Canada* (8th edn, Prentice Hall 2001) 431.

theory. Officials express this condition of deference perhaps most evocatively when they claim that they approach their provinces with 'cap in hand'.[52]

III. Federal Constitutional Theory, Constitutional Change, and Cities

The federal constitutional theory developed thus far is incomplete. In the previous section, I demonstrated that a portion of the theory applied to federations in which the constitutional status of cities is not entrenched. I argued that cities in these federations experience *consequences* of domination similar in kind to those a province subject to the acts of a constitutionally unconstrained federal government would undergo. I noted, however, that the theory's concept of domination did not apply in its entirety because one important aspect of the concept requires a breach of the constitution's provisions. Moreover, in section I, I argued that constitutional entrenchment of the division of powers is a defining feature of federations. Thus, it seems that we need to account for this feature—and more precisely, the *absence* of entrenched powers for cities—in order to develop a fully formed federal constitutional theory of the city.

This section will round out the theory by arguing that federal constitutions that do not entrench city powers should be amended so that they do. The first segment of this section will draw upon recent scholarship on constitutional amendments to argue that the Canadian Constitution should be reformed in this way. In the second segment of this section, I will focus on a Canadian case study to show how this form of entrenchment protects interests identified by the federal constitutional theory developed in section I. I will conclude by suggesting in broad outline how constitutional reform in this area might be undertaken in order to vindicate those interests.

A. Constitutional reform, Canadian fiscal federalism, and cities

Richard Albert has recently described the functions of constitutional amendment procedures. According to Albert, these procedures 'offer a way to respond to the changing political, social, economic, and other needs of the community—needs that the governing constitution may inadequately serve, whether as a result

[52] Steve Palkin, 'Is it time to get our big-city mayors out of the "short pants, begging cap-in-hand" business?' (*tvo*, 31 January 2017) <https://www.tvo.org/article/is-it-time-to-get-our-big-city-mayors-out-of-the-short-pants-begging-cap-in-hand-business> accessed 27 May 2021. For the purposes of this chapter, I will assume that cities cannot leverage their powers to overcome their disadvantage relative to the provinces.

of suboptimal constitutional design or new social circumstances'.[53] This view of constitutional amendment has supported arguments in favour of constitutionally entrenching city powers. Ran Hirschl, for instance, has claimed that because of recent social, economic, and environmental changes, cities around the world should be granted constitutional status.[54] In this section, I will focus on Canada. A brief political history of Canadian federalism will show how evolving social and economic circumstances justify amending the Constitution in order to entrench jurisdictional powers adequate to the needs of today's cities.

A vertical fiscal gap between the federal and provincial governments has become necessary to facilitate redistributive policies in the Canadian federation today.[55] Rod Macdonald has traced the origins of the expansive federal power to tax and spend to the economic shocks occasioned by the Great Depression. In the 1930s, Canada pursued policies 'to resuscitate the economy and protect the welfare of citizens',[56] and in response to the need to raise revenue in order to finance the war effort in the 1940s, the federal government deployed a range of policy instruments, including inter-provincial equalization transfers and constitutional amendments: s 91(2A) (unemployment insurance) and s 94A (old age pensions).[57] In the post-war period, the need grew for the institutions and programs of the welfare state. Yet as Macdonald notes, despite having constitutional jurisdiction to regulate these programs, 'few provinces had the tax base, the population and the government capacity to manage them. As a result, with the concurrence of most provinces, Ottawa took the initiative in developing social welfare policy initiatives.'[58]

The federal government's role in providing welfare state policies can be explained by the history surrounding the constitutional division of powers. In 1867, it was inconceivable that the 'social terrain occupied by religious and charitable institutions and by rural and neighbourhood collective assistance organizations'[59] would be occupied by governments. Therefore, neither legislative authority nor fiscal powers were allocated in the Canadian Constitution in a way that could respond to the policy needs of the welfare state. In response to this constitutional oversight, the federal government—which does not have jurisdiction to legislate directly in areas of provincial jurisdiction such as health and education—currently regulates and spends in these areas pursuant to its spending power.[60] Scholars have

[53] Richard Albert, *Constitutional Amendments: Making, Breaking and Changing Constitutions* (OUP 2019) 42.

[54] Hirschl (n 1) 181–97.

[55] Harvey Lazar, 'Trust in Intergovernmental Fiscal Relations' in Harvey Lazar (ed), *Canadian Fiscal Arrangements: What Works, What Might Work Better* (McGill-Queen's P 2005) 3, 12.

[56] Roderick A Macdonald, 'The Political Economy of the Federal Spending Power' (2008) 34 *Queen's L J* 249, 278.

[57] ibid, 279.

[58] ibid, 280.

[59] ibid.

[60] See Hoi L Kong, 'The Spending Power in Canada' in Peter Oliver, Patrick Macklem, and Nathalie Des Rosiers (eds) *The Oxford Handbook of the Canadian Constitution* (OUP 2017) 434.

argued for constitutional amendments in order to respond to this state of affairs and to align provincial powers with provincial fiscal capacity.[61]

The above constitutional history helps to explain why the Constitution should similarly be amended in order to provide municipalities with constitutionally entrenched powers. In response to the above developments, demand in the provinces for social services grew in the post-war period. But beginning in the latter decades of the 20th century, federal spending in this area declined and provincial governments downloaded onto cities the responsibility for providing some of these services.[62] Yet provincial legislation provides cities with limited sources of revenue: typically, charges, property taxes, and any additional taxing powers that the provinces delegate to them. Because cities rely on these limited sources, as well as discretionary transfers from the provinces or the federal government, they typically do not have the capacity to independently raise revenue sufficient to fund the services that their populations need.

Enid Slack has recently identified the high social spending needs that cities currently have[63] and examined cities' lack of revenue raising capacity to meet them.[64] She, along with scholars including Kristen Pue, has argued for policy changes that would better align the spending needs with the fiscal capacity of cities.[65] I suggest that if the Constitution were amended to entrench some of these fiscal powers and to specify subject matter over which cities and provinces would have exclusive jurisdiction, cities would no longer be vulnerable to provincial decisions to download service responsibilities, without providing adequate resources. A constitutional amendment of this kind would, in Albert's words, respond to 'changing political, social, economic and other needs of the community'[66] and correct 'an observed fault' in the Canadian Constitution.[67]

[61] See, eg, Andrew Petter, 'Federalism and the Myth of the Federal Spending Power' (1998) 68 *Can Bar Rev* 488.

[62] Michael Dewing, William R Young, and Erin Tolley, *Municipalities, the Constitution and the Canadian Federal System* (Parliamentary Library Background Paper BP 276–E, 2006) 17.

[63] Enid Slack, 'Financing Large Cities and Metropolitan Areas' (*Institute on Municipal Finance and Governance*, 3 Nov 2011) 8 <https://munkschool.utoronto.ca/wp-content/uploads/2012/07/Slack_FinancingLargeCities_IMFG_20111.pdf> accessed 27 May 2021.

[64] ibid 10.

[65] See, eg, Kristen Pue, 'A "Big City Charter" for Edmonton and Calgary: Explaining the Role of Municipalities in Canada's Federal Framework' (*Centre for Constitutional Studies*, 20 September 2018) <https://www.constitutionalstudies.ca/2018/09/a-big-city-charter-for-edmonton-and-calgary-explaining-the-role-of-municipalities-in-canadas-federal-framework/> accessed 27 May 2021.

[66] Albert (n 53) 42.

[67] ibid, 39.

B. Canadian cities in federal constitutional theory; effective constitutional reform

According to our republican constitutional theory of federalism, if a federal constitution does not entrench city powers, cities will be subject to the consequences of provincial domination. And the above application of Albert's theory of constitutional change suggests that developments in the history of the Canadian federation justify amending the Constitution to entrench the powers of cities. The tenor of these analyses has been normative and conceptual. By contrast, the remainder of this section will focus on concrete institutional questions. I will first examine how entrenching the powers of Canadian cities and Montréal, in particular, would satisfy what I called above the general and multinational cases for the republican theory of federalism. The section will conclude in a prescriptive register: I will recommend that Canadian courts clear away obstacles to constitutional reform.

1. Canadian illustrations

The general republican case for the division of powers would apply to any Canadian city whose powers were entrenched in the Constitution. Recall that according to the general case, citizenship is divided: for some jurisdictional matters, individuals in a federation are citizens of the federal level of government and for others, the provincial. As a consequence, the provincial and federal legislatures are loci of different facets of an individual citizen's democratic agency. Citizens elect members of provincial legislatures to represent their provincial interests and federal members to represent their federal interests. And, as we have seen, the division of powers protects the various facets of citizenship within a federation from domination. Entrenching city powers would offer constitutional protection to one more jurisdictionally defined facet of citizenship. This extension would be relatively straightforward, as a matter of constitutional law, since the Supreme Court of Canada has long recognized that city governments are important vehicles through which citizens exercise their democratic agency.[68]

The multinational republican case for the division of powers would apply only to those Canadian cities for which constitutional entrenchment would protect a distinct group's identity interest. In the standard multinational case, a province is allocated jurisdiction in order to protect from domination a group that is the majority population in that province, but a minority in the rest of the federation. For example, francophones are the majority in Québec but they are a minority relative to the majority anglophone population in Canada as a whole. Québec's entrenched constitutional status protects its minority population from domination by the majority represented in the federal Parliament.[69] By extension, a city's status could be

[68] *Shell Canada Products Ltd v Vancouver* [1994] 1 SCR 231, 243–5 (McLachlin J).

[69] See Kong, 'Division of Powers' (n 9).

entrenched in order to protect a population that is a majority within the city, but a minority relative to the population in the rest of that city's province.

Weinstock has argued that Montrealers, for example, have a distinctive bilingual and multilingual identity that is distinct from the conception that many Quebeckers outside of Montréal have of Québec as a unilingual francophone society that is threatened by bilingualism and multilingualism.[70] Entrenching the City of Montréal's powers in the Canadian Constitution would thus protect Montrealers' distinct identity from domination by the provincial legislature, which represents a population that is potentially antagonistic to facets of that identity.

2. A prescription for constitutional reform

A sympathetic reader may accept that constitutional reform in this context is necessary to secure the benefits that the theory of federalism has identified. Yet, the reader may be sceptical about the prospects for reform. Such scepticism is warranted. Cities in Canada play no role in constitutional amendment: in Weinstock's terms, they have no meta-jurisdictional authority since they have no 'say in the political processes that distribute jurisdiction among political entities'.[71]

By contrast, Canadian provinces, including Québec, do possess meta-jurisdictional authority. For certain matters, the Constitution requires unanimous consent of all the provinces and the federal Parliament in order for a constitutional amendment to pass.[72] In effect, the requirement of unanimity gives to each province a veto over any changes to the Constitution that would affect the entire federation. In addition, for any amendment that directly affects the specific interests of some, but not all, provinces, only the legislative assemblies of provinces to whom such an amendment applies and the 'two houses of the federal Parliament' need consent.[73] Here again, the affected provinces are granted constitutional authority to shape any changes to their jurisdiction. Finally, s 38(3) of the *Constitution Act, 1982* states that any amendment made in accordance with the formula that requires agreement among the federal Parliament, and seven provinces comprising 50 per cent of the national population 'shall not have effect in a province, the legislative assembly of which has expressed its dissent thereto by resolution supported by a majority of its members'. The provision ensures that if any provinces dissent to an amendment passed according to this formula, such an amendment will not apply to those provinces.

The provinces' role in constitutional amendment seems to present an insurmountable obstacle to constitutionally entrenching the powers of Canadian cities.

[70] Daniel Weinstock, 'Self-determination for (some) cities?' in Axel Gosseries and Yannick Vanderborght (eds), *Arguing about Justice: Essays for Philippe Van Parijs* (Presse Université de Louvain 2011) 377.

[71] ibid, [11].

[72] Constitution Act 1982 s 41, being schedule B to the Canada Act 1982 (UK) c 11.

[73] Constitution Act s 43.

Since any constitutional amendment to the status of cities would affect the provinces in which those cities were located, the affected provincial legislatures would play a decisive role under any of the relevant amending formulas. Yet we have seen that a key contributing factor to city residents' vulnerability to domination is their lack of equal representation in provincial legislatures. Provincial legislatures are, therefore, the institutions through which cities can—through constitutional amendment—escape domination, but those legislatures are also the very instruments by which cities are dominated. In the end, it seems highly unlikely that majorities of representatives in those legislatures—who are not predisposed to consider the interests of city dwellers during ordinary law-making processes—would amend the Constitution in order to protect those interests.

The solution to this problem lies outside of the division of powers provisions of the Canadian constitution. We have seen above that city residents are unequally represented in provincial legislatures, and this fact provides the starting point for the constitutional solution. Section 15 is the equality rights provision of the Canadian Charter of Rights and Freedoms[74] and expressly prohibits discrimination on the basis of race. In the parlance of Canadian constitutional law, race is an 'enumerated ground'. Moreover, Canadian equality jurisprudence specifies that a law can be found to discriminate in respect of an enumerated ground, even if that law does not explicitly mention the ground. In the Supreme Court of Canada's words: 'Adverse impact discrimination occurs when a seemingly neutral law has a disproportionate impact on members of groups protected on the basis of an enumerated . . . ground.'[75]

Application of this equality jurisprudence would likely lead a court to conclude that provincial electoral regulations are discriminatory. According to Michael Pal and Sujit Choudhry, the laws and policies that shape provincial electoral boundaries result in the votes of urban-dwelling racial minorities being under-represented in provincial legislatures.[76] The authors identify the potential harm that arises from these laws and policies: 'we should worry whether governments will discount the interests of this under-represented set of voters and be less responsive to their concerns than they would otherwise be under conditions of voter parity.'[77] Drawing on the jurisprudential principles set out above, Pal and Choudhry conclude that state action in this area 'results in adverse effects discrimination against a vulnerable minority protected by s 15'.[78]

[74] ibid, s 36(1).

[75] See *Fraser v Canada (Attorney General)* [2020] 450 DLR (4th) 1 [30] (Abella J).

[76] Michael Pal and Sujit Choudhry, 'Still Not Equal? Visible Minority Vote Dilution in Canada' (2014) 8 *Can Poli Sci Rev* 85 (hereafter Pal and Choudhry, 'Minority Vote Dilution in Canada').

[77] ibid 94. It is important to note that these potential consequences are serious, as they impact a fundamental constitutional interest, namely the right to vote. Canadian equality rights jurisprudence has traditionally held that if a law impacts a fundamental interest, this can be a strong indicator that the law is discriminatory. See *Law v Canada (Minister of Employment and Immigration)* [1999] 1 SCR 497, 538–9 [77] (Iacobucci J).

[78] Pal and Choudhry, 'Minority Vote Dilution in Canada' (n 76) 96.

If courts were to adopt this position (and assuming that the s 15 violation could not be justified under s 1),[79] they would address one source of domination that my application of republican theory has identified and remove an obstacle to constitutionally entrenching the status of cities. If courts were to strike down existing electoral laws and legislatures were to replace them with laws that accorded urban votes more equal weight, provincial legislatures would likely be more responsive to the interests of urban residents. The provinces would thus no longer be in a structural position to dominate cities: they would instead have electoral incentives to give due regard to city residents' interests. Moreover, if urban voters were more equally represented in provincial legislatures, and if those voters were to demand constitutional reform, amendments entrenching the status of cities might become a real possibility. Of course, there are many reasons why provincial legislators may choose not to pursue this kind of constitutional amendment but if courts were to accept the equality rights arguments advanced in this chapter, one obstacle to reform would be removed. As a consequence, Canada would be one step closer to giving institutional form to this chapter's federal constitutional theory of cities.

IV. Conclusion

This chapter has offered a republican version of a federal constitutional theory of cities. Other versions are, of course, possible. One prominent alternative theory of federalism relies on metaphors of the marketplace, and that theory was originally developed to analyse cities.[80] Prominent scholars, including Richard Briffault, have argued that the marketplace model, in its original form, does not fit easily with important facts about cities.[81] Others have argued that the model's factual assumptions do not hold when applied to federal states.[82]

I do not intend to enter deeply into this debate, but I will conclude by highlighting an essential feature of the theory that I have developed in this chapter and contrasting it with the marketplace view. We have seen that constitutional theory, especially in its republican form, seeks to ensure that the coercive power of the state

[79] For a fuller version of the argument that applies current constitutional doctrine under ss 15 and 1, see Hoi L Kong, 'Constitutional Amendment and the Canadian City' in Alexandra Flynn, Richard Albert, and Nathalie Desrosiers (eds), *Unlocking the Constitutional Handcuffs on Canadian Cities: New Possibilities for Municipal Power* (McGill-Queen's P, forthcoming). It is possible that some measure of inequality between urban and non-urban votes could be justified, in order to ensure that provincial legislatures would not disregard the interests of the non-urban electorate.

[80] See Roderick M Hills, 'Compared to What? Tiebout and the Comparative Merits of Congress and the States in Constitutional Federalism' in William A Fischel (ed), *The Tiebout Model at Fifty: Essays in Public Economics in Honor of Wallace Oates* (Lincoln Institute of Land Policy 2005) 239.

[81] See, eg, Richard Briffault, 'The Rise of Sublocal Structures in Urban Governance' (1997) 82 *Minn L Rev* 503.

[82] See, eg, Jacob T Levy, 'Federalism, Liberalism, and the Separation of Loyalties' (2007) 101 *Am Poli Sci Rev* 459, 460–2.

can be justified to those who are subject to it. According to this version of constitutional theory, citizens and officials are members of a community who seek to define and apply fair and just terms on which to interact. To the extent that marketplace theories of federalism—with their focus on consumer preferences and firm competition—deprecate these concerns, they fail in an important sense to offer a constitutional theory of the city, as opposed to an economic one.[83] It is for this reason that I doubt that these theories can offer what this collection promises: a federal *constitutional* theory of the city.

[83] See also, Hoi L Kong and Ron Levy, 'Deliberative Constitutionalism' in André Bächtiger and others (eds), *The Oxford Handbook of Deliberative Democracy* (OUP 2016) 626, 636.

7

Cities, Federalism, and Criminal Law Reform

William Partlett

I. Introduction

Federalism's decentralization has long been seen as serving important ends.[1] It can increase policy effectiveness by allowing local experimentation and flexibility, deepen democracy by enhancing the opportunities for citizens to engage in self-government, and protect individual rights by dividing power and enhancing deliberation. Many federations ignore these advantages, however, when discussing ways to improve the criminal justice system. For instance, in the country with one of the longest traditions of federalism (the United States), criminal justice reform is at the forefront of politics.[2] Yet discussions of the benefits of decentralizing power rarely feature in this debate.[3] In other federations with central criminal codes, federal decentralization is also rarely viewed as a resource for improving the functioning of the criminal justice system.

This is a problem: local participation can help to generate a more effective and just criminal justice system. It therefore should be a larger part of discussions of criminal justice reform in federations around the world. This chapter will focus on the important role that cities—and their populations—can play in the regulation and reform of criminal law. It will argue that cities are important sites for advancing the key ends of federal decentralization; as Richard Briffault, argues 'the case for federalism . . . tends to approach the case for localism'.[4] This is particularly true for

[1] See section II. The author would also like to thank the helpful comments at the conference convened on this topic at Melbourne Law School in 2019 (convened with the funding of the Australian Research Council). He also would like to thank Phapit Triratpan for her invaluable help in preparing the chapter for publication.

[2] 'An Unlikely Alliance of Left and Right' *The Economist* (Atlanta, 17 August 2013) <https://www.economist.com/united-states/2013/08/17/an-unlikely-alliance-of-left-and-right> accessed 1 June 2021; Jamiles Lartey, 'Trump Signs Bipartisan Criminal Justice Overhaul First Step Act Into Law,' *The Guardian* (22 December 2018) <https://www.theguardian.com/us-news/2018/dec/21/trump-prison-reform-first-step-act-signed-law> accessed 1 June 2021.

[3] William Partlett, 'Criminal Law and Cooperative Federalism' (2019) 56 *Amer J Crim L* 1663 (hereafter Partlett, 'Criminal Law') (describing how the federal government is seeking to undermine decentralization through multi-million dollar programmes such as Project Safe Neighborhoods).

[4] Richard Briffault, '"What About the 'Ism'?" Normative and Formal Concerns in Contemporary Federalism' (1994) 47 *Vanderbilt L Rev* 1303, 1312–17 (hereafter Briffault, 'Normative and Formal

William Partlett, *Cities, Federalism, and Criminal Law Reform* In: *Cities in Federal Constitutional Theory.* Edited by: Erika Arban, Oxford University Press. © William Partlett 2022. DOI: 10.1093/oso/9780192843272.003.0008

criminal justice systems because crime—and particularly violent crime—remains disproportionately an urban question; its main perpetrators and victims are urban residents.[5] But, although the study of cities is experiencing a renaissance,[6] cities remain largely objects of substantive criminal law.[7] One author has described cities as the 'forgotten stepchildren of both federal politics and scholarship'.[8] This chapter will therefore seek to remedy this problem by demonstrating that—at least in the area of criminal law—the theoretical justifications for federalism can be advanced by cities. Cities, therefore, should be considered as key institutional players in both the practice and theory of federalism.

This chapter will seek to understand the ways that cities can help to reform and therefore improve criminal law in federations. Although cities rarely play a formal role in formulating substantive criminal law norms, they can oversee and hold accountable the broad discretion exercised by police and prosecutors in the criminal justice system. This oversight and direction of executive discretion is already underway in many federations. In the sanctuary city movement, for instance, urban mobilization has pressured city governments to direct the discretion of prosecutors and police in line with urban priorities. Moreover, community-oriented policing and prosecution also gives urban populations an important role in overseeing the exercise of discretion.

This chapter will argue that these existing urban accountability mechanisms should be studied, supported, and expanded as part of ongoing efforts to reform criminal justice systems.[9] These mechanisms can in turn generate mechanisms for urban populations to hold their law enforcement officers accountable for the enforcement of criminal law. This decentralization can help achieve key benefits. Facing the reality of crime every day, urban communities have access to superior

Concerns') (suggesting that the small size and multiplicity of local governments allows them to advance the values of federalism more effectively than the states).

[5] See section II below.

[6] See, eg, Ernest Ballin and others (eds), *European Yearbook of Constitutional Law 2020: The City in Constitutional Law* (Springer P 2021); Ran Hirschl, *City, State: Constitutionalism and the Megacity* (OUP 2020); Alina Harkness and Bruce Katz, 'Why Urban Governance Matters—Now More than Ever' (*Brookings*, 12 April 2016) <https://www.brookings.edu/blog/metropolitan-revolution/2016/04/12/why-urban-governance-matters-now-more-than-ever/> accessed 1 June 2021. This debate is also international: Yun-Chung Chen and Mirana Szeto, 'The Forgotten Road of Progressive Localism: New Preservation Movement in Hong Kong' (2015) *16 Inter-Asia Cultural Studies* 436.

[7] Cities are generally the objects of subnational (state or province) constitutional law. The Canadian Constitution expressly delegates power to the provinces to manage municipalities/cities. The United States and Australian Constitution do not mention cities, but they have varying status in state constitutional law. See Gerald Frug, 'The City as a Legal Concept' (1980) 93 *Harv L Rev* 1057 (explaining the "powerlessness" of cities in the United States); Frank Stilwell and Patrick Troy, 'Multilevel Governance and Urban Development in Australia' (2000) 37 *Urban Studies* 909, 925 (hereafter Stilwell and Troy, 'Multilevel Governance') (exploring the "marginal status" of local governments in Australia).

[8] Loren King, 'Cities, Subsidiarity, and Federalism' in James E Fleming and Jacob T Levy (eds), *Federalism and Subsidiary* (NYU P 2004) 291, 295.

[9] William Stuntz, *The Collapse of American Criminal Justice* (Harv U P 2011) (arguing that centralization has caused serious problems for the American criminal justice system).

and context-specific information about criminal law. This information can help to craft and encourage more flexible, innovative, and effective approaches for tackling crime. This information advantage can also help to form more rights-protective criminal law policy because it is based on a first-hand understanding of the trade-offs between security and individual rights in the criminal justice system. Finally, increased urban participation can help overcome the legitimacy problem that many law enforcement officers face by improving trust for law enforcement. City empowerment can therefore help to strengthen the political safeguards of federalism for individual criminal defendants.[10]

To make this argument, this chapter will be divided into the following five sections. Section II will describe the central problem of this chapter: how federal decentralization is frequently ignored in discussions about improving criminal justice systems. Section III will explain why cities are ideal places for reviving the advantages of federalism and therefore making criminal justice systems fairer and more effective. Section IV will demonstrate that criminal law is about far more than substantive criminal law norms; it also necessarily includes vast discretion by police and prosecutors. Section V will demonstrate how cities are already developing accountability mechanisms to oversee and direct this use of criminal law discretion. The study and strengthening of these mechanisms should be an important part of discussions of criminal justice reform. Section VI will conclude.

II. Federalism, Decentralization, and Criminal Law Reform

Federalism theory argues that the decentralization of power is preferable because its advances key ends, including enhanced policy experimentation and effectiveness, deepened political participation, and stronger individual rights.[11] Yet, this decentralization agenda is rarely understood as a resource for improving criminal justice systems. When mentioned in criminal justice reform, federalism is generally no more than a 'slogan' that is used 'without thinking [it] through or testing them'.[12] This is a problem: decentralization can have important benefits in ongoing criminal law reform.

[10] Larry D Kramer, 'Putting the Politics Back into the Political Safeguards of Federalism' (2000) 100 *Colum L Rev* 215 (hereafter Kramer, 'Putting the Politics Back'); Herbert Wechsler, 'The Political Safeguards of Federalism: The Role of the States in the Composition and Selection of the National Government' (1954) 54 *Colum L Rev* 543 (hereafter Wechsler, 'The Political Safeguards').

[11] See further Arban, chapter 1 in this volume.

[12] Barry Friedman, 'Valuing Federalism' (1997) 82 *Minn L Rev* 317, 404.

A. The advantages of federalism

Courts, scholars, and constitution-makers have argued that federal decentralization carries a number of advantages. Although overlapping, these arguments can be divided into three categories.

Experimentation and effectiveness. One set of arguments for federal decentralization is pragmatic: well-functioning federalism allows different localities to craft different approaches to law. This in turn improves 'efficiency through experimentation'.[13] There are two key mechanisms at work. First, the diffusion of power places policy-making authority in the hands of communities that possess superior knowledge. Second, and relatedly, it allows inter-jurisdictional experimentation in tackling common problems.

In criminal law, for instance, a diffusion of policy-making power (particularly to cities) can help ensure the development of new and innovative ways for solving criminal law problems. Crime is a frequently a highly context-specific phenomenon, based on local factors. Local communities—city residents—have first-hand information about these particular factors and the best ways to counter it; this information frequently leads to policy that differs from conventional left–right political ideologies or accepted best practices. A decentralized approach will allow policy to be formulated with this specific contextual information in mind. In this approach, localities can experiment with 'novel social and economic solutions' to shared problems of crime and therefore 'serve as a laboratory' for other jurisdictions.[14] We can see examples of this operating in the United States, where some states have experimented with alternatives to mass incarceration by diverting some individuals away from the formal criminal law system. This American state-level example has helped lead to experimentation in the Australian state of Victoria, which has established an Assessment and Referral Court to divert criminal defendants with cognitive impairment or mental health issues away from the mainstream criminal justice system.[15]

Participation. Another set of arguments value federalism for its contribution to enhancing democratic participation. Well-functioning federalism moves government decision making closer to the citizen, which in turn 'increases opportunity for citizen involvement in democratic processes'.[16] In particular, decentralized government helps to increase participation by those who might not have the resources

[13] Brenner Fissell, 'Federalism and Constitutional Criminal Law' (2017) 46 *Hofstra L Rev* 489, 521.

[14] *New State Ice Co v Leibmann* 285 US 262, 311 (1932) (Brandeis J dissenting).

[15] Magistrates Court of Victoria, 'Assessment and Referral Court' (20 November 2018) <https//www.mcv.vic.gov.au/about-us/assessment-and-referral-court-arc> accessed 1 June 2021; Louis Schetzer, 'Value of a Justice Reinvestment Approach to Criminal Justice in Australia: A Submission to the Senate Legal and Constitutional Affairs References Committee' (Public Interest Advocacy Centre, 18 March 2013) 18 (discussing the influence of American local approaches in reforming the criminal justice system).

[16] *Gregory v Ashcroft* 501 US 452, 458 (1991).

to participate in a national (or transnational) process of policy formation.[17] This citizen involvement encourages key values at the centre of democracy and can help to rebuild trust for institutions.

This insight is critical for improving criminal justice systems. One of the key causes of crime is a breakdown of trust between local communities and law enforcement institutions.[18] The communities that face crime on a day-to-day basis—whether as victims or as perpetrators—are unable to participate in centralized criminal justice reform discussions (whether at state, national, or transnational level). In particular, this kind of centralized reform approach 'limit[s] the voice of groups who are most affected by crime and who frame crime as a public interest problem'.[19] Feeling voiceless, many are likely to view law enforcement officers and institutions with suspicion. Returning policy-making power about criminal law to the local level can improve the ability of these under-represented communities to participate in the criminal justice system and hold their executive officials accountable. This process is more likely to make local communities feel like active citizens and therefore improve trust between law enforcement and the local community.

In addition, this enhanced local participation can help to serve as a training ground for local activists interested in becoming involved in broader policy discussions.[20] This can help to ensure a broader and more diverse set of voices in the policy discussion. This is important as research shows that 'where people are situated in relation to crime, neighborhood, family status, class, race, and a whole host of other factors will probably influence attitudes toward crime and the police'.[21] These views can help to better inform the discussion of criminal justice reform.

Process-based rights protection. A final set of arguments suggests that federalism protects individual rights by dividing and devolving political authority. This understanding of rights-protection is grounded in process: it argues that political competition between different governments will help to increase the likelihood of rights-protective law. Scott Stephenson argues that federalism introduces 'additional participants' into the process which can improve 'deliberation on rights'.[22] The United States Supreme Court has long based its jurisprudence on this idea, writing in *New York v United States* that the Constitution does not divide power to ensure integrity of the states 'as abstract political entities ... To the contrary, the Constitution divides authority between federal and state governments for the

[17] Richard Briffault, 'Our Localism: Part l-Localism and Legal Theory' (1990) 90 *Colum L Rev* 346, 397 (noting how average citizens are more likely to believe that their voices are drowned out or ignored due to the greater number of constituents in national political processes).
[18] James S Coleman, 'Social Capital in the Creation of Human Capital' (1988) 94 *Amer J Sociology* S95 (arguing that crime reflects a breakdown in the 'social fabric' of a society).
[19] Lisa L Miller, *The Perils of Federalism: Race, Poverty, and the Politics of Crime Control* (OUP 2008) 6 (hereafter Miller, *The Perils of Federalism*).
[20] Friedman, 'Valuing Federalism' (n 12) 391–2.
[21] Miller, *The Perils of Federalism* (n 19) 160.
[22] Scott Stephenson, 'Federalism and Rights Deliberation' (2014) 38 *Melb U L Rev* 709.

protection of individuals.'[23] Finally, a long line of distinguished scholars have argued that the 'political safeguards' of federalism ensure rights.[24]

Federalism's diffusion of power can ensure that these political safeguards work in protecting rights in criminal justice systems. Criminal law discussions have increasingly migrated to the national level.[25] This centralization has distorted criminal law debates. Recent research from the United States has shown that this national, centralized policy formulation has a tendency to be particularly harsh because it is dominated by elites and special interest groups who view harsh penalties and streamlined criminal law procedures as the most effective way to combat violent crime.[26] Decentralization can give urban communities a voice in policy. This can help to protect rights. While these communities consistently demand effective and strong penalties to deter criminal activity and keep their streets safe, they also understand first-hand the rights-implications of intrusive policing techniques and overly harsh incarceration regimes. They are thus well-positioned to understand the trade-off between security and individual rights. Empowering their voice can thus help to advance the political foundations of rights protection.

B. Federalism and decentralization in criminal justice reform

These advantages of federalism, however, have played very little role in discussions of criminal justice reform. This stems in part from growing trends towards centralization in federations, particularly in discussions of legal reform.[27] For instance, even in the United States, with its tradition of federalism and local control of crime, the rhetoric of criminal law reform often focuses on national changes and fails to explore the benefits of diffusing power.[28] To make matters worse, leading federal criminal law programmes actively seek to undermine the central ideas of federalism.[29] In particular, these programmes provide millions of dollars to encourage

23 *New York v United States* 505 US 142, 181 (1992).

24 Kramer, 'Putting the Politics Back' (n 10) 215; Wechsler, 'The Political Safeguards' (n 10) 543.

25 Susan Ehrlich, 'The Increasing Federalization of Crime' (2000) 32 *Arizona St L J* 825 (discussing the United States). In Australia, national power over criminal law power has also expanded: see Parliament of Australia, 'History of Criminal Law' <https:www.aph.gov.au/About_Parliament/Parliamentary_Departments/Parliamentary_Library/Browse_by_Topic/Crimlaw/Historycriminallaw> accessed 1 June 2021.

26 Miller, *The Perils of Federalism* (n 19).

27 Eugenie Brouillet, 'Canadian Federalism and the Principle of Subsidiarity: Should We Open the Pandora's Box?' (2011) 54 *Sup Ct L Rev* 601, 602 (hereafter Brouillet, 'Canadian Federalism') (quoting Alain Delcamp that 'a natural tendency in every organized society [is] to strengthen its centre'). The centralization is also linked to the growing role of international law institutions in law reform who often (but not always) undervalue the importance of diffused power.

28 Friedman, 'Valuing Federalism' (n 12) (arguing that federalism has been largely ignored in the practice of judicial decision-making over the last one hundred years). Although beyond the scope of this chapter, federalism's reformist promise has been undervalued because of federalism's association with racism and exclusion during the post-WWII period.

29 Partlett, 'Criminal Law' (n 3); Miller, *The Perils of Federalism* (n 19).

prosecutors and police to circumvent local control of crime thereby weakening accountability and undermining individual rights. This approach stems from decades of the federalization of criminal law which simultaneously criminalizes the same conduct at both the state and federal levels. For instance, both the states and the federal government have criminal laws regulating street-level gun and drug crime. These overlapping laws, however, are adjudicated and punished in very different ways. In particular, federal criminal law is far 'harsher and offers fewer protections than state law'.[30]

In the United States, federal programmes such as Project Safe Neighborhoods ('PSN')—which was 'restored' under the Trump administration and is being continued by the Biden administration—take advantage of this overlap by encouraging cooperation between federal prosecutors and state and local police in circumventing state law.[31] An implementation guide for PSN describes how the 'partnership' is geared towards yielding the most 'effective and vigorous prosecution tools available'.[32] The guide explains how federal criminal law offers particularly 'effective' tools, including more restrictive pre-trial bail laws, far longer sentences, and evidentiary rules that are 'more favorable than controlling state law'.[33] One of the key techniques is for local prosecutors and police to leverage these more 'effective' federal policies to use 'the possibility of severe federal sanctions . . . as an incentive for a defendant to accept a strong state plea bargain'.[34]

These cooperative programmes are successful because executive law enforcement agents on both sides of the federal divide have strong incentives to pursue them. For federal prosecutors, cooperation with state and local law enforcement helps them enforce federal criminal statutes in the absence of a federal police force.[35] Thus, cooperation with state and city authorities allows them to pick a certain number of street-level crimes for prosecution and therefore show their superiors (and voters) a stellar statistical record of successful prosecutions.[36] On the other side, state and local police embrace federal involvement because the threat of transferring a case to the federal system makes it far easier to gain guilty pleas (and

[30] Partlett, 'Criminal Law' (n 3) 1670.

[31] Gerhard Peters and John T Woolley, 'Donald J Trump, Remarks at the Project Safe Neighborhoods National Conference in Kansas City, Missouri' (*The American Presidency Project*, 7 December 2018) <http://www.presidency.ucsb.edu/node/332793> accessed 1 June 2021 (discussing how the Trump White House is 'here today to restore one of the most effective crime prevention strategies in America: Project Safe Neighborhoods').

[32] United States Department of Justice, 'Project Safe Neighborhoods: America's Network Against Gun Violence Implementation Guide for PSN Partners' 2–16 <https://ww.bja.gov/programs/psn/psn_toolkit.pdf> accessed 1 June 2021.

[33] ibid, 2–17.

[34] ibid.

[35] Daniel Richman, 'Project Exile and the Allocation of Federal Enforcement Authority' (2001) 43 *Ariz L Rev* 369, 378.

[36] ibid.

improve their own conviction rates).[37] This has led to a system of codependence between executive branch enforcement agents from both levels of government.[38]

This cooperation attacks key ends of federalism. First, it explicitly signals disdain for local criminal law experimentation. In fact, in pursuit of 'effective' solutions, these programmes seek to circumvent local approaches to criminal law because they are viewed as too lenient. Secondly, these programmes weaken local participation and accountability by circumventing regulation in line with the views of the 'local electorate'.[39] These cooperative agreements undermine the ability of state voters and their legislative representatives to hold their own state and local officials accountable for drug and gun possession crimes. The ability to hold officials accountable is at the heart of a sovereign political entity. This is particularly true in a state's exercise of one of its core police powers: the power to prosecute non-economic street crime. Moreover, by depriving state voters of meaningful ways of controlling their own street-level criminal law policy, for instance by establishing drug courts as an alternative to harsh sentencing, such programmes weaken the accountability of state governments. As a Virginia district court stated, it 'lowers citizens' expectations of the Commonwealth's public servants, it insulates those officials from constructive criticism, and it dissipates political pressure that citizens might otherwise exert to improve the performance of local law enforcement'.[40]

Thirdly, and finally, cooperative prosecution programmes like PSN are a classic example of a 'departure' from the federal structure that undermines individual liberty.[41] By aggregating executive power across local, state, and federal government, these agreements undermine locally formulated checks that protect the rights of criminal defendants such as state law and criminal juries. Moreover, it allows executive branch agents vast discretion to pick and choose individuals for harsh federal punishment. Many have criticized these programmes for relying on race to make these determinations. These programmes therefore turn federalism against the individual, reversing the rights-protective nature of federalism overall.

Outside the United States. In other federations, federalism and decentralization are also rarely viewed as ways of improving criminal justice systems.[42] This also stems from the trend towards centralization in federations.[43] It also reflects the

[37] ibid.

[38] Daniel Richman, 'The Past, Present, and Future of Violent Crime Federalism' (2006) 34 *Crime & Just* 377, 407–26; Daniel Richman, 'Federal Criminal Law, Congressional Delegation and Enforcement Discretion' (1998) 46 *UCLA L Rev* 757 (hereafter Richman, 'Federal Criminal Law') (describing the vast amount of delegated power to federal prosecutors is a form of 'aid-in-kind to state enforcers').

[39] *New York v United States* (n 23) 169.

[40] *United States v Jones* 36 F Supp 2d 304, 313–14 (ED Va 1999).

[41] *New York v United States* (n 23) 181–2.

[42] Criminal law is the subject matter of concurrent jurisdiction between the Bund and the Länder: Basic Law for the Federal Republic of Germany, art 74. Article 72 says that 'on matters within the concurrent legislative power, the Länder shall have power to legislate so long as and to the extent that the Federation has not exercised its legislative power by enacting a law'.

[43] Brouillet, 'Canadian Federalism' (n 27) 602 (quoting Alain Delcamp that 'a natural tendency in every organized society [is] to strengthen its centre').

fact that many European and Latin American federations such as Germany, Brazil, Argentina, and Canada centralize criminal law in national codes. Underlying these national codes is a belief—particularly strong in the civilian legal tradition—that criminal law should be formulated centrally on the principles of uniformity and rationality. In this form, as Reinhard Zimmerman states, the law 'can be reduced to a rational and organized system'.[44] Criminal justice reform is therefore generally underpinned by two concepts.

First, criminal justice reform is viewed as the rational improvement of the general criminal law that applies comprehensively across the whole polity. In particular, code improvement allows the rational and systematic reform of criminal law principles or procedures founded on deeply rooted prejudices. If law can be rationalized, then it should be rationalized for all—and not just a particular subdivision of the country. This centralization in turn ensures an improved and rationally fairer system of criminal law for every citizen facing criminal proceedings. Thus, the reform rationale underpins the codification justification in the civil law system itself. Second, these codes seek to reflect a rule of law value that law is accessible and equally applied. A single code 'facilitates [the law's] comprehensibility',[45] makes clearer to the individual the criminal sanction that she will face if she violates the law. This is viewed as making it far easier for citizens to actually understand the potential sanctions for specific violations.

This centralizing mindset is also driven by key institutions in criminal justice reform. In Europe, trans-European institutions and norms are at the centre of criminal reform discussions. These institutions frequently view reform as a process of rationalization and harmonization. For instance, the Council of Europe has stated that over recent years 'reform' has involved 'bring[ing] their criminal justice system in line with Council of Europe standards'.[46] In Latin America, the Organization of American States and the United Nations are similarly engaged in standard-setting as a way to reform criminal justice systems.[47]

This kind of centralized reform is not on its own problematic; in fact, it could suggest devolving power. But conflating reform with standard-setting and uniformity fails to meaningfully draw on local knowledge or participation in the formulation of new policies. In this way, it ignores the value of subsidiarity—a key principle in many code-based federations which are grounded in the federal principle of the diffusion of power.[48] In fact, subsidiarity principles in many federations

[44] Reinhard Zimmermann, 'Codification: History and Present Significance of an Idea' (1995) 3 *Eur Rev Private L* 95, 97–8.

[45] ibid, 98.

[46] Council of Europe, 'Criminal Justice Reform' <https://ww.coe.int/en/web/national-implementation/thematic-work/criminal-justice-reform> accessed 1 June 2021.

[47] See, eg, United Nations, 'United Nations Latin American Institute for the Prevention of Crime and the Treatment of Offenders (ILANUD)' <https://www.unodc.org/unodc/en/commissions/CCPCJ/PNI/institutes-ILANUD.html> accessed 1 June 2021.

[48] See further Cahill and O'Sullivan, chapter 3 in this volume.

suggest that although the law might be centralized, it should be applied in a way that is sensitive to local differences. Subsidiarity mandates that 'action should be taken at the lowest level of government at which particular objectives can adequately be achieved'.[49] Some have argued that subsidiarity should be taken more seriously in code-based federations.[50]

Finally, even in other federations without uniform codes such as Australia, federalism is rarely viewed as a resource for reforming the criminal justice system. Instead, reformist tendencies once again tend to be centralizing. A good example is the reformist move to create a national uniform criminal code that would lead to harmonization in Australia in the early 1990s. The goal was to draft a 'more perfect' criminal law that would ultimately have been 'free from the restrictions of a particular case and unsullied by political or policy considerations'.[51] This Model Criminal Code ('MCC') was 'produced with the objective of providing all nine Australian jurisdictions—Commonwealth, states and territories—with the opportunity to enact uniform criminal legislation (or at least consistent legislation)'.[52] Although this ultimately failed, the MCC remains an example of the centralizing nature of criminal law reform.

III. Cities and Criminal Law Reform

The failure to value federalism in criminal law reform is a significant problem; decentralization can help to improve both the effectiveness and fairness of criminal justice systems. Enhancing the role of cities—where most crime takes place—in the regulation of criminal law can help to solve this problem. In fact, the diffusion of power to the city can yield a more effective criminal justice system: cities have superior information and therefore can help formulate more effective policies; enhanced urban participation can improve trust between local communities and criminal law enforcement; and cities can help overcome the rights-reducing distortions of centralized criminal law policy-making.

Cities have an intimate relationship with crime. Although cities were first built in the medieval period to provide sanctuary from violence and crime,[53] they have since become the most common site for criminal activity.[54] This is particularly true

[49] George A Bermann, 'Taking Subsidiarity Seriously: Federalism in the European Community and the United States' (1994) 94 *Colum L Rev* 332, 338–9.

[50] Brouillet, 'Canadian Federalism' (n 27).

[51] ibid.

[52] Stella Tarrant, 'Building Bridges in Australian Criminal Law: Codification and the Common Law' (2014) 39 *Monash U L Rev* 838, 840.

[53] Henri Pirenne, *Medieval Cities: Their Origins and the Revival of Trade* (Princeton U P 1952).

[54] Edward L Glaeser and Bruce Sacerdote, 'Why is There More Crime in Cities?' (1999) 107 *J Pol Econ* S225; Pablo Fajnzylber, Daniel Lederman, and Norman Loayza, 'What Causes Violent Crime?' (World Bank, Washington, DC, 1998).

in North and South America. In the United States, for instance, metropolitan areas have 79 per cent more violent crimes and 300 per cent more violence than rural areas.[55] Furthermore, studies from Latin America—one of the most urbanized regions in the world—suggest that crime increases in response to city size.[56] An expert report on Latin American cities estimated that households located in cities with more than one million inhabitants had a 70 per cent higher likelihood of experiencing violence than those in cities of between 50,000 and 100,000.[57] Crime has also played a critical role in shaping the development of cities by effecting city population flows.[58]

Scholars have posited reasons for why crime rates are higher in cities. A number of studies have linked increased poverty and inequality in cities with crime rates.[59] These factors are frequently linked with entrenched histories of racial injustice. Others argue that urban crime rates are related to a breakdown in trust and the more unstable and anonymous nature of city life.[60] Wilson and Hernstein argue that many temporary residents in cities fear neither recognition nor community reprisals.[61] Glaeser and Sacerdote argue that crime rates tend to be higher in cities because of the presence of higher value 'targets', lower probabilities of arrest, and the composition of residents.[62] One World Bank study paraphrased the problem as 'rapid growth of cities feeds the chaotic formation of slums, in which overcrowding and competition for scarce resources combine with weak state security presence to foster criminality and violence'.[63]

Given that crime is predominantly an urban problem, there are strong reasons to think that cities can advance the decentralizing benefits of federalism.[64] First, urban communities have better, first-hand information on the particular causes and approaches to crime than non-urban populations or centralized bureaucrats and planners. They are therefore critical in helping to generate evidence-based policies that respond to real problems on the ground. H. Geoffrey Moulton writes that this can lead to 'significant benefits in terms of … governmental efficiency'.[65] This

55 Glaeser and Sacerdote, 'Why is There More Crime in Cities?' (n 54) S225.

56 Alejandro Gaviria and Carmen Pagés, 'Patterns of Crime Victimization in Latin America' (1999) Inter-American Development Bank, Working Paper No 408 <https://papers.ssrn.com/sol3/papers.cfm?abstract_id=192590> accessed 1 June 2021.

57 Alejandro Gavíria and Carmen Pagés, 'Patterns of Crime Victimization in Latin American Cities' (2002) 67 *J Development Econ* 181, 181–203.

58 Julie B Cullen and Steven D Levitt, 'Crime, Urban Flight, and the Consequences for Cities' (1999) 81 *R Econ & Stat* 159 (discussing the empirical evidence for a strong connection between rising crime rates and urban flight).

59 Ellen Brennan-Galvin, 'Crime and Violence in an Urbanizing World' (2002) 56 *J Intl Affairs* 123 (hereafter Brennan-Galvin, 'Crime and Violence').

60 Louis Wirth, 'Urbanism as a Way of Life' (1938) 44 *Amer J Sociology* 1, 1–24.

61 James Q Wilson and Richard J Hernstein, *Crime and Human Nature* (Simon and Schuster 1985).

62 Glaeser and Sacerdote, 'Why is There More Crime in Cities?' (n 54).

63 The World Bank, 'Violence in the City' <https://openknowledge.worldbank.org/handle/10986/27454> accessed 11 April 2022.

64 Brennan-Galvin, 'Crime and Violence' (n 59).

65 H Geoffrey Moulton Jr, 'The Quixotic Search for a Judicially Enforceable Federalism' (1999) 83 *Minn L Rev* 849, 852.

kind of policy formulation has led to worldwide success. For instance, in Brazil, co-ordination with local communities and groups has played a critical role in undermining the problems of urban crime.[66]

Secondly, enhancing urban involvement in criminal law policy has important effects as well. From a democratic point of view, it transforms urban populations from objects of the criminal justice system (as many are now) into citizen subjects who are actively creating criminal law policy. This can help to improve a key problem in many criminal law systems around the world: a lack of trust between urban communities and police. Numerous studies show trust between police and local communities to be a key factor in crime reduction.[67] Urban participation in the actual regulation of criminal law can help to boost this trust and cooperation. Finally, it can help to train leaders. For instance, in the United States, city mayors are leading the way in experimenting with new ways of reforming the criminal justice system.[68]

Finally, and relatedly, cities can help to ensure a better balance between the rights of criminal defendants and the safety of the community. For urban populations, criminal law policy is not an abstract question of political ideology; on the contrary, it affects their everyday life. On one hand, they are frequently the direct victims of crime. They therefore know the central importance of effective punishment and deterrence for maintaining order and security on the streets.[69] On the other hand, they also feel the effects of harsh policing and criminal law punishment. In particular, they understand the costs of incarceration versus other forms of punishment. They are therefore well-placed to understand the tradeoffs between enforcement that is sufficiently harsh to deter crime (and protect the innocent) while also sufficiently fair to avoid creating even larger problems for the community.

IV. Criminal Law and the Importance of Discretion

Despite the advantages of enhancing urban involvement in the legal regulation of crime, cities have few legal mechanisms for participating in *substantive* criminal

[66] Rodrigo R Soares and Joana Naritomi, 'Understanding High Crime Rates in Latin America: The Role of Social and Policy Factors' in Rafael Di Tella, Sebastian Edwards, and Ernesto Schargrodsky (eds), *The Economics of Crime: Lessons for and from Latin America* (U Chicago P 2010) 52 <https://ww.nber.org/chapters/c11831.pdf> accessed 1 June 2021.

[67] Tom R Tyler and Jeffrey Fagan, 'Legitimacy and Cooperation: Why Do People Help the Police Fight Crime in the Their Communities' (2008) 6 *Ohio St J Crim L* 231.

[68] Collier Meyerson, 'A Crop of Reform-Minded Mayors is Trying to Fix Policing and Fight Mass Incarceration' *The Nation* (12 March 2018) <https://www.thenation.com/article/archive/a-crop-of-reform-minded-mayors-are-trying-to-fix-policing-and-fight-mass-incarceration/> accessed 11 April 2022.

[69] Alec MacGillis, 'The Tragedy of Baltimore' *The New York Times* (12 March 2019) <https://www.nytimes.com/2019/03/12/magazine/baltimore-tragedy-crime.html> accessed 1 June 2021 (discussing how the local community is demanding additional police to reduce spiking crime rates).

lawmaking. Even in federations without national criminal codes, the locus of substantive criminal lawmaking is the state government, which is frequently as 'remote and non-participatory' from the city as the federal centre.[70] This reflects what many have characterized as the general powerlessness of cities in federal systems.[71] Almost one hundred years ago, the United States Supreme Court described this position, stating that cities 'have no inherent right of self-government which is beyond the legislative control of the state' and that 'the state may withhold, grant or withdraw powers and privileges as it sees fit'.[72]

But just because cities play very little role in *substantive* criminal lawmaking does not mean that they cannot play an important role in the regulation of criminal law. Criminal law is about far more than substantive legal norms. Criminal justice systems involve the exercise of significant discretion by executive law enforcement officers—prosecutors and police—in the enforcement of criminal law.[73] This discretion is inescapable, stemming from the fact that both prosecutors and police have limited resources and therefore must 'choose how to allocate investigative and prosecutorial resources'.[74] The amount of discretion varies between different criminal justice systems. On one end, in the United States, for instance, vast discretion is explicitly given to police and (especially) prosecutors. This has led one leading academic to argue that 'law enforcers, not the law, determine who goes to prison and for how long'.[75] On the other end, in Germany, central codes seek to limit the discretion of police and prosecutors. But even in this system, the exercise of discretion is central to criminal law enforcement.[76]

A. Police discretion

It has long been known that the full enforcement of the law by police is impossible; police exercise broad discretion in the implementation of criminal law.[77] A leading historian has written that '[e]very level of police work, especially at the micro level,

[70] H Jefferson Powell, 'The Oldest Question of Constitutional Law' (1993) 79 *Va L Rev* 633, 688, fn 262.

[71] See Frug, 'The City as a Legal Concept' (n 7) (explaining the 'powerlessness' of cities in the United States); Stilwell and Troy, 'Multilevel Governance' (n 7) 925 (exploring the 'marginal status' of local governments in Australia).

[72] *City of Trenton v New Jersey* 262 US 182, 187 (1923).

[73] Here I follow Roscoe Pound in defining discretion as 'authority conferred by law to act in certain conditions or situations in accordance with an official's ... own considered judgment and conscience'. Roscoe Pound, 'Discretion, Dispensation, and Mitigation: The Problem of the Individual Special Case' (1960) 35 *NYU L Rev* 925.

[74] Zachary Price, 'Enforcement Discretion and Executive Duty' (2014) 67 *Vanderbilt L Rev* 682.

[75] William J Stuntz, 'The Pathological Politics of Criminal Law' (2001) 100 *Mich L Rev* 505, 509.

[76] Richman, 'Federal Criminal Law' (n 39) (discussing the vast enforcement discretion given in United States criminal law).

[77] Sanford Kadish, 'Legal Norm and Discretion in the Police and Sentencing Process' (1961) 75 *Harv L Rev* 904.

involves choice on part of the police officer'.[78] Responding to these multifaceted and varied encounters therefore requires that police officers exercise considerable discretion in the course of their everyday activities. But this discretion is an 'unavoidable and ubiquitous feature' of all police work.[79] Scholars have classified the multifaceted ways in which police exercise discretion, including the choice of (1) objectives; (2) methods of intervention; (3) how to dispose of cases; (4) investigative measures; and (5) field procedures.[80]

These forms of police discretion are common to all criminal justice systems.[81] In some federations like Germany, there have been legislative attempts to limit police discretion through legislation. But even in Germany there is a recognition that this discretion is unavoidable and can lead to different approaches. For instance, the state police in some German Länder have been encouraged to become involved in the charging decisions involving individuals that they have apprehended for certain types of criminal conduct. In particular, in the state of Saxony, police have been encouraged to create the conditions legally required for a conditional withdrawal of criminal proceedings in cases of shoplifting.[82]

B. Prosecutorial discretion

Prosecutors also exercise significant discretion in enforcing substantive criminal law.[83] The scope of this prosecutorial discretion varies. In some systems, prosecutors are purposely delegated vast power.[84] In the United States, for instance, prosecutors have broad power to determine who they are going to prosecute. The United States Supreme Court has stated that 'the Executive Branch has exclusive authority and absolute discretion to decide whether to prosecute a case'.[85] In other federations, the law tries to limit prosecutorial discretion. In Germany, for instance, the Criminal Procedure Code attempts to centralize control over the actions of the prosecutor. This includes, most importantly, the conception of compulsory prosecution under the 'principle of legality'. Prosecutors are part of

[78] Mark Finnane, 'Police and Politics in Australia—The Case for Historical Revision' (1990) 23 *Aust & NZ J Criminology* 218, 218.

[79] Katherine Beckett, 'The Uses and Abuses of Police Discretion: Toward Harm Reduction Policing' (2016) 10 *Harv L & Pol Rev* 77, 77.

[80] Herman Goldstein, *Policing a Free Society* (Ballinger P 1977) 95–100.

[81] Gregory H Williams, 'Police Discretion: A Comparative Perspective' (1989) 64 *Indiana L J* 873.

[82] Michael Jasch, 'Police and Prosecutions: Vanishing Differences Between Practices in England and Germany' (2004) 5 *German L J* 1207, 1213.

[83] Sanford C Gordon and Gregory A Huber, 'Citizen Oversight and the Electoral Incentives of Criminal Prosecutors' (2002) 46 *Amer J Pol Sci* 334.

[84] John Langbein, 'Controlling Prosecutorial Discretion in Germany' (1974) 41 *U Chicago L Rev* 439 (hereafter Langbein, 'Controlling Prosecutorial Discretion').

[85] *Nixon v United States* 418 US 683, 693 (1974).

a centralized institution, which is meant to 'permit a unitary interpretation of the law to be propounded for the whole state'.[86]

Prosecutorial discretion is, however, unavoidable. One of the most common ways in which prosecutors exercise discretion is through agreements in which defendants admit their guilt in return for a reduced sentence. In the United States, this process of deal-making—known as plea bargaining—is so widespread that many scholars argue that substantive criminal law has very little to 'no effect' on a plea bargain. In this plea-bargaining process, the law provides the prosecutor with a 'menu' of choices. The prosecutor gets to choose which one she wants to charge with and which not to. One scholar explains how this creates a situation where '[t]he law-on-the-street—the law that determines who goes to prison and for how long—is chiefly written by prosecutors, not by legislators'.[87]

Even in the most centralized system, prosecutors exercise discretion in making agreements with defendants prior to trial.[88] In Germany, where prosecutors are legally bound to prosecute under the principle of legality, the 'increased volume' of cases in many centralized systems 'wreaks havoc with the principle of legality'.[89] In these cases, it is necessary to dispose of some cases 'summarily'.[90] When this happens, prosecutors are no longer rule-bound clerks, but instead are a 'key actor who decides, for many defendants, whether or not they will face the most severe available criminal penalties'.[91] Thus, even in Germany, one of the most significant ways in which prosecutors exercise their discretion is through making agreements with criminal defendants in return for pleading guilty.[92]

V. Controlling Discretion through Accountability Mechanisms

This discretion presents an opportunity for cities to exercise control over the criminal justice system. In particular, urban populations can seek to shape the exercise of this discretion. In some cases, cities already are doing so. Two examples are illustrative: the spread of the sanctuary city movement and community-oriented policing and prosecution.[93] Criminal justice reformers should take note of these

[86] Langbein, 'Controlling Prosecutorial Discretion' (n 84) 449.

[87] William J Stuntz, 'Plea Bargaining and Criminal Law's Disappearing Shadow' (2004) 117 *Harv L Rev* 2548, 2549.

[88] See Jenia Turner, 'Plea Bargaining and Disclosure in Germany and the United States: Comparative Lessons' (2016) 57 *Wm & Mary L Rev* 1549.

[89] Ronald F Wright and Marc L Miller, 'The Worldwide Accountability Deficit' (2010) 67 *Wash & Lee L Rev* 1587, 1596.

[90] ibid.

[91] ibid.

[92] Regina E Rauxloh, 'Formalization of Plea Bargaining in Germany: Will the New Legislation Be Able to Square the Circle?' (2011) 34 *Fordham Intl L J* 296.

[93] Harald E Pepinsky, 'Better Living Through Police Discretion' (1984) 47 *L & Contemporary Problems* 249.

developments and seek to strengthen and expand these forms of urban accountability. These mechanisms can then help to further deepen the federalism benefits in criminal justice reform.

A. Sanctuary cities and traditional political accountability: the interests of cities

In declaring themselves sanctuaries, cities provide important lessons on how urban communities can help to inject the advantages of federalism into the criminal justice system. The sanctuary city movement draws its name from a desire for cities to provide 'sanctuary' for undocumented migrants from central immigration law. One of the central strategies in sanctuary cities has been the use of city ordinances to divert the discretionary apportionment of police resources away from the enforcement of federal immigration laws. These policies can be seen as 'acts of defiance by municipal policy makers against federal immigration laws and policies'.[94]

The United States sanctuary city movement began in California in the 1980s.[95] In San Francisco, the city government passed a local 'City of Refuge' ordinance that prohibited the use of city funds and police resources to assist in the enforcement of federal immigration law. Since then, other cities have introduced concrete policies such as Don't Ask, Don't Tell (DADT) policies which prohibit city police from requesting, recording, or disseminating the immigration status of detained individuals.[96] For instance, in 2004, in Toronto, Canada, activists launched a DADT campaign, after which Toronto's city administration and School Board adopted a range of DADT policies.[97] These policies were the product of a Solidarity City Network that pushed the City Council to adopt a set of by-laws.

These types of actions advance key ends of federalism. Most obviously, this movement demonstrates the role that local knowledge and participation can play in criminal justice reform. Cities built their sanctuary status in response to a key reality of city-based law enforcement: Overly zealous enforcement of immigration laws can ultimately aggravate violent crime by reducing trust and cooperation between the police and immigrant communities. Directing local police not to enforce immigration law will increase trust between the authorities and the immigrant community and therefore enhance the chances that immigrant communities will

[94] Harald Bauder, 'Sanctuary Cities: Policies and Practices in International Perspective' (2016) 55(2) *Intl Migration* 174, 179 (hereafter Bauder, 'Sanctuary Cities').

[95] Peter Mancina, 'The Birth of a Sanctuary-City: A History of Governmental Sanctuary in San Francisco' in Randy Lippert and Sean Rehaag, *Sanctuary Practices in International Perspectives: Migration, Citizenship and Social Movements* (Routledge 2013) 205.

[96] Bauder, 'Sanctuary Cities' (n 94) 176.

[97] ibid, 179.

assist in crime reduction. This in turn is likely to increase the effectiveness of criminal law enforcement overall.

B. Community-oriented policing and prosecution

Another important accountability mechanism at the city level is institution-building that attempts to build links between local communities and police and prosecutors. The deepest-rooted examples come from the community-oriented policing movement. For decades (particularly in South and North America), there have been attempts to enhance the role of cities in the oversight of police.[98] Underlying these initiatives has been a desire to increase trust between urban populations and the police. Many of these initiatives date back decades. In Atlanta, a Citizen Review Board was put into place by the Police Commissioner in 2007 after the death of an elderly woman during the service of an arrest warrant. After controversy about the circumstances of her death, the Chief of Police recommended that a civilian board be created to review individual complaints.[99] Seattle created the Office of Police Accountability that operates within the Seattle Police Department and also reviews individual complaints.[100] President Barack Obama's 2014 Task Force on 21st Century Policing declared the importance of bringing the community into policing. It stated that law enforcement should seek to adopt policies that 'reinforce the importance of community engagement in managing public safety'.[101] In Latin America, as violence in cities spiked during the 1990s, community-oriented policing grew in influence. These policies were in some cases borrowed from Anglo-American countries.[102] In Rio de Janeiro, a centre-left government brought in a pilot programme that focused on 'building good relations with residents' and 'hold[ing] police accountable'.[103]

A less well-known but similarly important initiative is *community-oriented prosecution*. These programmes reflect the belief that criminal justice systems work best when prosecutors work with community members to identify priority areas for prosecution.[104] In the United States, this started with the reorganization of the

[98] Samuel Walker, *Police Accountability: The Role of Citizen Oversight* (Wadsworth Thompson Learning 2001) 19.

[99] Darrel W Stephens, Ellen Scrivner, and Josie F Cambareri, 'Civilian Oversight of the Police in Major Cities' (Office of Community Oriented Policing Services, United States Department of Justice, 2018) 14–15 <https://cops.usdoj.gov/RIC/Publications/cops-w0861-pub.pdf> accessed 1 June 2021.

[100] ibid, 16.

[101] ibid, 42.

[102] Markus-Michael Müller, 'Community Policing in Latin America: Lessons from Mexico City' (2010) 88 *Eur R of Latin Amer & Caribbean Studies* 21.

[103] Enrique D Arias and Mark Ungar, 'Community Policing and Latin America's Citizen Security Crisis' (2009) 41 *Comparative Pol* 409, 418.

[104] John S Goldkamp, Cheryl Irons-Guynn, and Doris Weiland, 'Community Prosecution Strategies: Measuring Impact' (Bureau of Justice Assistance, November 2002) <https://www.ncjrs.gov/pdffiles1/bja/192826.pdf> accessed 1 June 2021.

Montgomery County, Maryland state district attorney office along regional lines so that prosecutors could better understand the needs of particular communities in the early 1990s. Since then, this movement has expanded around the United States.

C. Accountability mechanisms

These types of accountability mechanisms should be studied, supported, and expanded. Although this chapter only has space to begin this project, some preliminary ideas can be highlighted. First, the sanctuary city example shows how urban communities frequently have different interests in the exercise of police and prosecutorial power than the central government. This is an insight that is not just confined to immigration law and policy; it also cuts across the entire criminal law area. National politics can become the product of malapportioned political voting rules that give disproportionate power to low-crime, rural areas that have far greater trust in law enforcement officials (and a fear of crime). In these contexts, national elections can tend towards law-and-order campaigns and slogans, which often contain only thinly veiled racial undertones.[105] City representatives, by contrast, are shaped by a more realistic understanding of crime. Accountability mechanisms can therefore help to ensure that interests of cities are taken into account in the practical operation of the criminal justice system.

The sanctuary city model, however, will not work in all contexts. Because it is grounded in electoral mobilization, it is less appropriate to cities that do not have their own elected self-government and accountable officials. Moreover, in some jurisdictions, one of the model's central mechanisms—city-wide ordinances—is vulnerable to pre-emption by either state or federal law.[106] For instance, in the United States, many state legislatures are increasingly using their constitutional powers to block cities and local governments from adopting local ordinances on immigration policy or gun control.[107] This is leading to long and complex court battles about the proper extent of local autonomy. Despite these challenges, this movement represents an important model for beginning to understand how cities can participate in the reform of their criminal justice systems.

Second, community-oriented policing and prosecution suggest that it is possible to build cooperative relationships between local communities and executive-branch police and prosecutors. Most importantly, these initiatives demonstrate that prosecutors and police do not inevitably view themselves as antagonistic to

[105] Katherine Beckett, *Making Crime Pay: Law and Order in Contemporary American Politics* (OUP 1997).

[106] See also Briffault, chapter 5 in this volume.

[107] Emily Badger, 'Blue Cities Want to Make Their Own Rules and States Won't Let Them' *The New York Times* (6 July 2017) <https://www.nytimes.com/2017/07/06/upshot/blue-cities-want-to-make-their-own-rules-red-states-wont-let-them.html> accessed 1 June 2021.

local communities; instead, they perceive the importance of local engagement in enhancing the effectiveness of their activities. Accountability mechanisms should be built on this kind of cooperation. Thus, this cooperation is built on the idea that the local population share the same goal as police and prosecutors: an effective and fair criminal justice system. Building on these lessons, this chapter will suggest some additional design features for accountability institutions stemming from the decentralizing benefits of federalism.

Real cooperation and meaningful oversight. First, accountability mechanisms need to be more than just symbolic. Instead, they should be designed to afford urban populations sufficient power to gather information and oversee how police and prosecutors are exercising their discretion. In other words, cooperation must reflect a serious commitment by executive branch agents to be transparent and cooperate in good faith. This can raise some difficult questions that need to be worked out. For instance, some jurisdictions prize prosecutorial discretion to such an extent that they will not tolerate interference. Accountability mechanisms—as best they can—should seek to respect important limitations yet also reflect the values of real cooperation.

This kind of authority is critical to ensuring the effective goals of federalism. In particular, by giving urban communities real power, police and prosecutors in the system can actually benefit from the enhanced information that local populations frequently possess about the development of criminal law policy. This can enable context-specific and more rights-protective approaches that focus on particular threats in a particular city.[108] Furthermore, it is useful in advancing the participation goals of federalism. In particular, it helps to ensure that urban participation is more than just symbolic and that a real forum for urban communities to actively participate in discussions about policing and prosecutorial practices in their cities is provided. In an important way, these institutions will serve as a powerful bridge between the communities affected by crime and the executive agents charged with enforcing the law. There is strong evidence that linking law enforcement resources to local government is likely to increase trust and reduce crime. In Australia, there is considerable evidence that local solutions can help to ensure effectiveness.[109]

Effective representation. Accountability mechanisms should also be designed to ensure that these mechanisms include broad-based participation from the individuals who are best situated to comment on criminal law policy. As part of designing representation, reformers should seek to study the ways that participation

[108] Australian Institute of Criminology, 'Why Local Government Has a Major Role in Crime Prevention' (AIC Crime Reduction Matters No 19, 2004) <https://ww.aic.gov.au/publications/crm/crm19> accessed 1 June 2021.

[109] Adrien Cherney, 'The Role of Local Government in Crime Prevention: An Overview' (2006) 5(3–4) *Local Government Reporter* 25–8.

has been structured in other places. This design should be oriented in a way that allows for the training and participation of individuals who are able to actually contribute to critical policy goals. Finally, in designing representation, these accountability mechanisms should also consider structuring their representation to allow collaboration with other city-wide, criminal justice institutions such as public defender offices to better play a role in holding the exercise of discretion to account.

VI. Conclusion

This chapter has argued that federations should not ignore the benefits of decentralization in improving their criminal justice systems. These benefits—which draw on federalism literature—focus on the diffusion of power to build more effective and fair criminal justice systems. Cities are the ideal sites to lead this federalism revival. By expanding accountability mechanisms, urban communities can exercise more local control over the discretion exercised by both police and prosecutors and therefore help to improve their own criminal justice systems. In so doing, they can help to reform the criminal justice system on the basis of both superior, first-hand knowledge of criminal law problems and the improvement of relations between law enforcement and local communities.

This argument is a reminder of the importance of cities in realizing the benefits of decentralization that underpin theories of beneficial federalism.[110] Local government is the unit of government providing the most realistic opportunities for meaningful participation. Andrzej Rapaczynski writes that 'if there is some genuine room for instrumental participation in American political life, it can realistically exist only on the local level'.[111] Richard Briffault argues that the case for federalism is 'served, and perhaps better served, by local governments'.[112] This chapter suggests that if the federalism case for localism is strong, it is perhaps even stronger for cities. This finding therefore suggests a broader research agenda to discover other ways in which urban empowerment can advance the values of federalism.

This argument also shows the ways in which federalism should contribute to ongoing discussions of criminal justice reform. In many federations, particularly in North and South America, criminal justice systems have become captured by national politics and become overly punitive and tough on crime. In fact, amidst

[110] Matthew J Parlow, 'Progressive Policy-Making on the Local Level: Rethinking Traditional Notions of Federalism' (2008) 17 *Temple Pol & Civil Rights L Rev* 371.

[111] Andrzej Rapaczynski, 'From Sovereignty to Process: The Jurisprudence of Federalism After Garcia' [1985] *Sup Ct Rev* 341, 402.

[112] Briffault, 'Normative and Formal Concerns' (n 4) 1315.

national 'war on drugs' campaigns, police search and arrest policies have hardened and incarceration rates have spiralled out of control. Future work should seek to build on this chapter and further explore how cities can use accountability mechanisms to reform these dysfunctional systems; in so doing, the benefits of federalism can play an important role in helping to build both fairer and more effective criminal justice systems.

8

Cities and the Environment on the Constitutional Stage

Victims and Villains

Rebecca Nelson[*]

I. Introduction

Globally, human influence on the environment is now widely considered in both academic and popular settings to be so significant as to constitute a new geological epoch, the Anthropocene.[1] The rapidly accelerating pace, scale, and impact of urbanization makes it a critical driver of that influence,[2] so much so that some prefer the term 'Astycene'—an era altered and characterized by the 'astos', or urban dweller.[3] The widespread adoption of modern constitutional environmental rights provisions speaks to the scale and severity of contemporary environmental threats in general. However, the centrality of cities in causing and experiencing environmental threats, and the corresponding constitutional implications, remain substantively unaddressed by constitutions and their scholars. This chapter applies an environmental lens[4] to the key questions of whether constitutions should recognize cities, and what any such recognition should seek to accomplish in terms of the role, powers, and visibility of cities. Related to these questions are considerations of

* This work is based on research funded by the Australian Research Council (#DE180101154). It benefited from thoughtful comments and discussions with Erika Arban, Amanda Cravens, A R Siders, and Nicola Ulibarri, and attendees of the University of Melbourne School of Law Centre for Comparative Constitutional Studies' Brown Bag Seminar Series, and research assistance by Lucas Volfneuk and L M Shirley. All errors remain those of the author.

[1] Simon L Lewis and Mark A Maslin, 'Defining the Anthropocene' (2015) 519 *Nature* 171, 171.

[2] Tariq Banuri and others, 'Drivers of Environmental Change-Global Environment Outlook (Geo-6): Healthy Planet, Healthy People' in Paul Ekins, Joyeeta Gupta, and Pierre Boileau (eds), *Global Environment Outlook (Geo-6): Healthy Planet, Healthy People* (United Nations Environment Programme 2019) 21.

[3] Karen C Seto, Roberto Sánchez-Rodríguez, and Michail Fragkias, 'The New Geography of Contemporary Urbanization and the Environment' (2010) *35 Annual Rev Environment & Resources* 167, 168.

[4] This perspective is offered while recognizing that other, non-environmental values are also relevant to decisions about constitutionally recognizing cities, for example social and economic factors. This chapter does not seek to exclude, but rather to add to, these other perspectives.

Rebecca Nelson, *Cities and the Environment on the Constitutional Stage* In: *Cities in Federal Constitutional Theory.*
Edited by: Erika Arban, Oxford University Press. © Rebecca Nelson 2022. DOI: 10.1093/oso/9780192843272.003.0009

how cities need to respond to challenges posed by environmental change, and how cities may be defined for the purposes of federal constitutional law.

Existing consideration of the constitutional status of cities tends to address environmental issues only in passing, and chiefly from a socio-economic, rather than ecological, perspective. Scholars focus on political diversity, democratic self-governance, and the implications of constitutionally recognizing cities (or not) for their environmental ambition. Hirschl argues that electoral arrangements that under-represent the population of cities, relative to non-urban areas, result in under-representing progressive political views at the scale of national politics.[5] Conversely, over-representing rural views may mean over-representing apathy or even active antipathy to environmental concerns.[6]

A second environmental focus of the discussion on constitutionally recognizing cities is its fiscal dimension. Some argue that greater fiscal autonomy for cities brought about by constitutionally recognizing them would empower them to pursue environmental protection free from influences perceived to diverge from environmental aspirations.[7] Autonomy could reduce cities' current reliance on big business to finance city spending, which may promote corporate over public interests, and trigger a 'race to the bottom' of regulatory protections that are perceived as burdensome to business[8] (noting that the race to the bottom hypothesis is not without challenge in the environmental context).[9] Some existing experience suggests that increasing constitutional autonomy may increase environmental ambition.[10]

This chapter seeks to build on these discussions by centring the ecological and environmental context of cities in territorial rationales for formally recognizing cities within constitutional systems, considering federalism as 'an idea, rather than a particular institutional model'.[11] While it may seem unorthodox to use environmental conditions as a focus for considering constitutional matters, doing so is consistent with accounts of federalism that recognize the 'constitutional salience of territory',[12] and seek to recognize and protect territorial specificity while fostering one common polity.[13] Fundamentally, the territorial dimension of federal

[5] Ran Hirschl, *City, State: Constitutionalism and the Megacity* (OUP 2020) 175–7.
[6] ibid, 178.
[7] ibid, 175.
[8] ibid, 182–3, 191.
[9] See, eg, T Levy Jacob, 'Federalism, Liberalism, and the Separation of Loyalties' (2007) 101 *Amer Pol Sci Rev* 459, 461–2.
[10] Hirschl (n 5) 179.
[11] Stephen Tierney, 'Federalism and Constitutional Theory' in Gary Jacobsohn and Miguel Schor (eds) *Comparative Constitutional Theory* (Edward Elgar P 2018) 45; Sonja Walti, 'Multi-Level Environmental Governance in Henrik Enderlein, Sonja Walti, and Michael Zurn (eds), *Handbook on Multi-Level Governance* (Edward Elgar P 2010) 411, 419. See also Arban, chapter 1 in this volume.
[12] Tierney, (n 11) 64.
[13] ibid, 62.

constitutional theory ought to consider territory, not in the abstract, but territory comprised of land, water, and linked social-ecological systems.[14]

This chapter uses the metaphor of the constitutional stage to advance a theoretical argument about the value of constitutionally recognizing cities where 'recognition' is understood with respect to the environmental functions that constitutional recognition would facilitate. Section II describes the environmental backdrop to that stage in physical and institutional terms. Section III argues that a city can act in the role of both environmental victim and villain, each of which has implications for whether it is desirable to recognize cities in constitutions, and if so, how to do so. Section IV argues that the action on stage should unfold using dialogues and improvisation—in other words, that constitutional arrangements for recognizing cities should focus on intergovernmental coordination mechanisms that can adapt to changing circumstances, rather than the 'constitutional monologues' of exclusive powers and rigid constitutional formulations. Section V explores factors relevant to the casting call—determining what counts as a city for the purposes of an environmentally informed constitutional narrative.

II. Backdrop

The curtains rise on a complex backdrop of environmental challenges and a busy institutional scene . . .

The question of constitutionally recognizing cities requires first considering the physical and institutional environmental backdrop to the constitutional stage. This involves reflecting on the nature of contemporary environmental challenges and what makes them difficult to address; and the ways in which existing, constitutionally recognized levels of government exercise environment-related powers. These reflections reveal the theoretical and practical centrality of multi-level governance of contemporary environmental problems as a key feature of the backdrop to the constitutional stage.

A. Cumulative environmental problems

Our most important contemporary environmental problems are not the challenges that emerge from the singular environmental catastrophes—oil spills or nuclear meltdowns—that make the front pages of newspapers. Rather, the most important environmental problems that form the backdrop to our constitutional stage are cumulative, complex, and insidious. They are caused by the aggregate effect of many,

[14] As for the benefits of considering environmental policy for 'territorially complex natural systems' in multi-level governance theory: Enderlein, Walti and Zurn (eds), (n 11) 411, 420.

sometimes innumerable, activities, including individually minor effects, which interact and aggregate in scientifically complex ways to produce cumulatively significant environmental effects.[15] Cumulative environmental problems at all scales build slowly and insidiously—from the effects of global climate change producing sea level rise and heat waves that will threaten many cities, but particularly coastal cities;[16] to the regional accumulation of urban and peri-urban land use changes that endanger species;[17] to the local expansion of urban paved areas increasing flooding risks.[18]

These characteristics of cumulative environmental problems carry important challenges for designing legal and institutional interventions to address them. Their complexity entails high requirements for environmental information and scientific expertise to detect and predict problems,[19] and sufficient funding to secure these requirements. Their slow buildup makes shifts in environmental conditions difficult to discern not only for the public, but also for experts with long experience.[20] This makes long-term data collection about environmental conditions critical to reveal dangerous trends in accumulated environmental harm, preferably insulated from the potential for funding changes to create discontinuities in collection that would fundamentally compromise the value of the data.[21] A slow buildup also threatens the salience of cumulative environmental problems when people, and politicians, face more immediate, headline-grabbingly obvious concerns that evoke strong visceral reactions.[22] The insidious nature of cumulative problems means that there is a risk that problems will not remain sufficiently politically salient to ensure enduring efforts to address them. This suggests the benefits of involving multiple levels of government, including cities, as 'norm sustainers'.[23] Similarly, characteristics related to requirements for funding and technical

[15] Scholars have offered various definitions and typologies of cumulative environmental effects. For a review of these, see Peter N Duinker and others, 'Scientific Dimensions of Cumulative Effects Assessment: Toward Improvements in Guidance for Practice' (2013) 21 *Environmental Reviews* 40, 42–3: An influential regulatory definition of cumulative effects is 'the impact on the environment which results from the incremental impact of [an] action when added to other past, present, and reasonably foreseeable future actions regardless of what agency ... or person undertakes such other actions'.

[16] See n 50 and accompanying text.

[17] See n 79 and accompanying text.

[18] See nn 77 and 78 and accompanying text.

[19] In relation to cumulative effects on water resources, see, generally, Rebecca Nelson, 'Water Data and the Legitimacy Deficit: A Regulatory Review and Nationwide Survey of Challenges Considering Cumulative Environmental Effects of Coal and Coal Seam Gas Developments' (2019) 23 *Australasian J Water Resources* 24.

[20] See, generally, S K Papworth and others, 'Evidence for Shifting Baseline Syndrome in Conservation' (2009) 2 *Conservation Letters* 93.

[21] Nelson (n 19) 25. See, generally, Gary M Lovett and others, 'Who Needs Environmental Monitoring?' (2007) 5 *Frontiers in Ecology and the Environment* 253.

[22] See, generally, Elke U Weber, 'Experience-Based and Description-Based Perceptions of Long-Term Risk: Why Global Warming Does Sot Scare Us (yet)' (2006) 77 *Climatic Change* 103.

[23] See, generally, Sharmila L Murthy, 'States and Cities as "Norm Sustainers"' (2019) 37 *Virginia Environmental L J* 1.

resources have implications for desirable institutional elements of the backdrop to our constitutional stage.

B. Cumulative problems and the inevitability, benefits, and risks of multi-level government

Addressing cumulative environmental problems inherently involves multiple levels of government in a complex institutional-environmental backdrop to the constitutional stage. The characteristics of cumulative environmental problems suggest that it will rarely be possible or desirable to address them using a single level of government, whether at a local or higher level. This is an extension to the observation of Justice La Forest, speaking for the majority in a leading Canadian constitutional case: 'the protection of the environment is a major challenge of our time. It is an international problem, one that requires action by governments at all levels'.[24]

Cumulative environmental problems involve diverse interacting activities that are commonly regulated by different levels of government. Taking water resources as an example: in the United States, the federal government regulates water pollution and protects endangered aquatic species, while individual states allocate water resources, the cumulative effects of which (over-use of water) can threaten endangered species[25] and exacerbate water pollution;[26] and land use regulation, which affects both water quality and quantity, is a matter of state law, the implementation of which states delegate to local governments, including cities.[27] Cumulative environmental problems may be so complex, interconnected, and disrespectful of territorial boundaries that it would be impossible and undesirable to eliminate duplication and 'vertical' and 'horizontal' interdependence.[28]

In practice, multiple levels of government, including cities, commonly have powers relevant to dealing with cumulative environmental problems. Even without constitutional recognition, cities have long played important environment-related

[24] *R v Hydro-Québec* [1997] 3 SCR 213 [127].

[25] Rebecca Nelson, 'Groundwater, Rivers and Ecosystems: Comparative Insights into Law and Policy for Making the Links' (2013) 28 *Aust Environment Rev* 558, 562.

[26] This can occur, for example, by causing seawater to intrude into fresh aquifers, or causing a groundwater contaminant plume to spread: Rebecca Nelson and Philippe Quevauviller, 'Groundwater Law' in Anthony J Jakeman and others (eds), *Integrated Groundwater Management: Concepts, Approaches and Challenges* (Springer 2016) 189, 191.

[27] Barbara A Cosens and Craig A Stow, 'Resilience and Water Governance: Addressing Fragmentation and Uncertainty in Water Allocation and Water Quality Law' in A S Garmestani and C R Allen (eds), *Social-Ecological Resilience and Law* (Columbia U P 2014) 152.

[28] That is, they cannot be addressed by a single agency or ministry: John A Hoornbeek and B Guy Peters, 'Understanding Policy Problems: A Refinement of Past Work' (2017) 36 *Policy & Society* 365, 378; Francesco Palermo and Karl Kössler, *Comparative Federalism: Constitutional Arrangements and Case Law* (Hart P 2017) 391–3; R Hollander, 'Rethinking Overlap and Duplication—Federalism and Environmental Assessment in Australia' (2010) 40 *Publius* 137, 139, 151–3.

law-making roles under traditional city functions related to environmental health and safety, land use zoning and water supply, for example.[29] Cities continue to adapt these areas of power to contemporary environmental problems, such as climate change.[30] However, questions of cities' vulnerability to pre-emption by state[31] and federal governments may arise where cities seek to regulate controversial local activities, like greenhouse gas emissions, the use of genetically modified organisms in agriculture, and the practice of hydraulic fracturing in producing energy resources.[32] Whether or not pre-emption is an issue in a particular jurisdictional context, the fact remains that the backdrop to the stage may feature both state and federal actors. Lessons from their interactions usefully inform the desirable role of cities as an actor against this backdrop (section III).

Trends in the vertical allocation of regulatory competency over the environment and natural resources have changed over time, from pre-1970s global preferences for centralized, top-down natural resources governance to 'decentralization euphoria' in the 1990s.[33] Vertical allocations of environmental law-making authority at the constitutional level are highly varied across jurisdictions and environmental subject matters. In some cases, power is shared between federal and state governments, as in Germany.[34] In other cases, significant exclusive national powers accompany grants of autonomy to sub-national governments and some areas of concurrent power, as in Italy.[35] In others, national powers are limited and patchwork-like, overlying a 'carpet' of broader state powers, as in Canada,[36] and may change with time and with constitutional interpretation, as in Australia.[37] In some jurisdictions (the United States, Australia, Germany, Brazil, and Canada, for example), federal law overrules inconsistent state law under doctrines of

[29] See, generally, Sarah Fox, 'Localizing Environmental Federalism' (2020) 54 *UC Davis L Rev* 133, 137–8. Note that this varies between jurisdictions, for example Indian cities lack land use and water supply powers: David Simon and others, 'Responding to Climate Change in Small and Intermediate Cities: Comparative Policy Perspectives from India and South Africa' (2021) 13 *Sustainability* 1, 11.

[30] See, eg, Katherine A Trisolini, 'All Hands on Deck: Local Governments and the Potential for Bidirectional Climate Change Regulation' (2010) 62 *Stanford L Rev* 669, 694–734.

[31] This chapter uses the generic word 'state' to refer to sub-national levels of government that are typically recognized by constitutions. For further discussion of preemption, see Briffault in this volume.

[32] See, generally, Jonathan Verschuuren, 'Hydraulic Fracturing and Environmental Concerns: The Role of Local Government' (2015) 27 *J Environmental L* 431; Rita Barnett-Rose, 'Judicially Modified Democracy: Court and State Pre-Emption of Local GMO Regulation in Hawaii and Beyond' (2015) 26 *Duke Environmental L and Policy Forum* 71.

[33] Krister P Andersson and Elinor Ostrom, 'Analyzing Decentralized Resource Regimes from a Polycentric Perspective' (2008) 41 *Policy Sciences* 71, 72.

[34] Palermo and Kössler (n 28) 391–3.

[35] ibid, 393–6.

[36] Sari Graben and Eric Biber, 'Presidents, Parliaments, and Legal Change: Quantifying the Effect of Political Systems in Comparative Environmental Law' (2017) 35 *Virginia Environmental L J* 357, 374, citing Meinhard Doelle and Chris Tollefson, *Environmental Law: Cases and Materials* (2nd edn, Thomson Reuters 2013).

[37] Lee Godden and Jacqueline Peel, *Environmental Law: Scientific, Policy and Regulatory Dimensions* (OUP 2010) 127.

pre-emption,[38] though concurrent regulation of the same type of environmental effect may still exist in some settings.[39]

Theorists argue that overlapping competencies offer both benefits and risks. On one hand, overlapping environmental regulatory competency insures against agency capture, facilitates policy experimentation and diffusion, boosts democracy, and acts as a valuable check and balance in a politically controversial area.[40] This multi-level check and balance is especially valuable in the case of cumulative environmental problems because the scale of the problem may affect whether, and how, it is perceived. Some environmental problems may only manifest at a larger scale (for example, protecting species that are nationally endangered, but locally common). Conversely, local-scale analysis may reveal important contributors to cumulative environmental problems that become 'lost' when considered at a larger spatial scale, because 'more other sources of effect get captured in the analysis'.[41] In both cases, the true significance of the cumulative problem may go unnoticed if there is no information collection and sharing process to aggregate and analyse data at the scale at which the effects become environmentally significant. Consideration by one level of government alone may miss environmental harms that are significant at a different jurisdictional scale.

Overlapping power also carries risks. Environmental regulation may be ineffective where a lower-level government is reluctant to enforce centrally mandated law because it lacks capacity or enthusiasm;[42] where it breeds 'conflict, stalemate and inaction' due to blame-shifting or the need to reach consensus;[43] where one level ceases regulating but overlooks important inadequacies in the other level's actions;[44] or where there is simply confusion and tension.[45] An important lesson from these observations is that the risks associated with overlapping or interdependent powers necessitate coordination that is designed to minimize these difficulties.

[38] Sandra Zellmer, 'Federal Pre-Emption and Displacement of Environmental Statutes and Common Law Claims' in Michael Faure (ed), *Elgar Encyclopedia of Environmental Law* (Edward Elgar P 2016) 99.

[39] *Water Act 2007* (Commonwealth of Australia) s 40; Palermo and Kössler (n 28) 385.

[40] Hollander (n 28) 153–6; Joyeeta Gupta and Claudia Pahl-Wostl, 'Global Water Governance in the Context of Global and Multilevel Governance—Its Need, Form, and Challenges' (2013) 18 *Ecology & Society* 53, 55; Andersson and Ostrom (n 33) 76; Erin Ryan, 'Negotiating Environmental Federalism: Dynamic Federalism as a Strategy for Good Governance' (2017) *Wisconsin L Rev* 17, 37; Cosens and Stow, (n 27) 156–7; Enderlein, Walti, and Zurn (n 11) 411, 415.

[41] Riki Therivel and Bill Ross, 'Cumulative Effects Assessment: Does Scale Matter?' (2007) 27 *Environmental Impact Assessment Rev* 365, 382.

[42] Sara Dillon, 'The Mirage of EC Environmental Federalism in a Reluctant Member State Jurisdiction' (1999) 8 *NYU Environmental L J* 1, especially 13–17; Huiyi Zhao and Robert Percival, 'Comparative Environmental Federalism: Subsidiary and Central Regulation in the United States and China' (2017) 6 *Transnational Environmental L* 531, 536 (in relation to local-level implementation of central Chinese laws).

[43] Enderlein, Walti and Zurn (n 11) 414.

[44] Dillon (n 42) 13–15.

[45] Louise Tait and Megan Euston-Brown, 'What Role Can African Cities Play in Low-Carbon Development? A Multilevel Governance Perspective of Ghana, Uganda and South Africa' (2017) 28 *J Energy in Southern Africa* 43, 48.

In addition to the complexity that arises from the inevitability of overlapping regulatory competency, the nature of the overlap can be highly dynamic, for diverse reasons: evolving statutory implementation of explicit constitutional environmental provisions;[46] negotiated federalism in the case of more ambiguous powers;[47] or the implications for national powers of ratifying international environmental treaties.[48] Accordingly, coordination mechanisms should allow for changing relationships (see further section IV).

The environmental backdrop to our constitutional stage can be characterized, then, as involving cumulative, complex, and insidious environmental challenges that manifest at multiple geographic scales; and the messy and interdependent exercise of environment-related powers that underscores the value of intergovernmental coordination, both theoretically and practically. Against this backdrop, we turn to considering the question of constitutionally recognizing cities by understanding the nature of cities as environmental actors on the constitutional stage.

III. The City as Environmental Victim and Villain and Constitutional Implications

The backdrop set, this section turns to exploring the characters of cities in the environment and contends that they may be both collective environmental 'victims' and 'villains'. That is, cities may both suffer from and cause environmental harm. Which is the case may vary with the specific environmental issue and over time and space, even within a single national jurisdiction. Examining the characteristics of the hypothetical 'victim-city' and 'villain-city' at each end of this spectrum helps draw out insights relevant to the questions of whether it would be desirable to constitutionally recognize cities, and what any such recognition ought to accomplish. It also further confirms the value of intergovernmental coordination demonstrated in section II.

A. The city as environmental victim

The victim-city limps onto the stage, an environmentally benign and ambitious, but resource-poor, city. It suffers from cumulative socio-environmental stresses beyond its control, exacerbated by dense city living and, to the city's great concern, stresses that are experienced unequally across its territory.

46 Roderic O'Gorman, 'Environmental Constitutionalism: A Comparative Study' (2017) 6 *Transnational Environmental L* 435, 437.

47 Ryan (n 40) 37.

48 Godden and Peel (n 37) 127.

The effects of key global and regional environmental trends are likely to be especially pronounced in cities because of the realities of dense urban living. In particular, climate change effects are increasing vulnerability 'in urban centres of all sizes, economic conditions and site characteristics'.[49] Key vulnerabilities relate to increased peak temperatures exacerbated by urban 'heat islands', water shortages, coastal flooding caused by sea level rise, and inland flooding caused by extreme rainfall events.[50] Urban infrastructure for water, sanitation, energy, transport, and communication will face increasing stresses, especially where cities have dense and aging infrastructure, or have under-invested in infrastructure either generally or in informal neighbourhoods.[51] These impacts interact with socio-economic stressors that are likely to be more pronounced in cities than elsewhere, including 'rapid population growth, political instability, poverty and inequality, ineffective local governments, [and] jurisdictional fragmentation'.[52] Climate change will also increase migration to cities,[53] with migration considered to provide independent support for constitutionally recognizing cities.[54]

It can be expensive to collect data about, and respond to, these diverse and serious environmental concerns, and this is problematic, since cumulative environmental problems have high data demands[55] and cities around the world bear increasing financial burdens of responsibilities transferred from higher government levels.[56] The urban effects of climate change are a case in point. Adapting to predictions of coastal sea level rise may involve providing better drainage to prevent flooding, building seawalls, better maintaining roads, investing in cooling capacity for transport infrastructure, enhancing medical services, and improving green spaces to reduce the urban heat island effect.[57] Such action relies on the unique local environmental knowledge of cities,[58] but also requires high-cost, sophisticated science. There appears little evidence that cities have any advantage or reliable capacity in relation to complex scientific knowledge, which may be less obtainable with often limited local resources.[59]

[49] A Revi and others, 'Urban Areas' in C B Field and others (eds), *Climate Change 2014: Impacts, Adaptation, and Vulnerability Part A: Global and Sectoral Aspects Contribution of Working Group II to the Fifth Assessment Report of the Intergovernmental Panel on Climate Change* (CUP 2014) 537, 538.

[50] ibid, 552–6.

[51] ibid, 557–9.

[52] ibid, 549.

[53] Banuri (n 2) 21, 49-50.

[54] Hirschl (n 5) 174.

[55] See section II.

[56] Seto, Sánchez-Rodríguez, and Fragkias (n 3) 180; Tait and Euston-Brown (n 45) 44–5.

[57] Revi (n 49) 571, 572–3, 575, 591.

[58] Andersson and Ostrom (n 33) 75; Jonathan H Adler, 'When is Two a Crowd—The Impact of Federal Action on State Environmental Regulation' (2007) 31 *Harv Environmental L Rev* 67, 77; Daniel C Esty, 'Revitalizing Environmental Federalism' (1996) 95 *Mich L Rev* 570, 648; Ryan (n 40) 24.

[59] Daniel L Millimet, 'Environmental Federalism: A Survey of the Empirical Literature' (2014) 64 *Case Western Reserve L Rev* 1669, 1746; Andersson and Ostrom (n 33) 76.

The need for both local environmental information and local environmental action reveals the benefit of constitutionally recognizing cities in a way that ensures a stable, independent funding base that does not rely on offering incentives to attract mobile industrial capital that would further increase local environmental harms.[60] Greater fiscal autonomy would help meet these costs, and intra-city inequalities could be addressed by a constitutional fiscal equalization strategy (giving more federal tax money to cities with less), made possible by constitutionally recognizing cities.[61] Handouts to cities from higher-level governments are unlikely to solve the problem. Political considerations aside, local environmental perceptions and preferences may differ from those of higher-level governments. Cities may prefer bolder action on climate change than federal governments because they expect reduced local air pollution, increased green business opportunities, or perceive greater voter demand.[62] Where local governments need to rely on federal environmental funding programs, those initiatives may have different goals that do not adequately respond to local perceptions of the most important problems.[63] Constitutionally guaranteed funding would avoid this.

The cumulative effects of environmental and socio-economic vulnerabilities in the victim-city give rise to unique and pronounced environmental justice concerns across multiple environmental domains.[64] Air pollution, for example, is mainly experienced in large urban areas, as a result of road emissions and industrial pollutants.[65] Poorer and minority populations may experience disproportionate impacts for several reasons: an environmental stressor may occur more commonly in poorer areas (eg poor sanitation in informal neighbourhoods of mega-cities); the environmental harm may accumulate with other sources experienced by the poor (eg outdoor air pollution compounding exposure to indoor air pollution caused by cooking with wood fuel);[66] and environmental stresses may compound other forms of disadvantage (eg poor health) that are less prevalent in wealthier or majority populations. Environmental problems and socio-economic stressors in cities have cumulative, compounding effects on relevant populations.

[60] Hoi Kong, 'Toward a Federal Legal Theory of the City' (2012) 56 *McGill L J* 473, 490-1.

[61] Hirschl (n 5) 218.

[62] Stepan Wood and Kevin Thompson, 'Transnational Voluntary Climate Change Initiatives for Local Governments: Key Variables, Drivers and Likely Effects' in Benjamin J Richardson (ed), *Local Climate Change Law: Environmental Regulation in Cities and Other Localities* (Edward Elgar P 2012) 55–9.

[63] Chloe B Wardropper, Chaoyi Chang, and Adena R. Rissman, 'Fragmented Water Quality Governance: Constraints to Spatial Targeting for Nutrient Reduction in a Midwestern USA Watershed' (2015) 137 *Landscape and Urban Planning* 64, 70.

[64] See, generally, Charles Lee, 'A Game Changer in the Making: Lessons from States Advancing Environmental Justice through Mapping and Cumulative Impact Strategies' (2020) 50 *Environmental L Reporter* 10203.

[65] See, generally, Phillip Dickerson and others, 'Air' in Paul Ekins, Joyeeta Gupta, and Pierre Boileau (eds), *Global Environment Outlook (Geo-6): Healthy Planet, Healthy People* (United Nations Environment Programme 2019) 21.

[66] Ioannis Manisalidis and others, 'Environmental and Health Impacts of Air Pollution: A Review' (2020) 8 *Frontiers in Public Health* 1, 2, 3.

This arguably justifies shielding the attempts of enlightened cities to improve environmental protections for their most vulnerable populations from pre-emption. Constitutional recognition could establish this shield for cities that pursue them as part of environmental justice initiatives.

Good intergovernmental coordination is also required to deal with cumulative environmental problems experienced by the victim-city. Horizontal, inter-city coordination is needed to deal with spatially continuous environmental problems, like flooding.[67] Vertical coordination is needed to deal with the potential for cities to be unduly constrained by higher-level governmental decisions about such matters as funding, land use, and infrastructure planning decisions.[68] Equally, vertical coordination could facilitate the transfer of information and expertise from other levels of government. Through vertical coordination, cities could also voice their experiences of regional and global environmental stresses to inform regional and global interactions undertaken by higher levels of government, for example, in treaty negotiations.

B. The city as environmental villain

The stage darkens, the victim-city retreats, and the villain-city looms. This resource-hungry city causes cumulative environmental damage outside its boundaries and is unresponsive to its under-represented communities, which suffer disproportionately from environmental stresses.

Cities may cause environmental harms at multiple spatial scales: to distant areas, to their surrounding regional environments, and to their own local urban environments. Cities often source resources from beyond their limits, and potentially far afield, with corresponding distant environmental impacts.[69] Individual city dwellers place more pressure on natural resources than their rural counterparts.[70] Globally, cities produce a high proportion of global greenhouse gas emissions,[71] and 25 cities produce 52 per cent of urban emissions.[72] Urbanization drives potentially distant land use changes and environmental impacts, known as 'urban land teleconnections' in urban geography scholarship,[73] for example land conversion to agriculture to sustain urban food demands. Regionally, sprawling urbanization[74]

[67] Revi (n 49) 577.

[68] ibid.

[69] See, generally, Benjamin Goldstein and others, 'Surveying the Environmental Footprint of Urban Food Consumption' (2017) 21 *J Industrial Ecology* 151; for an interactive presentation of academic data relating to urban sourcing of food, energy, and water, see <https://fewsion.dtn.asu.edu/>.

[70] But note that cities use resources more efficiently per unit of income generated: Banuri (n 2) 21, 31.

[71] Revi (n 49) 535, 538.

[72] Ting Wei, Junliang Wu, and Shaoqing Chen, 'Keeping Track of Greenhouse Gas Emission Reduction Progress and Targets in 167 Cities Worldwide' (2021) 3 *Frontiers in Sustainable Cities 1*, 3.

[73] See, generally, K C Seto and others, 'Urban Land Teleconnections and Sustainability' (2012) 109 *Proceedings of the National Academy of Sciences* 7687.

[74] Banuri (n 2) 35.

may threaten the often high ecological value of urban peripheries.[75] Cities also often use surrounding regions to source freshwater and dispose of wastewater, with the potential for environmental damage, including changing stream hydrology and chemistry, building dams, and over-pumping groundwater.[76] Within cities, urbanization damages rivers when large areas of impermeable surfaces—roads, roofs, carparks—and their drainage systems increase polluted stormwater, runoff, and flooding,[77] which existing laws do not effectively address.[78] Cities may overlook environmental protections for charisma-challenged endangered species within city limits.[79] More indirectly, the current COVID-19 pandemic shows that urbanization and dense living can create ideal conditions for the extensive spread of zoonotic and other emerging infectious diseases from urban centres to surrounding regions and the world at large.[80]

In view of the environmental risks that cities pose, granting cities constitutionalized 'negative autonomy' would seem unwise if there is a risk that cities might not reliably consider or deal with their environmental harms. Most charitably, a city may simply not perceive as significant an environmental problem that is highly significant at a different scale.[81] Less charitably, a city may have fewer electoral incentives than higher-level governments to control environmental externalities from which it perceives a benefit. This could include protecting habitat that would constrain city development or reducing city access to water supplies to protect regional rivers. The need for US federal legislative intervention to allow funding for municipal wastewater treatment in the 1950s was a case in point: cities had been reluctant to invest in benefits they perceived as accruing mainly to downstream areas.[82] The multi-scalar and cumulative nature of environmental problems—to which cities contribute, but for which they may not be solely responsible—suggests the value of collaborative problem-solving through intergovernmental coordination, rather than leaving cities out of regulatory or other actions to address environmental harm (see further section IV).

Cities may also lack strong incentives to address environmental harm, like locally severe air pollution, which may affect only a subset of politically

[75] Andrea Olive and Alexa Minichiello, 'Wild Things in Urban Places: America's Largest Cities and Multi-Scales of Governance for Endangered Species Conservation' (2013) 43 *Applied Geography* 56, 57.

[76] Michael J Stewardson and others, 'Understanding Hydrological Alteration' in Avril Horne and others (eds), *Water for the Environment: From Policy and Science to Implementation and Management* (Elsevier 2017) 37, 42–5, 57.

[77] ibid.

[78] See, eg, Rebecca Nelson, 'Sick City Streams: New Approaches to Legal Treatments' (2020) 43 *Melbourne U L Rev* 748.

[79] Olive and Minichiello (n 75) 56, 58, 64–5 (eg endangered bats in suburban Indianapolis): in the United States, 22 per cent of endangered species live in urban areas.

[80] See, generally, Tong Wu, 'The Socioeconomic and Environmental Drivers of the COVID-19 Pandemic: A Review' (2021) 50 *Ambio* 822.

[81] See n 41 and accompanying text.

[82] Zhao and Percival (n 42) 533.

disempowered urban dwellers who have little scope to obtain redress at the ballot box. These concerns highlight the value of constitutional environmental rights provisions, which are relatively commonplace in modern constitutions,[83] though arguably poorly implemented, at least in terms of direct judicial enforcement.[84] Disadvantaged urban communities would gain the greatest benefit from these provisions if they were defined or interpreted so as to recognize the cumulative effects of both socio-economic and environmental stresses, recognizing that urban socio-economic vulnerability can increase the impact of a given level of environmental harm.[85] Constitutional environmental protections could also apply specifically to urban dwellers, who are arguably most likely to find these protections under threat, by framing constitutional duties on governments, specifically including cities, to adopt legislative measures or policies to protect the environment.[86] This could also be the foundation for an accompanying constitutional duty on cities to report on how they deliver this obligation. This would at least build the potential for political pressure in response to governmental failures to deliver on obligations, even in the absence of a judicially enforceable right. Such a reporting duty would be consistent with the imposition of constitutional duties on governments to raise public awareness about environmental concerns.[87] Lastly, intergovernmental coordination (see further section IV) could help improve implementation of environmental rights, given the intersectoral (eg health, industry, transport) concerns that accumulate to pose environmental justice risks. Indeed, in finding a breach of a constitutional environmental right associated with an industrial pollution incident in Valparaiso, Chile, in 2019 its Supreme Court required a large array of public agencies to coordinate their actions to address it.[88]

1. Stage to reality

Real cities are neither the caricatured victim nor villain, but some mixture of both. Urban and regional environmental risks differ across space and time, and cities may have greatly varying degrees of ambition to address environmental problems, even within a single jurisdiction and in relation to a single issue.[89] Nonetheless,

[83] Lael K Weis, 'Environmental Constitutionalism: Aspiration or Transformation?' (2018) 16 *Intl J of Constitutional L* 836, 837.

[84] See, generally, ibid.

[85] See nn 64 to 66 and accompanying text.

[86] See, eg, art 90(2) of the Constitution of the Republic of Mozambique: 'The State and the local authorities, with collaboration from associations for environmental protection, shall adopt policies to protect the environment . . .', discussed in Ed Couzens and Meda Couzens, 'A Comparison of Constitutional Provisions on Water-Related Rights in Southern African States' in J Hollo Erkki (ed), *Water Resource Management and the Law* (Edward Elgar P 2017) 68, 77–8.

[87] ibid, 68, 79 (Seychelles), 84 (Zambia).

[88] Francisco Chahuan Chahuan contra Empresa Nacional de Petroleos Enap S.a, Corte Suprema de Chile, Case N° 5888-2019 (28 May 2019).

[89] In relation to the responses of US cities to climate change, see, generally, Armin Jeddi Yeganeh, Andrew P McCoy, and Todd Schenk, 'Determinants of Climate Change Policy Adoption: A Meta-Analysis' (2020) 31 *Urban Climate* 100547.

considering these ends of the spectrum supports a theoretical argument for recognizing cities in constitutions, regardless of their 'victimhood' or 'villainy'. Recognition would help address cumulative environmental problems in both situations.

In summary, seeing cities as environmental 'victims' carries three constitutional implications. Firstly, cities would benefit from a stable (constitutionalized) funding base to deal with the costs of predicting, detecting, and responding to growing environmental problems. Secondly, acute and unevenly experienced cumulative urban environmental stresses warrant constitutional protection from pre-emption for local environmental regulation that exceeds standards set centrally. Finally, structures for intergovernmental coordination that include cities would help cities to address inter-local problems as well as voice their concerns to influence how higher-level governments exercise powers relevant to cumulative environmental problems at higher spatial scales.

Seeing cities as environmental 'villains' supports Blank's caution against granting cities 'negative autonomy' in allocating any constitutional powers,[90] except to increase environmental protection within their boundaries. It would be preferable to address the environmental externalities of cities with mutual oversight and coordination. Secondly, it recommends giving cities a voice in the exercise of environment-related powers by higher-level governments, recognizing the potential for cities to help resolve externalities to which they contribute. It also supports constitutionalizing protective environmental rights standards that recognize the cumulative effect of environmental harms and socio-economic disadvantage that are pronounced for some urban populations. A formalized coordination mechanism would improve the delivery of these rights to urban dwellers and others.

IV. A Flexible Script with Improvised Dialogues

The set is in place, the characters are sketched, and the constitutional scriptwriter drafts a narrative of relationships and dialogues, inviting improvisation and change.

Section II highlights the value of intergovernmental coordination from the lessons of federal-state interaction related to the environment. Section III confirmed this value in considering the environmental roles of cities, whether victims or villains. In other words, the constitutional script requires flexible constitutional dialogues, not rigid soliloquys, to address the environmental problems from which cities suffer and to which they contribute. This speaks to intergovernmental relationships more akin to subsidiarity than federalism: it embraces overlapping

[90] Yishai Blank, 'Federalism, Subsidiarity, and the Role of Local Governments in an Age of Global Multilevel Governance' (2010) 37 *Fordham Urban L J* 509, 530.

jurisdiction, refrains from granting primacy to any one territorial sphere (other than to secure environmental rights and environmental justice), allows for more than two levels of government, and promotes duties of assistance rather than non-intervention and non-interference.[91] Overall, it produces a system in which governments 'work[] in tandem … as overlapping and cooperating rather than as negating one another'.[92]

Formalized legal mechanisms for coordination help address the challenging characteristics of cumulative environmental problems: their slow build, incremental nature, long time horizons, high information costs, and the potentially minor nature of individual contributing effects.[93] These characteristics are relatively unlikely to reflect important conditions that are theorized to promote coordination. These conditions include: leaders perceiving that their interests are served by incurring the 'high … transaction costs of initiating a collaborative effort'; a starting appreciation of the salience of the issue among all participants;[94] and shared beliefs about environmental values (given how these can differ at different scales),[95] the proper role of experts, and 'the relative seriousness and causes of policy problems'[96] (which can be complex and unclear without good environmental data).[97] Accordingly, dealing with cumulative environmental problems would benefit from formal intergovernmental coordination structures under which any government—including a city—could trigger a coordination process and action to address the problem. Such a 'trigger' feature would allow a federal or state government to require city involvement in a process designed to address the environmental impacts of cities; or a city could require state or federal involvement in resolving diverse factors that aggregate to cause cumulatively significant social-environmental harm among its residents, or to push for relevant national policy to help address the harm at a higher scale. A formal coordination mechanism also provides a vehicle for information-sharing between levels of government that have different environmental roles and specialized areas. Inadequate environmental information is a notorious obstacle to dealing with cumulative environmental problems,[98] and analysis of intergovernmental coordination in relation

[91] See, generally, ibid, especially 511.
[92] ibid, 512.
[93] See above section II.
[94] Kirk Emerson, Tina Nabatchi, and Stephen Balogh, 'An Integrative Framework for Collaborative Governance' (2012) 22 *J Pub Admin Research & Theory* 1, 9.
[95] Above n 41 and accompanying text.
[96] John C Calanni and others, 'Explaining Coordination in Collaborative Partnerships and Clarifying the Scope of the Belief Homophily Hypothesis' (2014) 25 *J Pub Admin Research & Theory* 901, 904, citing Paul A Sabatier and Hank C Jenkins-Smith, 'The Advocacy Coalition Framework: An Assessment' in Paul A Sabatier (ed), *Theories of the Policy Process* (Westview 1999) 117.
[97] See section II.A.
[98] Zhao Ma, Dennis R Becker, and Michael A Kilgore, 'Assessing Cumulative Impacts within State Environmental Review Frameworks in the United States' (2009) 29 *Environmental Impact Assessment Rev* 390, 391.

to cumulative problems suggests local governments can often be left out of this process.[99]

The stability offered by constitutionalizing coordination to structure intergovernmental interactions is a significant advantage over relying on legislation or formal policy as the basis for a coordination mechanism. Formal, non-constitutional intergovernmental mechanisms are certainly common.[100] They include executive forums, joint institutions and specialized agencies, and intergovernmental agreements.[101] However, policy dynamism can prove destabilising. Recent experience in Australia demonstrates the potential vulnerability of even well-established formal coordination mechanisms. Amid the COVID-19 pandemic, May 2020 saw the disbanding of the Council of Australian Governments, which had served as the long-running vehicle for federal-state coordination on environmental and water policy.[102] Its replacement 'National Cabinet' lacks a dedicated institutional focus on environmental issues, in favour of social and economic issues.[103] Even legislatively supported coordination can be brittle. Baulking at national environmental goals, states periodically threaten to withdraw[104] from a cooperative federal legislative scheme to manage Australia's most important interstate river basin, where the scheme relies on states voluntarily referring their powers to the federal government under a provision of Australia's Constitution.[105]

While ensuring the stability of some form of intergovernmental coordination, a constitutional coordination mechanism ought also to accommodate change. Experience suggests that not only are the domains of government problem-solving for cumulative environmental problems interdependent,[106] but the nature of

[99] ibid, 396.

[100] Johanne Poirier and Cheryl Saunders, 'Comparative Experiences of Intergovernmental Relations in Federal Systems' in Johanne Poirier, Cheryl Saunders, and John Kincaid (eds), *Intergovernmental Relations in Federal Systems* (OUP 2015) 440, 479.

[101] See, generally, ibid. Anika Klafki, 'Legal Harmonization through Interfederal Cooperation: A Comparison of the Interfederal Harmonization of Law through Uniform Law Conferences and Executive Intergovernmental Conferences' (2018) 19 *German L J* 1437, 1451–4; Arlene Kwasniak, 'Environmental Assessment, Overlap, Duplication, Harmonization, Equivalency, and Substitution: Interpretation, Misinterpretation, and a Path Forward' (2009) 20 *J Environmental L & Practice* 1, 29-30; Walter F Carnota, 'Intergovernmental Relations in Argentina: Systematic Confusion and Predominance of the Centre' in Johanne Poirier, Cheryl Saunders, and John Kincaid (eds), *Intergovernmental Relations in Federal Systems* (OUP 2015) 14, 29–31.

[102] Hollander (n 28) 144, 147–51. The Intergovernmental Agreement on the Environment, which settled national and state roles and responsibilities, was signed on 1 May 1992 <https://www.environment.gov.au/about-us/esd/publications/intergovernmental-agreement>.

[103] See *National Cabinet Reform Committees* <https://federation.gov.au/national-cabinet/national-cabinet-reform-committees>. See also Selena Bateman and Adrienne Stone, 'Australia: Covid-19 and Constitutional Law' in José María Serna de la Garza (ed), *Covid-19 and Constitutional Law: Covid-19 Et Droit Constitutionnel* (Universidad Nacional Autónoma de México 2020) 223, 224–5; J R Murphy and E Arban, 'Assessing the Performance of Australian Federalism in Responding to the Pandemic' (2021) 4 *Publius* 627.

[104] For example, Adam Webster, 'Reflecting on the Waters: Past and Future Challenges for the Regulation of the Murray-Darling Basin' (2019) 40 *Adelaide L Rev* 249, 254.

[105] ibid.

[106] See section II.B.

desirable coordination can change. Japanese compensation schemes for city air pollution illustrate this dynamism in the context of multi-level government, if not a federal system. In that case, responsibility for addressing the problem has shifted from local, to locally informed national, to cooperative national-metropolitan efforts spanning multiple sectors. Initial city-level healthcare programs for air pollution-affected residents became financially overwhelmed by the cost of large numbers of patients. Japan's national Pollution-Related Health Damage Compensation Law of 1973 was then introduced to deal with the health effects of air and other pollution. The implementation of this law occurred at multiple levels: to be eligible to receive compensation in relation to air pollution, a person was required to reside in, or commute to, a locally polluted area designated at the prefectural level.[107] Compensation was funded by a levy on polluting industries and an automobile tax.[108] National cancellation of the designated areas in 1987 triggered litigation. The resulting settlements required several national ministries to cooperate with the Tokyo metropolitan government to achieve air quality standards and required the Aichi prefectural government and national ministries to take action in relation to automobile pollution.[109]

The analysis above, together with the characteristics of cumulative environmental problems discussed in section II.A, suggest that a constitutional coordination mechanism to address environmental problems should assist governments at different levels using measures that help facilitate three key functions: building a shared understanding of the complex problems and their potentially disputed causes; establishing structures for collecting and sharing relevant information; and establishing triggers for intervening to prevent or remedy the problems. These functions could be advanced by multiple practical models of coordination and mechanisms for resolving disputes between the coordinating entities, for which the appropriate institutional model will be influenced by the jurisdictional context.[110] For present purposes, generalized insights are that constitutionalizing coordination in a way that recognizes cities ensures a stable pathway (albeit one that must accommodate flexibility and dynamism) for multiple levels of government to coordinate efforts to both understand and respond to contemporary environmental problems that cities cause or experience.

[107] Eri Osaka, 'Reevaluating the Role of the Tort Liability System in Japan' (2009) 26 *Arizona J Intl & Comp L* 393, 405.

[108] ibid.

[109] ibid 408, 419, 421.

[110] Considering these contexts lies outside the scope of this chapter, but for existing work on the more general topic of structures for intergovernmental relations in federal systems, see, eg, Johanne Poirier, Cheryl Saunders, and John Kincaid (eds), *Intergovernmental Relations in Federal Systems: Comparative Structures and Dynamics* (OUP 2015).

V. Casting Call

The set and script are complete, and the casting process begins: which cities make the cut?

If considering environmental concerns provides support for constitutionally recognizing cities, the question remains: which areas should be counted as 'cities'?[111] Urban research grapples with this question, producing debates about defining cities in numerous ways as social and economic entities and built, non-'natural' entities.[112] Interdisciplinary urban scholarship provides no easy, off-the-shelf answer.

If a rationale for constitutionally recognizing cities is that this facilitates action to deal with environmental problems involving cities, the changing nature of these problems makes it difficult to construct a static list of cities eligible for recognition. However, the analysis offered above points to several factors that are relevant to determining what counts as a city for the purposes of constitutional recognition to facilitate environmental problem-solving. This points to the desirability of a constitutional formula that could allow for change. Considering environmental 'victimhood' suggests that factors such as vulnerability to threats for example sea level rise and flooding and adequacy of basic infrastructure are relevant to defining a city. It also counsels against adopting a definition with a high population threshold: small and medium cities are growing at the fastest rate,[113] and experience more risk from natural hazards than megacities and big cities,[114] with fewer resources to cope.[115] Considering environmental 'villainy' suggests that factors such as an urban area's endowment of endangered species and the environmental vulnerabilities of its key regional resources, such as water supply and potential waste disposal sites, will be relevant to defining a city for present purposes.

Issues of spatial scale, diversity, and number are also salient. Defining cities at too fine-grained a scale risks inter-local fragmentation and competition.[116] Territorial environmental diversity also emerges as a relevant factor, analogous to traditional rationales for federal structures based on social (for example, ethnic) diversity.[117] A state, province, canton, or other subnational unit (in a federal system) or a nation (in a unitary system) in which cities experience highly diverse environmental issues would benefit most from constitutionally recognizing cities. At

[111] See also Cahill and O'Sullivan, chapter 3 in this volume, andDaniel Weinstock, 'Cities and Federalism' in James E Fleming and Jacob T Levy (eds), *Federalism and Subsidiarity* (NYU P 2014) 259.

[112] See, generally, Peter J Marcotullio and William Solecki, 'What Is a City? An Essential Definition for Sustainability' in Christopher G Boone and Michail Fragkias (eds), *Urbanization and Sustainability: Linking Urban Ecology, Environmental Justice and Global Environmental Change* (Springer 2013) 11.

[113] Banuri (n 2) 32.

[114] ibid, 21, 32.

[115] See eg, Simon (n 29) 11.

[116] Blank (n 90) 517.

[117] ibid 529.

higher scales of consideration, those cities' diverse environmental problems may be overlooked or treated by higher-level governments with insufficient local expertise. Conversely, a greater degree of environmental homogeneity among cities within an already constitutionally recognized unit reduces the need for recognition because there is reduced need for tailored local approaches to environmental problem-solving. Finally, if a central purpose of constitutionally recognizing cities is to facilitate intergovernmental coordination to address environmental problems, the practical challenges of large coordination efforts are also relevant.

VI. Curtains

In an era of climate change and other cumulative environmental problems, the temporal farsightedness required of constitutions demands closer attention to the constitutional implications of the ways that cities interact with their environments at multiple spatial scales. Cities face environmental problems that are sufficiently acute and complex as to warrant, and benefit from, constitutional recognition. But recognition to what end? The considerations advanced here are ambivalent as to allocating cities regulatory primacy in relation to environmental problems, even within their local areas: they may act as environmental villains, as well as victims. Rather than negative autonomy in relation to environmental regulatory authority, as a general matter, constitutions should support cities' fiscal autonomy. They should also provide minimum environmental safeguards by protecting high environmental standards from state and federal pre-emption and adopting constitutional environmental rights. Such rights are especially valuable in cities to deal with the cumulative nature of urban socio-environmental vulnerability. Without coordination, the cumulative nature of contemporary environmental threats carries risks of fragmented and ineffective legal responses to those threats. A constitutional coordination mechanism will be critical to genuine attempts to deliver these rights, as well as effectively deal with environmental problems from which cities suffer, and to which they contribute. The cumulative nature of environmental problems involving cities necessitates stable, yet flexible, formal mechanisms for intergovernmental coordination to understand and respond to them. Constitutions offer a promising pathway.

Curtains close.

9

Privacy and the City

Towards Progressive Urban Cosmopolitanism

*Bilyana Petkova**

I. Introduction

What are the laws of privacy in urban settings? Legal scholars have begun discussing privacy in the narrow context of smart cities,[1] but the topic has yet to penetrate the federalism and localism debates. The study of privacy in the city demonstrates that as new data-fuelled business models emerge in the urban environment, analysis of the legal powers of the city may benefit from insights into the relationship not only among levels of government but also between the private and the public sector. In federal and otherwise decentralized systems, cities' power or powerlessness is not solely defined by doctrines of preemption, but might be influenced by a city's general fiscal autonomy (including dependence on federal and state grants), and the policies cities adopt when entering into partnerships with private corporations.

In this chapter, I ask whether technology is now changing the conventional wisdom about city life habitually linked to privacy.[2] As cities take on the role of technology testbeds, in ways never seen before, they become sites for ever more intrusive surveillance and newer forms of what many refer to as 'datafication', which is different from, and less familiar than, 'digitization'. The latter refers to the use of computing devices to record, quantify, format, or store data as a series of digits. In contrast, 'datafication' refers to 'long-term storage in a format that is searchable, computationally manipulable, and [that] may be aggregated with information

* This chapter builds on and expands upon Ira Rubinstein and Bilyana Petkova, 'Governing Privacy in the Datafied City' (2020) 47 *Fordham Urb LJ* 755. For inspirational talks and insights, I am especially indebted to my co-author and collaborator, Ira Rubinstein. The project has been facilitated by the UK Data Trusts Initiative at Cambridge University that I joined at the final stages of this endeavour. Finally, I am thankful to Julia Pöschl for invaluable research assistance. All errors are mine

[1] See generally Kelsey Finch and Omer Tene, 'Welcome to the Metropticon: Protecting Privacy in a Hyperconnected Town' (2015) 41 *Fordham Urb L J* 1581; Liesbet van Zoonen, 'Privacy Concerns in Smart Cities' (2016) 33 *Government Information Q* 472.

[2] In Richard Sennett's interpretation of Benjamin Constant, 'a city of solitudes as well as communities': see Pablo Sendra and Richard Sennett, *Designing Disorder: Experiments and Disruptions in the City* (Verso 2020) 13.

Bilyana Petkova, *Privacy and the City* In: *Cities in Federal Constitutional Theory*. Edited by: Erika Arban, Oxford University Press. © Bilyana Petkova 2022. DOI: 10.1093/oso/9780192843272.003.0010

from other' sources.[3] Datafication thus makes it possible for organizations to use data in ways that may have been unanticipated or even technologically infeasible at the time of collection and are qualitatively different from the original purposes of the collection.

Cities are 'data-rich environments'[4] because their large populations generate vast amounts of data as they interact with IoT[5] devices and sensors in public spaces; utilize city services that collect, analyse, and optimize personal data;[6] and encounter the special-purpose technologies deployed by law enforcement to maintain public safety and safeguard citizens against terrorist attacks.[7] This ubiquitous collection of data about all aspects of city living and the near-constant monitoring of public spaces erodes the anonymity of urban living. It also threatens the 'marvel of balance'[8] between wanted and unwanted interaction with other people and government officials (especially local law enforcement), without which the diversity and tolerance of city life become untenable. Further, anonymity is but one aspect of privacy—the advent of big data has seen the emergence of broader concerns intertwined with privacy, such as lack of algorithmic fairness, accountability, and transparency. Questions inevitably arise as to how to best counteract these trends at the local level.

Although the interconnection of the above contexts in which cities are data-rich environments for law enforcement purposes is acknowledged, in the chapter I zoom in on civic uses of data in a handful of North American and European cities. Importantly, the comprehensive notion of data privacy adopted in the chapter allows for the conceptualization of data privacy as a lever of both regulation and deregulation. In legal terms, urban privacy is instrumentalized for the pursuit of traditional consumer protection and political participation goals that stretch beyond municipal boundaries, making cities participants in nation-wide debates of regulation and deregulation that reverberate across the country and may even have global implications. In the United States, for example, rather than the enactment of

[3] See Katherine Strandburg, 'Monitoring, Datafication, and Consent: Legal Approaches to Privacy in the Big Data Context' in Julia Lane and others (eds), *Privacy, Big Data, and the Public Good: Frameworks for Engagement* (CUP 2014) 11.

[4] Ira S Rubinstein, 'Privacy Localism' (2018) 93 *Wash L Rev* 1961, 1964.

[5] IoT (the 'Internet of Things') refers to the information networks comprised of sensors and other technologies embedded in physical objects and linked via wired and wireless networks. See Future of Privacy Forum, 'Comments of the Future of Privacy Forum on Connected Smart Technologies in Advance of the FTC "Internet of Things" Workshop' (*Federal Trade Commission*, 21 May 2013) <https://perma.cc/UHW8-4DFJ> accessed 25 September 2021.

[6] See generally Stephen Goldsmith and Susan Crawford, *The Responsive City: Engaging Communities Through Data-Smart Governance* (Jossey–Bass 2014); Stephen Goldsmith and Neil Kleiman, *A New City O/S: The Power of Open, Collaborative and Distributed Governance* (Brookings Institution P 2017).

[7] These include video security cameras, automatic licence plate readers ('ALPRs'), shot detectors, body-worn cameras, and facial recognition technology. See, generally, Task Force on Facial Recognition Surveillance and Jake Laperruque, 'Facing the Future of Surveillance' (*Project on Government Oversight*, 4 March 2019) <https://www.pogo.org/report/2019/03/facing-the-future-of-surveillance/> accessed 25 September 2021.

[8] See generally Jane Jacobs, *The Death and Life of Great American Cities* (Random House 1961) 59.

new legislation, public interest litigation plays a role in these cases. Simultaneously, privacy can also be instrumentalized by private actors—for example, in the sharing economy—that want to avoid regulation of any kind. I consider whether several cities, at the same moment in time, will reach different outcomes when faced with similar policy challenges or converge on policies across the board. Another question tackled is to what extent the level of privacy protection in the city is dependent on general federal constitutional and statutory frameworks.

Given that privacy is a multifaceted concept, I find that the same cities may protect certain aspects of it in some areas while undermining it in others. There are not (yet) clear privacy frontrunners and privacy laggards. Instead, I identify two main roles for data-rich cities: privacy activists and data stewards.

First, through data privacy activism, cities raise a voice in nation-wide political and consumer protection debates as illustrated in the Census 2020, Cambridge Analytica, and Equifax cases. As privacy activists, cities assume a role most closely aligned with a traditional public law institution acting to utilize innovation in the service of citizens. Second, cities act as data stewards when they take steps to govern a new datafied urban space.[9] This role extends from pooling data among city agencies to improve the delivery of services, to managing data-sharing agreements with private actors in discrete contexts (such as ride- or bike-share data), to ceding control over data governance as an element of huge real estate development deals.[10] As privacy stewards, cities may reorient the very understanding of 'public interest' from privacy protections to open data sharing practices and behave more like commercial actors. The case studies suggest that data stewardship is best understood on a spectrum spanning both highly protective intracity data agreements and commercial giveaways, with 'data collaboratives' (or 'data trusts') occupying a middle ground. Thus, cities-as-data stewards attempt to regulate their urban environments through data, which may occur at the expense of privacy. Finally, I find that the privatization of public services is morphing into the privatization of public spaces, as data collected in communal areas is co-owned or coopted by private companies.

Through this analysis, the chapter also contributes to broad theoretical questions such as how cities deal with the challenges posed by new technologies and the relationship between federalism, subsidiarity (or localism) and cities.

This chapter proceeds as follows: section II situates urban data initiatives and related privacy issues in the context of federalism and localism. Section III examines the city as a privacy activist through the lens of the Census 2020 litigation and lawsuits against major corporations (such as Facebook and Equifax). Section IV examines the city as a data steward using detailed case studies about the impact on the privacy of data-sharing agreements among city agencies and commercial

[9] Strandburg (n 3) 10–11.
[10] See section IV.B.4 below.

agreements with a number of urban innovation firms. Section V also contrasts instances of data governance arrangements in business-friendly environments, specifically comparing Toronto and Barcelona's efforts to preserve public interest while embracing smart city concepts.

II. From Federal to Local, Urban, and Cosmopolitan Values

Often the study of large, cosmopolitan cities falls in between the cracks of federalism and localism. Federalism often centres on the relationship between the federal government and the states while localism examines the relationship between states and localities. Granted, both scholarly work and constitutional doctrine recognize overlaps. Federalism and localism coincide on the values of decentralization: for example, Gerken spells out the normative case for federalism as promoting 'choice, competition, participation, experimentation, and the diffusion of power'.[11] But should what is true for localities in general apply *a fortiori* to big cities that compete for resources and human capital and, thanks to a sizeable market share, are maybe even more able to offer viable democratic experiments across a range of policies?

The role of cosmopolitan cities in a federal or a local constellation of actors is rarely studied separately since from a constitutional standpoint, the debates on cities tend to focus on issues such as power or powerlessness[12] or, at least in the US, on the longstanding dichotomy between home rule and Dillion's rule or new preemption measures.[13] No doubt, in thinking about depolarizing conflict in a charged political environment, questions of legal autonomy across all localities are essential for planting the seeds of a legal doctrine.[14]

However, as Schragger has pointed out in regard to the US (but similar conclusions can be reached for other jurisdictions), the lasting shift from rural to urban in demographics is yet to be encapsulated in law and power distribution.[15] Beyond the rural/urban divide, there are a small number of major cities that can be singled out because of their sheer size or cultural, technological, or political leadership. These cities arguably define a progressive urban cosmopolitanism.

Yet progressivism remains a loosely defined and fuzzy concept that gets intertwined with yet another unbounded and vague notion—that of cosmopolitanism.

[11] Heather Gerken, 'Foreword: Federalism All the Way Down' (2010) *125 Harv L Rev* 4, 6 (hereafter, 'Federalism All The Way Down'). See further Arban, chapter 1 in this volume, and Arban and Saunders, chapter 2 in this volume.

[12] Richard Schragger, *City Power: Urban Governance in a Global Age* (OUP 2016).

[13] See Briffault, chapter 5 in this volume;

[14] Nestor M Davidson, 'The Dilemma of Localism in an Era of Polarization' (2019) 128 *Yale L J* 4.

[15] Richard C Schragger, 'The Attack on American Cities' (2018) 96 *Tex L Rev* 1163.

If traditionally progressivism might have been associated with a top-down governmental welfare regulation that curbs business power and advances a human rights agenda, trends of globalization, technological advances, and the spread of neo-libertarianism infuse progressivism with new elements. It is this pedigree of cosmopolitan progressivism—selectively public-minded and business-friendly—that one can observe in urban settings. Technology firms both have a penchant for and contribute to the construction of that ethos. In terms of demographics, global cities like New York, Toronto, London, and San Paolo are home to very diverse populations; in terms of economic power, not only do such cities get a significant market share of their respective states and the national economy as a whole, but often their gross metropolitan product exceeds that of many states.[16] That said, local and cosmopolitan big cities' financial dependence on private investment to create and maintain infrastructure results in a special symbiosis with businesses.[17] This is interesting to explore in the context of the important transformation of law that Cohen compellingly traces as both businesses and governmental institutions transition from industrial to data-intense, informational capitalist models.[18] Cosmopolitan cities exemplify that transition: they function as a hybrid between a public institution seeking to act in the public interest and a business corporation seeking to maximize profits.

Further, I discuss other cities that have undertaken important smart city and data stewardship experiments—namely, Toronto and Barcelona.[19] The cosmopolitan ambitions of diverse and populous urban centres, like Canada's Toronto, are comparable to those of New York City, illustrated in the next section. In contrast, Barcelona, Spain—a middle-sized city in Europe that struggles for a cosmopolitan flavour—provides an example of an alternative vision of the public sector's engagement with technology firms. Moreover, a federalist and localist framing remains apt for these cities since Toronto is embedded within a federal system, while Barcelona is a part of Spain's highly decentralized government.

[16] The United States Conference of Mayors and The Council on Metro Economies and the New American City, 'US Metro Economies: Economic Growth and Full Employment, Annual GMP Report' (*Untied States Conference of Mayors*, June 2018) <http://www.usmayors.org/wp-content/uploads/2018/06/Metro-Economies-GMP-June-2018.pdf> accessed 25 September 2019.

[17] Schragger, 'The Attack on American Cities' (n 15) 1179. For similar arguments, see also Ran Hirschl, *City, State. Constitutionalism and the Megacity* (OUP 2020) 181–2.

[18] Julie Cohen, *Between Truth and Power: The Legal Constructions of Informational Capitalism* (OUP 2019). See also Shoshana Zuboff, *The Age of Surveillance Capitalism: The Fight for a Human Future at the New Frontier of Power* (Profile Books 2019).

[19] See section IV.B.4 and section V below.

III. The City as a Privacy Activist

Next to efforts to ensure privacy-as-anonymity in the context of internal public administration services, the cities I examine have been active in trying to safeguard privacy-as-political-participation as an issue with national ramifications.

A. Data wars: The census 2020 litigation through the prism of sanctuary cities

Data is power. By trying to protect the personal information of their immigrant populations, US states and cities are trying to safeguard local autonomy. As Somin remarks: 'State and local governments have extensive information about hundreds of millions of people that the federal government could abuse in many ways'.[20] Such abuse of data could serve the federal government to stifle what Gerken has called 'the loyal opposition': federalism's institutional structure for allowing minorities to take part in governance.[21] Gerken defines cities as the institutions that most resemble states, 'because states and cities enjoy general policymaking authority, a measure of autonomy, perhaps even a robust political identity'.[22] All this is true for large, cosmopolitan sanctuary cities that are homes to diverse immigrant communities that shape cities' political identities and that cities try to make use of local autonomy to protect. Cities do not exist separate from their inhabitants though. Urban power measured in political representation and the disbursement of state and federal funds depends on cities' populations.

In May 2017 President Trump established the (now defunct) Presidential Advisory Commission on Election Integrity. The Commission was supposed to collect a large pool of voter's personal data from election officials in the states which was supposed to fight voter fraud but was seen by many as an ill-masked attempt to restrict voting rights. Therefore, forty-four states, including many Republican-led state governments, and the District of Columbia invoked privacy, among other reasons, to reject some or all of the government's demands, which led to the government's decision to discontinue the existence of the Commission.[23]

More recently, the Trump administration crackdown on immigration has been countered by local efforts to oppose the federal government's deportation of undocumented immigrants. In turn, the federal government has fought back by

[20] Ilya Somin, 'Making Federalism Great Again: How the Trump Administration's Attack on Sanctuary Cities Unintentionally Strengthened Judicial Protection for State Autonomy' (2019) 97 *Tex L Rev* 1247, 1283 (hereafter Somin, 'Making Federalism Great Again').

[21] Heather K Gerken, 'The Loyal Opposition' (2014) 123 *Yale L J* 1958.

[22] Gerken, 'Federalism All The Way Down' (n 11) 8.

[23] Ilya Somin, 'Demise of Trump Voter Fraud Commission Is a Victory for Federalism' (*Reason: The Volokh Conspiracy*, 4 January 2018) <https://reason.com/volokh/2018/01/04/demise-of-trump-voter-fraud-commission-i> accessed 25 September 2021.

leveraging new data wars that threaten to significantly curtail local autonomy. Arguably, the Census 2020 litigation, whereby states and cities were the first to file a case against the Department of Commerce's decision to insert a citizenship question in the 2020 census, is best understood against the backdrop of the former administration's attempts to discipline sanctuary jurisdictions.

1. Background to the census 2020 litigation: sanctuaries' protection of immigrants' data and local autonomy

In 2017 California declared itself 'a sanctuary state.' As part of its sanctuary policies, the state passed Senate Bill 54 restricting the range of information state and local governments are allowed to share with federal immigration enforcers.[24] Also, California Assembly Bill 450 was passed to prohibit employers from voluntarily allowing a federal immigration enforcement agent to enter 'nonpublic' areas of their workplaces or to access, review, or obtain the employees' records.[25]

In response, the Trump administration sought to enforce 8 USC § 1373, a federal law mandating that a federal, state, or local government entity or official may not prohibit, or in any way restrict, any government entity or official from sending to, or receiving from, the Immigration and Naturalization Service information regarding the citizenship or immigration status, lawful or unlawful, of any individual.[26] The case has been framed as about local enforcement of immigration law and federalism,[27] but these issues closely intersect with privacy in as much as the challenged laws in effect present California's legal attempts to safeguard its immigrant population's personal information.

The Census 2020 litigation, in which many sanctuary cities have taken part, is not directly about federalism much like the sanctuary cities' litigation is not directly about the protection of personal information. No matter the legal framing, the context of the litigation in the Census 2020 cases reveals a pattern: for local autonomy to exist, the privacy of national minorities—that make up for the majority in big urban centres—needs to be preserved.

2. Census 2020 litigation

The US Constitution explicitly mandates the government to conduct a census every ten years.[28] The federal government collects census data on all persons residing in the US, regardless of their legal status, to apportion state representatives to the House of Representatives, to draw political districts and allocate power to them, as well as to allocate hundreds of billions of dollars in federal, state, and local funds. Simultaneously, census data is used for demographic purposes and has habitually

[24] California Government Code §§ 7284.6(a)(1)(C) and (D).
[25] ibid.
[26] 8 USC § 1373(a).
[27] Somin 'Making Federalism Great Again' (n 20) 1249.
[28] US Const, amend XIV, § 2 ('Enumeration Clause').

included respondents' race, sex, age, and whether they own or rent a home, but the national census excluded a question on citizenship.

In March 2018, Secretary of Commerce Wilbur Ross announced that he would reinstate a citizenship question in order for citizenship data to better assist the Department of Justice ('DOJ') with the enforcement of the Voting Rights Act ('VRA') against racial discrimination in voting. Litigation ensued; the question of whether the inclusion of a citizenship question is lawful was going to be reviewed by the Supreme Court.

The first case to be decided, by the District Court for the Southern District of New York,[29] set the tone that other lower courts then followed.[30] Two sets of plaintiffs initiated the litigation: the first to file a case was a coalition of eighteen states and the District of Columbia, together with fifteen cities and counties, and the United States Conference of Mayors. Among the city plaintiffs, San Francisco, New York City, Chicago, and Seattle—all the big cosmopolitan cities that participated in the sanctuary cities litigation—took part. The second plaintiff was a coalition of non-governmental organizations that support immigrants.[31] Together, the two groups raised two challenges: first, they contended that Ross's decision to reinstate the citizenship question violated the Administrative Procedure Act ('APA'), which prohibits federal agencies from acting in a manner that is arbitrary; second, they alleged that the decision violated the Due Process Clause of the Fifth Amendment of the US Constitution because the decision was motivated in part by invidious discrimination against immigrant communities of colour.

For big cities that are home to a disproportionate share of their states' noncitizen populations, the consequences of an undercount might be grave, for they would result in diluting such cities' political power within their states. In addition, under any undercount scenario states and cities might suffer significant losses in federal funding. The Court accepted New York City's and Chicago's diversion of resources to counteract the potentially harmful effects of data distortion caused by inserting a citizenship question as a relevant injury.

In substance, the Census 2020 litigation is about making available to the federal government the personal information of vulnerable immigrant populations concentrated in big urban centres. The legal battle in the Supreme Court against inserting such a question was finally won on administrative law grounds, and the Biden administration has since quashed other attempts by former President Trump to reinsert a citizenship question through executive orders. Although the dispute

[29] *New York v US Department of Commerce*, 315 F Supp 3d 766 (2018) ('*New York*').

[30] *California v Ross*, 358 F Supp 3d 965 (2019), *Kravitz v US Dept of Commerce*, 366 F Supp 3 545 (2018). See, generally, Brennan Center for Justice, '2020 Census Litigation' (*Brennan Center for Justice*, 2021) <https://www.brennancenter.org/issues/gerrymandering-fair-representation/fair-accurate-census/2020-census-litigation> accessed 25 September 2021.

[31] New York Immigration Coalition, CASA de Maryland, American-Arab Anti-Discrimination Committee, ADC Research Institute, and Make the Road New York.

has been muted since, in practice it is not unfathomable that the havoc it created might have resulted in immigrants not reporting their resident status anyway. As a result, in 2021 sanctuary jurisdictions like New York State and California both lost a congressional seat while the consequences for New York City and San Francisco in terms of state and federal grants are at the time of writing yet unclear.

B. City attorneys general as data privacy enforcers

Cities have litigated to protect the public interest against the federal government in order to preserve the personal information of city dwellers and safeguard local autonomy, but cities have also fought in court to protect the public interest against private parties that violate the privacy of their residents. Although state attorneys general have a proven track record in privacy enforcement,[32] also city attorneys general are emerging now as new players at the forefront of consumer privacy enforcement. States have their own versions of the Federal Trade Commission ('FTC') Act,[33] as well as other privacy and consumer protection laws that city attorneys general can invoke in court.

The participation of city attorneys general in privacy enforcement actions that assert public interest reveals certain patterns. First, the cases that they chose to litigate are usually high-profile ones—both the Cambridge Analytica incident[34] and the Equifax breach are prime examples of high-profile cases with significant nation-wide and global impact. Although legally speaking all cases fall within consumer privacy protection, thematically they can be divided into two types. In the electoral context—the Cambridge Analytica suit brought by the attorneys general of Chicago and Washington DC against Facebook, much like in the context of political representation and local autonomy—the Census 2020 litigation, preserve democratic values. In turn, the Equifax cases brought by the city attorneys general of San Francisco and Chicago were against a credit reporting agency (Equifax) that in 2017 suffered a major data breach. The breach resulted in compromising

[32] Bilyana Petkova, 'The Safeguards of Privacy Federalism' (2016) 20 *Lewis & Clark L Rev* 595; Danielle K Citron, 'The Privacy Policymaking of State Attorneys General' (2017) 92 *Notre Dame L Rev* 747.

[33] 15 USC § 45, prohibiting unfair or deceptive practices in or affecting commerce.

[34] In 2014, Facebook permitted a researcher, Alexander Kogan, to allow Facebook users to download his app designed as a personality quiz. Around 270,000 users did so but the app not only collected their data, it also harvested the information of all their friends, giving access to the profiles of an estimated 50–70 million people. Kogan then sold this information to a company called Cambridge Analytica, a political data firm that offered to identify the preferences of voters based on their personality traits, friend networks, and Facebook 'likes' in order to influence their behaviour with targeted election advertisements. The involvement of Cambridge Analytica in the 2016 election of President Trump has been widely publicized. The Cambridge Analytica scandal has been widely followed in Europe where it became apparent that Cambridge Analytica might have affected the Brexit vote: Sue Halpern, Why the UK Condemned Facebook for Fueling Fake News', *The New Yorker* (22 February 2019).

the personal information of 145.5 million Americans. The city lawsuits aimed at improving consumer protection standards in data-intense sectors, and were based on a broad interpretation of harm.

In both examples, cities were the first governmental actor to file an action in court. This contrasts with expertise-heavy data breach cases where the FTC firsts invest resources into investigation, and state and local authorities participate at the end stages of litigation, and share in any settlement.[35] Moreover, data privacy litigation shows a harmonious city-state relationship of well-resourced, big cities working shoulder-to-shoulder with their states. That dynamic might be exemplary of what Schragger dubs as 'our federalism's anti-urbanism' or the tendency of US-state-based federalism to disfavour decentralization to sub-state governments to the effect that to exert any real-life influence, often cities need to be in synchrony with their states.[36] In this sense, large, cosmopolitan cities' privacy activism is emerging within blue states and opposition seems more likely to come from a conservative federal administration. Certainly, city litigation with data privacy implications fits neatly into the wider partisan dynamics in which local actors stage opposition and serve as checks on federal power through the institutional venue of federalism. In these first cases, as an embodiment of urban progressivism, cities are also using their enforcement powers to protect the public interest while filling in the municipal coffers with whatever settlements they are able to reach throughout the litigation. Even subsequent action by the federal tier does not preclude cities further progressing on their claims and winning a separate settlement.[37]

IV. Cities as Data Stewards

At every level of government—federal, state and local—agencies amass personal data and must manage their data assets in the public interest. US cities, for example, collect and utilize a very wide range of personal and sensitive data with relatively few encumbrances from superior levels of government. They have the most control and highest degree of data stewardship when they process data incidental to delivering city services and share it among city agencies. They face greater challenges in protecting data and serving the public interest when they interact with powerful commercial actors motivated by private interests.

35 Interview David Vladeck, former FTC Director (23 March 2019).

36 Schragger, 'The Attack on American Cities' (n 15) 1184.

37 Kathy Fieweger, 'City of Chicago Reaches Settlement with Equifax' (*City of Chicago*, 7 April 2020) <https://www.chicago.gov/city/en/depts/dol/provdrs/lit/news/2020/april/settlement-with-equifax.html> accessed 25 September 2021.

A. Interagency data sharing agreements

In offering services to their residents, cities amass huge quantities of data. The emphasis is on making these services more efficient and effective via data integration and analysis, especially for traditional social services. Many families receive services and benefits from multiple public and private programmes. Yet, often caseworkers working with the same families are not even aware of one another in part because they maintain their data in siloed databases. Data integration and analysis not only allows caseworkers to coordinate services for clients but to do a better job of matching individual clients with existing services and improve policy decisions and programme development more generally.[38] This data-oriented approach raises numerous privacy issues. Integrated social service programmes depend on the collection, sharing, and repurposing of highly personal data and therefore require very tight controls over data access, use, disclosure, and retention to avoid privacy violations. One way to handle such issues is by developing standardized data-sharing agreements with strong privacy provisions. New York City offers an excellent example of this approach, although over time it has supplemented the use of data agreements with local privacy ordinances as well.

The policies governing the collection, retention, and disclosure of identifying information by city agencies and certain city contractors and subcontractors define personally identifiable information very broadly, outline strong confidentiality requirements for 'sensitive identifying information',[39] require city agencies to adhere to specific privacy protection principles, and establish additional requirements such as data minimization and anonymization. New York City has done a very good job of addressing the privacy issues associated with data integration and analysis, evolving from data-sharing agreements to a local ordinance requiring comprehensive citywide privacy policies and protocols. In its zeal to improve city life by processing and analysing massive amounts of data, however, the city has been less successful in identifying and correcting issues related to algorithmic fairness, accountability, and transparency.

B. Commercial agreements

Apart from any constraints accompanying federal and state social programmes, US cities operate with a very free hand in governing local data.[40] Nor are the city's

[38] See, eg, Robert M Goerge, 'Data for the Public Good: Challenges and Barriers in the Context of Cities' in Julia Lane and others (eds), *Privacy, Big Data, and the Public Good: Frameworks for Engagement* (CUP 2014) 153.

[39] New York City Mayor's Office of Information Privacy, *Citywide Privacy Protection Policies and Protocols* (24 February 2021) s 3.2.5.

[40] See Rubinstein, 'Privacy Localism' (n 4) 2031–5, 2046–7.

regulatory powers preempted by federal or state law, given that the federal Privacy Act applies exclusively to personal data held by federal agencies, while most states lack comparable laws, and the minority states with such laws limit their scope to state, as opposed to local, agencies.[41] When cities enter into commercial agreements with private firms, however, they must contend with the privacy practices and norms of some very large and powerful firms. And these market forces may exert greater sway over cities than any statutory rules from higher levels of government. In this next section, I discuss two sectors of great importance to 21st-century cities: broadband and the sharing economy.

1. Broadband: low-cost and high-speed, but privacy is optional

In 2012, New York City announced a design challenge to replace just over 7,500 outdated pay phones with up to 10,000 digital kiosks across its five boroughs.[42] Each kiosk would offer 24/7 free internet access at gigabit speeds and a range of other popular services such as free public Wi-Fi phone calls, device charging, and a tablet for access to city services, maps, and directions.[43] A consortium called CityBridge won the bid by proposing a kiosk called 'Links'. CityBridge agreed to lay cable, install infrastructure, and operate the 'LinkNYC' network in exchange for splitting advertising revenues with the city, valued at $1 billion over the life of the twelve-year franchise agreement.[44]

However, LinkNYC raises several privacy concerns. The first is the risk of security breaches and unwanted surveillance of users and passersby. To begin with, LinkNYC requires users to register with an email address and agree to allow CityBridge to gain access to their Web traffic. The kiosks also contain video cameras that capture a 360-degree view of the surrounding streets and sidewalks.[45] The New York Civil Liberties Union ('NYCLU') has argued that the sheer volume of information these devices gather 'will create a massive database of information that will present attractive opportunities for hackers and for law enforcement surveillance, and will carry an undue risk of abuse, misuse and unauthorized access'.[46]

[41] ibid, 2020.

[42] See generally Maren Maier, Mary McBride and Paul McConnell, 'LinkNYC: Redesigning Telecommunication to Activate the Twenty-First-Century Creative City' in André Corrêa d'Almeida, *Smarter New York City: How City Agencies Innovate* (Columbia U P 2018) 79.

[43] See Joshua Brustein, 'Building a Smart City? Have You Thought About Porn and Privacy?' (*Bloomberg*, 15 September 2016) <https://www.bloomberg.com/news/articles/2016-09-15/building-a-smart-city-have-you-thought-about-porn-and-privacy> accessed 25 September 2021.

[44] Maier, McBride, and McConnell (n 42) 91.

[45] Ava Kofman, 'Are New York's Free LinkNYC Internet Kiosks Tracking Your Movements?' (*The Intercept*, 8 September 2018) <https://theintercept.com/2018/09/08/linknyc-free-wifi-kiosks/> accessed 25 September 2021.

[46] NYCLU, 'City's Public Wi-Fi Raises Privacy Concerns' (*New York Civil Liberties Union*, 16 March 2016) <http://www.nyclu.org/news/citys-public-wi-fi-raises-privacy-concerns> accessed 25 September 2021.

A second concern is that LinkNYC collects information about users for advertising purposes under a privacy policy that, despite revisions, leaves too many questions unanswered and offers too few protections against the harms associated with online targeting and profiling. As the Electronic Frontier Foundation has noted, the original CityBridge privacy policy governing use of LinkNYC kiosks 'allowed nearly limitless retention of user data, including browsing history'.[47]

The third concern is that LinkNYC is but the first stage in Alphabet/Sidewalk Lab's plans to extend the monetization of personal data from the online world to the physical landscape.

Of course, at the end of the day, LinkNYC and its boosters can always fall back on the argument that those who object to the kiosks are welcome not to use them. But this is false dichotomy based on an illusory choice. What it really amounts to is forcing citizens to comply with the (private) terms and conditions of their own surveillance or to stay off the (public) streets. As Nick Pinto points out, 'there is a different issue at play here: the right of the City of New York to surrender [citizens'] data for us'.[48]

2. The sharing economy: data sharing—litigation or data collaboratives?

One might expect that big cities would show across-the-board, natural preferences for enabling data-driven companies of the shared economy to operate on their territory: above all, the shared economy epitomizes cosmopolitan progressivism. As Daniel Rach and David Schleicher have it: 'the presence of bike- or car- or home-sharing services conveys something important about how progressive, how technologically advanced, and indeed how "world class" a city is.'[49] Presence does not necessarily mean lack of any regulation, however.[50] When cities interact with data-intense companies to design their urban spaces, the quest to improve the municipal services, whether well-intended or catering to incumbent industry's interests,[51] may leave them less aware of whether their efforts raise privacy issues. This is the background of the lawsuit discussed below, which is an example of a not very optimal way of addressing data exchanges in the sharing economy. After reviewing this litigation, I turn to more collaborative forms of data sharing, focusing on a model spearheaded in Seattle.

[47] Shahid Buttar and Amul Kalia, 'Link NYC Improves Privacy Policy, Yet Problems Remain' (*Electronic Frontier Foundation*, 4 October 2017) <https://www.eff.org/deeplinks/2017/09/linknyc-improves-privacy-policy-yet-problems-remain> accessed 25 September 2021.

[48] Nick Pinto, 'Google is Transforming NYC's Payphones into a "Personalized Propaganda Engine"' (*Village Voice*, 6 July 2016) <https://www.villagevoice.com/2016/07/06/google-is-transforming-nycs-payphones-into-a-personalized-propaganda-engine/> accessed 25 September 2021.

[49] Daniel E Rauch and David Schleicher, 'Like Uber, but for Local Government Law: The Future of Local Regulation of the Sharing Economy' (2015) 76 *Ohio St L J* 901, 946 (citations omitted).

[50] ibid, 943.

[51] ibid.

Two home-sharing platforms, Airbnb and HomeAway, filed motions to preliminary enjoin a New York City Ordinance ('the Ordinance') that would have required them to turn over on a monthly basis extensive personal data on customers who use their platforms to advertise short-term rentals ('hosts').

After the New York City mayor signed the Ordinance into law, Airbnb and HomeAway initiated legal actions asserting that the Ordinance violated the First and Fourth Amendments of the US Constitution and that it conflicted with the *Stored Communications Act* ('SCA') that regulates the disclosure to governmental authorities of stored electronic communications. The US Court for the Southern District of New York found that the Ordinance violated the Fourth Amendment.

Both at statutory and constitutional level, privacy should be considered without necessarily constraining cities' legitimate attempts to harness the sharing economy. The New York City Ordinance might have benefited from the application of data minimization principles and from clearly restricting access to the data; it is, however, doubtful whether such improvements would have satisfied the requirement for pre-compliance review that the District Court emphasized under the Fourth Amendment.[52] Eventually, Airbnb and HomeAway won on appeal as well. Cities' drive towards progressive urban cosmopolitanism of which privacy is an integral part shows that the private sector can sometimes reinforce the trend in a non-predatory fashion.

3. From data sharing agreements to data collaboratives and data trusts

Although some cities have had to resort to litigation to gain access to home-share data as described in the previous section, cities have fared somewhat better in obtaining ridership data from ride-hailing firms like Uber and Lyft as well as bicycle sharing systems like Blue Bike (Boston), Citi Bike (NY metro area), and Lime, Ofo and Spin (Seattle).

New York City's Taxi and Limousine Commission (TLC) has long required ride-hailing firms to provide the agency with information such as pick-up times and locations, licence plate numbers, and base information. In May 2016, however, the TLC issued a 'driver fatigue rule' that additionally required such firms (including Uber, its competitors, and other for-hire vehicles) to share more detailed information including the duration and destinations of drivers' trips.[53] Uber objected on

[52] Albeit choosing different regulatory paths, big cities in Europe face similar problems. For example, since 2014 the City of Amsterdam has had in force a city ordinance that limits Airbnb rentals to sixty days per year and four persons per property. City officials negotiated an agreement requiring cooperation from the platform. Airbnb refused to execute the agreement, but it adjusted its platform settings and complied accordingly. In 2018, the City Board of Amsterdam cut the permitted rental stays to thirty days, effective as of 2019. Airbnb has not yet complied with the new rules by adjusting its platform settings.

[53] Vincent Barone, 'Uber, NYC at Odds Over Data Collection for New Safety Rule' (*AMNY*, 5 December 2016) <https://www.amny.com/transit/uber-nyc-at-odds-over-data-collection-for-new-safety-rule-1.12707850> accessed 26 September 2021.

both privacy and trade-secret grounds and even tried to avoid the rule by releasing a free tool allowing cities and developers to track car travel times,[54] but despite these concerns, the TLC proceeded with the new rule and as of 1 February 2019, ride-share companies must provide TLC 'the date, time, and location of pickups and drop-offs, the vehicle's license number, the trip mileage, itemized trip fare, route and how much the driver was paid'.[55]

Some ride-share and bike-share firms have entered into voluntary agreements with major cities to provide trip data in support of city transportation policy and planning goals. For example, in January 2015, Uber agreed to provide Boston with 'quarterly, anonymous data about the duration, general locations, and times of rides that start or end in the city'.[56]

In July 2017, the City of Seattle began a pilot programme for 'dockless-bikes' under which bike-share operators had two options for sharing granular data about their riders with the city: they may provide the city with anonymized trip information as specified in Seattle's Bike Share Permit Requirements, or they may share data under a signed agreement with the Transportation Data Collaborative ('TDC') located at the University of Washington ('UW').[57] The TDC is a protected and linked data repository of sensitive information from regional public and private transportation providers. It allows partnering agencies to create data-driven policy, support research uses, and provide individuals with authenticated access to their own transportation records.[58]

A recent paper co-authored by TDC staff members at UW makes the case for data collaboratives by observing that researchers and the public are very poorly served by the usual dichotomy between open (publicly available) and closed (proprietary) data systems.[59] Institutions are reluctant to make 'sensitive' data openly available to researchers mainly on privacy and intellectual property grounds, and therefore restrict access to such data or its linkage with other data sets and instead share less interesting and useful information with the research community.

[54] Aarian Marshall, 'The Secret Uber Data That Could Fix Your Commute' (*Wired*, 3 February 2017) <https://www.wired.com/2017/02/ubers-coughing-data-nyc-fix-commute/> accessed 26 September 2021.

[55] Aarian Marshall, 'NYC Knows More Than Ever About Your Uber and Lyft Trips' (*Wired*, 31 January 2019) <https://www.wired.com/story/nyc-uber-lyft-ride-hail-data/> accessed 26 September 2021.

[56] The ride-share data from Uber would be stripped of identifying information and exact locations: see Nicole Dungca, 'In First, Uber to Share Ride Data With Boston' (*Boston Globe*, 14 January 2015) <https://www.bostonglobe.com/business/2015/01/13/uber-share-ridership-data-with-boston/4Klo40KZREtQ7jkoaZjoNN/story.html> accessed 26 September 2021.

[57] 'Bike Share Permit Requirements' (*City of Seattle*, 30 June 2017) <https://www.seattle.gov/Documents/Departments/SDOT/BikeProgram/BicycleSharePermitRequirements.pdf> accessed 26 September 2021.

[58] See 'What is the Transportation Data Collaborative?' (*UW Transportation Data Collaborative*) <https://www.uwtdc.org/about> accessed 26 September 2021.

[59] Meg Young and others, 'Beyond Open vs Closed: Balancing Individual Privacy and Public Accountability in Data Sharing' in Association for Computing Machinery, *FAT* '19: Proceedings of the Conference on Fairness, Accountability, and Transparency* (ACM 2019) 191.

As noted, this tension is apparent in the transportation sector, where city agencies want more granular access to firm data than ride-hailing and bike-share firms wish to supply. Building on their work in creating the TDC, the co-authors describe the design of a 'legal-technical infrastructure' they call Collaborative Data Trusts ('CDTs'), which they offer as an alternative to the open/closed dichotomy.

One important way in which data trusts achieve privacy goals is by relying on differential privacy and synthetic datasets, which allow responsible use of sensitive data by removing causal relationships between variables while preserving relationships in all other cases.[60] The use of customized synthetic datasets also allows researchers to remove signals that could expose proprietary data (and hence competitive advantage for the data providers) or preserve biases that could reinforce discriminatory policies.[61] Finally, the integrated legal–technical infrastructure utilizes data sharing and use agreements to specify in advance the data to be shared and the scope of research and the legal recourse of the data trust if data quality is deficient and of the data sources in the event of unauthorized disclosure.[62] As an intermediary that embodies the values of independent stewardship, institutional safeguards and collective action, data trusts, properly understood[63] hold enormous promise for cities engaged in data management activities because they enable city governments to maintain their role as data stewards while benefiting from data-driven activities even as they interact with the private sector in a highly collaborative manner.

4. From data sharing to Toronto's outsourcing of data governance

The largest and most controversial smart city project in which data trusts play a prominent role is Sidewalk Lab's efforts to build a smart city of the future in Toronto.[64] In the spring of 2017, Waterfront Toronto ('WT'), a Canadian redevelopment agency established in 2002 by the government of Canada, the government of Ontario, and the City of Toronto to oversee the revitalization of Toronto's eastern waterfront, issued a Request for Proposal ('RFP') for the Quayside Development project.[65] It sought an 'Innovation and Funding Partner' to help create and fund

[60] ibid.

[61] ibid.

[62] ibid.

[63] Sylvie Delacroix and Neil D Lawrence, 'Bottom-Up Data Trusts: Disturbing the "One Size Fits All" Approach to Data Governance' (2019) 9 *Int'l Data Privacy L* 236, 240–1.

[64] Sidewalk Labs announced that it was no longer pursuing this project, attributing its decision to the 'unprecedented economic uncertainty' both worldwide and in the Toronto real estate market. See Daniel L Doctoroff, 'Why We're No Longer Pursuing the Quayside Project—And What's Next for Sidewalk Labs' (*Medium*, 7 May 2020) <https://medium.com/sidewalk-talk/why-were-no-longer-pursuing-the-quayside-project-and-what-s-next-for-sidewalk-labs-9a61de3fee3a>.

[65] See Waterfront Toronto, 'Request for Proposals: Innovation and Funding Partner for the Quayside Development Opportunity' (*Quayside Toronto*, 17 March 2017) <https://quaysideto.ca/wp-content/uploads/2019/04/Waterfront-Toronto-Request-for-Proposals-March-17-2017.pdf> accessed 27 September 2021. See also Acting City Manager, 'Waterfront Strategic Review' (*City of Toronto*, 2015) <https://www.toronto.ca/legdocs/mmis/2015/ex/bgrd/backgroundfile-81763.pdf> accessed 27

'a globally-significant community that will showcase advanced technologies, building materials, sustainable practices and innovative business models that demonstrate pragmatic solutions toward climate-positive urban development'.[66] Sidewalk Labs was selected by WT.

This section examines Sidewalk Labs' original data governance and privacy proposal for Sidewalk Toronto as set out in its Master Innovation and Development Plan issued in June 2019.[67] In a chapter devoted to 'Digital Innovation', the firm proposed the creation of an independent 'trust' with broad authority over data governance issues within both Quayside and the much larger adjacent site that Sidewalk Labs refers to as the 'IDEA District'.[68] The proposed Urban Data Trust ('UDT') would establish privacy guidelines and a related assessment process administered by its Chief Data Officer who reviews and approves projects using data collected in the physical environment of the IDEA District. In developing a 'trusted process for responsible data use', Sidewalk Labs sought to respond to three concerns raised during the public consultations: first, that data collection in the public realm amounted to a form of surveillance; second, that the collection and use of such data should be treated as a public resource (provided privacy risks have been addressed) and not solely benefit the private or public sector; and, third, that Sidewalk Labs should not enjoy any special advantages in developing the core digital services for the IDEA District.[69] The company sought to address these concerns by creating a new category of 'urban data'[70] and giving it additional privacy protections by treating urban data as a 'collective' asset that would not be owned 'in the traditional sense' but rather managed by an independent entity (the UDT) and made publicly accessible by default; and applying consistent processes and guidelines to all entities collecting urban data in the district including Sidewalk Labs. While this strategy sounds reasonable at first glance, it suffers from many shortcomings. The most severe among them is a democratic deficit or lack of political legitimacy.

To begin with, the RFP called upon the partner to work closely with WT in creating 'the required governance constructs to stimulate the growth of an urban innovation cluster, including legal frameworks (e.g., Intellectual Property, privacy, data sharing)'.[71] As many commentators have observed, it is highly problematic

September 2021. See, generally, Ellen P Goodman and Julia Powles, 'Urbanism Under Google: Lessons from Sidewalk Toronto' (2019) 88 *Fordham L Rev* 457.

[66] Waterfront Toronto (n 65).

[67] Sidewalk Labs, 'Master Innovation and Development Plan' (*Quayside Toronto*, 2019) ch 5 <https://quaysideto.ca/wp-content/uploads/2019/09/MIDP-Volume-2-Chapter-5-Digital-Innovation-Accessible.pdf> accessed 27 September 2021 (hereafter Sidewalk Labs, 'Master Innovation and Development Plan').

[68] See ibid, 377–9.

[69] ibid, 416–19.

[70] Defined as 'information gathered in the city's public realm, its publicly accessible spaces, and even some private buildings': ibid, 377.

[71] Waterfront Toronto (n 65) 17.

for a vendor 'to propose the structure, operation, and regulatory power' of the governing entity with authority over the vendor.[72] A lack of legitimacy also undermines Sidewalk Lab's conception of a data trust. According to the MIDP, the final agreement between WT and Sidewalk Labs would set up the structure of the UDT and authorize the creation of a non-profit entity with 'the charter to address the digital governance challenges related to urban data while also promoting data-driven innovations that benefit individuals and society',[73] but have very little to say about the basics of governance and the source of funding for the UDT. This lack of legitimacy has two probable consequences for Sidewalk Labs' data governance proposal. First, although the RDU Guidelines incorporate well-established privacy principles and outline an RDU Assessment process covering any collection or use of urban data, it is not at all clear how the CDO will handle the difficult choices he or she will likely encounter.

Second, this democratic deficit leaves Sidewalk Labs in a weak position to mitigate any controversies resulting from its creation of a new category of urban data. The company asserts that it heard public concerns over the collection of such data and responded by laying out the guidelines and assessment process described above.[74] Absent from this response is any discussion of simply restricting the collection of urban data or strengthening Canadian privacy law.[75] Critics have dismissed the very notion of urban data as 'an elaborate contortion aimed at giving Sidewalk Labs the regulatory cover it needs to collect data without consent in public places that it quasi-owns'.[76] Nor does Sidewalk Labs allay these concerns by emphasizing open standards and open data. To its credit, the company offered a plan to ensure a digitally open city. This plan was laudable, yet it seemed disingenuous given that Sidewalk Labs already enjoyed advantages that few other companies can ever match, even if Quayside achieves the status of a digitally open city. These include deep expertise with collecting and using urban data, ownership interests or investments in other companies that have already developed many of the tools needed to make Quayside successful,[77] and access to the financial resources and technical sophistication of its multi-billion-dollar sister firm, Google.

[72] Natasha Tusikov, '"Urban Data" & "Civic Data Trusts" in the Smart City' (*Centre for Free Expression*, 6 August 2019) <https://cfe.ryerson.ca/blog/2019/08/%E2%80%9Curban-data%E2%80%9D-%E2%80%9Ccivic-data-trusts%E2%80%9D-smart-city> accessed 27 September 2021. See also Goodman and Powles (n 65) 474, asking 'why is a vendor making policy?'.

[73] Sidewalk Labs, 'Master Innovation and Development Plan' (n 68) 420–1.

[74] See ibid, 416.

[75] See Tusikov (n 72).

[76] Sean McDonald, 'MIDP: The Data Governance Proposal' (*Medium*, 27 June 2019) <https://medium.com/swlh/midp-the-data-governance-proposal-55272767dd40> accessed 27 September 2021; see also Goodman and Powles (n 65) 473.

[77] These include Flow Inc (traffic-management system), Intersection (public Wi-Fi networks), and Cityblock Health, Inc. (innovative healthcare to low-income neighborhoods). See Marianna Valverde, 'Mystery on the Waterfront: How the "Smart City" Allure Led a Major Public Agency in Toronto into a Reckless Deal with Big Tech' (Centre for Free Expression, 3 December 2018) <https://cfe.ryerson.ca/blog/2018/12/mystery-waterfront-how-smart-city-allure-led-major-public-agency-toronto-reckless-deal> accessed 27 September 2021.

Following the release of the MIDP, the Chair of WT issued an open letter identifying concerns with the size, scope, and funding of Sidewalk Labs proposal, and seeking additional information on data governance issues.[78] On 31 October 2019, the Chair released a second open letter announcing that the parties had reached 'alignment' on these and other 'threshold issues' based on Sidewalk Labs' confirmation that it would scale back the proposal from the 190-acre IDEA District to the original 12-acre Quayside site; switch to a new, WT-led approach to data governance based on existing Canadian privacy law; partner with other real estate developers rather than act as lead developer and modify its revenue-sharing plans with WT; and make various other concessions.[79] Sidewalk Labs agreed that going forward, WT will act as the lead on any future discussions with governmental entities; comply with all existing and future privacy legislation, regulations, and policy framework; accept that relevant municipal provisions and federal laws will determine data governance; store all personal information collected in its digital operations within Canada; and not use 'Urban Data' as a term and otherwise eliminate the UDT from its proposal.[80] Eventually, public outcry and ensuing litigation about the competence of WT to enter into agreement with Sidewalk Labs, as well as the coronavirus pandemic, all contributed to the project been temporarily muted and Sidewalk Labs' withdrawal.

In sum, the above case studies establish that cities vary widely in their attitudes towards data stewardship: some cities are quite inconsistent in their privacy awareness, depending on their desired goals. For example, New York City's local laws protecting personal data held by city agencies is a model of data stewardship with its strong embrace of privacy principles and internal management programmes using a risk-based approach. In sharp contrast, the LinkNYC broadband initiative allows a private firm to set the terms of engagement. Conversely, New York City wanted and got sharing economy data from the likes of Uber and Airbnb by relying on aggressive rulemaking that sparked lawsuits while in the process it almost completely disregarded data stewardship. Seattle and several other cities have experimented with alternative approaches to data stewardship by embracing the idea of data trusts, with Seattle demonstrating leadership by developing both the technical and legal aspects of such trusts. Finally, Toronto offered a plan that equated UDT data governance with absolute monopoly by a private developer (Sidewalk

[78] See Stephen Diamond, 'Open Letter from Waterfront Toronto Board Chair' (*Waterfront Toronto*, 24 June 2019), <https://www.waterfrontoronto.ca/nbe/portal/waterfront/Home/waterfronthome/newsroom/newsarchive/news/2019/june/open+letter+from+waterfront+toronto+board+chair%2C+stephen+diamond+regarding+quayside> accessed 27 September 2021.

[79] Stephen Diamond, 'Open Letter from Waterfront Toronto Board Chair' (*Waterfront Toronto*, 31 October 2019) <https://www.waterfrontoronto.ca/nbe/portal/waterfront/Home/waterfronthome/newsroom/newsarchive/news/2019/october/open+letter+from+waterfront+toronto+board+chair+-+october+31%2C+2019> accessed 27 September 2021.

[80] See Letter from Waterfront Toronto to Sidewalk Labs (29 October 2019).

Labs), thereby compromising citizen's agreement on the governance of their data in public (or quasi-public) spaces.

V. The Rhetoric of Barcelona: The Promise of a 'Public' Smart City

Critics of smart city solutions have pointed to the neoliberal turnaround which municipalities have started to converge worldwide. The heart of the criticism goes into the very framing of the smart city concept, dominated by a logic of inevitability and an aura of a self-evidently progressive project.[81] Can we reimagine the relationship between technology companies and cities in which technology is used for the benefit of citizens instead of big companies? In which Sidewalk Labs does not use the data from Quayside simply to perfect its AI but to build digital solutions that promote citizen participation, help personalize services, and de-bureaucratize national and local governments, all the while preserving privacy and creating a more enjoyable local environment that stimulates growth? A Spanish city in Europe—Barcelona—is branding itself as the alternative smart city, one in which the municipality retains control over critical urban infrastructure and services.

After a pan-European financial crisis, in 2010 the Spanish model of deep decentralization came under severe pressure. The initial reaction to the 2009 financial crisis of the Spanish government was to draw up an expansionist programme of €25 billion. The programme, known as 'Plan E', involved funding projects that were to be carried out by local governments, including small to medium investments in infrastructure and other specific policies like technological development. However, in May 2010, the central government adopted a strict economic stability package in close adherence to the criteria laid down by the European economic authorities. This programme sought to cut public debt from 9.2 per cent of GDP in 2010 to just 3 per cent by 2013 and incorporated a wide range of austerity measures that hit especially hard the local governments in Spain.[82] It is against this background that in 2015 Barcelona—the capital of Catalonia and the second-largest city in the country—elected a mayor with a radically progressive agenda centred around the principle of data sovereignty. Ada Colau ran her first election campaign with slogans on the re-municipalization of water and energy, social housing, and promises about turning Barcelona into a commons-based digital city built from the bottom-up.[83] The Mayor's Committee on Digital Innovation came up with a Digital Plan, putting emphasis on data ownership by the city, open-source code,

[81] See Evgeny Morozov and Francesca Bria, *Rethinking the Smart City: Democratizing Urban Technology* (Rosa Luxemburg Stiftung 2018) 23–4.
[82] ibid, 92.
[83] See, generally, Morozov and Bria (n 81).

and the publication of a technology procurement handbook that specifies contractual clauses mandating ethical standards—fostering a culture of transparency that encourages whistleblowers against corruption and crowdsourcing of ideas for dealing with urban problems.[84] Francesca Bria, Barcelona's Chief Digital Officer, has even been called 'the Robin Hood of data'.[85]

Although privacy and data protection are enshrined as separate human rights both on the level of European law[86] and in the Spanish Constitution,[87] they have not been central to Barcelona's vision of data sovereignty. The European statutory framework that could potentially challenge the commodification of data—the GDPR—allows the processing of personal data only when under a legitimate basis. Furthermore, smart city business models that rely on consent as a default legal basis (such as LinkNYC or Quayside to some extent) may run into trouble given the high bar the GDPR places on establishing that consent is valid.[88] For example, most recently, the German Federal Cartel Office (FCO)—the country's antitrust watchdog—partnered with data protection authorities in other European countries to raise a legal challenge against Facebook for abuse of its dominant position. The FCO claimed that the all-embracing consent sought from Facebook users for the collection of their personal data through third-party websites and applications that are embedded in Facebook's interface (eg, through its 'Like', 'Share', and 'Login' buttons) did not meet the criteria for informed consent because users were not made aware of the extent of Facebook's data-sharing practices.[89] Moreover, in 2019 on data protection grounds alone, in France, Google was fined €50 million for breaching the GDPR requirements of 'informed', 'specific', and 'unambiguous' consent in providing personalized advertisements.[90] Instead of referring to the GDPR however, Bria emphasized the advent of blockchain technology for ensuring the privacy of Barcelona's residents who contribute their personal data to the city's data commons.[91] The statement chimes in with recent academic interpretations that place blockchain technology outside the scope of the GDPR.[92] Future reliance on

[84] Andrew Dowling, 'A Tale of Two Cities: Barcelona and Madrid in Spain' in Alistair Cole and Renaud Payre (eds), *Cities as Political Objects: Historical Evolution, Analytical Categorisations and Institutional Challenges of Metropolitanisation* (Edward Elgar P 2016) 92.

[85] Amy Lewin, 'Barcelona's Robin Hood of Data: Francesca Bria' (*Sifted*, 16 November 2018) <https://sifted.eu/articles/barcelonas-robin-hood-of-data-francesca-bria/> accessed 27 September 2021.

[86] See, generally, Charter of Fundamental Rights of the European Union, arts 7 and 11. See also Joined cases C-293/12 and C-594/12, *Digital Rights Ireland Ltd v Minister for Communications* [2014] ECR I-238; Case C-131/12, *Google Spain v Agencia Española de Protección de Datos* [2014] ECR 317; Case C-362/14, *Schrems v Data Protection Commissioner* [2015] ECR I-650.

[87] See Constitution of Spain 1978, arts 18.1, 18.2.

[88] See Council Regulation (EC) 2016/679 of 27 April 2016 on the protection of natural persons with regard to the processing of personal data and on the free movement of such data [2016] OJ L 119/1.

[89] Adrian Künzler, 'Facebook Under Investigation' (Speech to Yale Information Society Project, 3 September 2019).

[90] 'The CNIL's Restricted Committee Imposes a Financial Penalty of 50 Million Euros Against Google LLC' (*CNIL*, 21 January 2019) <https://www.cnil.fr/en/sanctions-issued-cnil> accessed 30 September 2021.

[91] Francesa Bria, 'Smart Cities and Strategy for Digital Sovereignty' (Pictet Talk, 20 January 2020).

[92] See Georgios Dimitropoulos, 'The Law of Blockchain' (2020) 95 *Wash L Rev* 1117.

blockchain for the rollout of smart city applications in Europe might thus mean that, in spite of its differentiating rhetoric, the 'European' data stewardship model exemplified by Barcelona is, in fact, steadily converging with North American data practices in the urban context.

In many ways, Europe and North America 'remain two worlds apart because of their very different understandings of the role that the public and the private sector should play in society'.[93] Since Europeans place their trust in the public sector, a narrative centred around public data ownership seems intuitively appealing to European sensitivities, and in Spain, it was also embedded into the discourse of local anti-austerity opposition. However, in June 2019, Barcelona's Mayor Colau was very narrowly re-elected, and it remains to be seen to what extent she can keep up with her electoral promises and go beyond the rhetoric of Barcelona as a 'neoliberal city with a human face'.[94] The idea of advancing public interest goals through procurement seems well-intentioned, although achieving purely public ownership of data generated through the use of devices supplied by private companies might prove next to impossible. Moreover, much like the synchronized action of state and city actors in the United States that has a better chance of achieving regulatory experimentation, the interlocking nature of Spain's 'non-institutional' federalism makes coordination and close cooperation between the regional, provincial, and municipal level essential. With independence and nationalist demands (mostly in rural Catalonia but increasingly spreading also in Barcelona) clashing with the urban agenda of Colau, the actual outcome of the data sovereignty brand remains unsure.

VI. Conclusion

Urbanization is here to stay, and so is the growing interest in the city. Jane Jacob's evergreen account of organic urban development remains relevant in the era of technology-driven datafication: '[C]ities may fairly be called natural economic generators of diversity and natural economic incubators of new enterprises.'[95] Privacy, broadly conceptualized, becomes an intrinsic part of a global city's progressive cosmopolitan identity as it intersects with the social capital that characterizes big cities—diversity and economic growth. This chapter has sought to blend insights from the literature on global cities, federalism, and localism studies, as well as on smart cities and privacy scholarship to show that cosmopolitan urbanism intersects privacy activism with data stewardship.

93 Bilyana Petkova, 'Privacy as Europe's First Amendment' (2019) 25 *Eur L J* 119, 153.
94 See Morozov and Bria (n 81) 27–8.
95 Jacobs (n 8) 148.

Cities use their legal arsenal to litigate under federal, state, or city law in order to protect the personal information of their city dwellers in a variety of contexts ranging from political participation to consumer protection. Regardless of whether such experiments turn out to be successful—and they sometimes may well be[96]—in the US cities' privacy activism, likely amplified by the stance of their states, may serve as a trigger for bipartisan policy debates and a catalyst for enforcement. Regarding technology's courtship with the city, privacy may be respected to a certain degree by local agencies, but privacy concerns increasingly give way to open data practices worldwide. Privacy is also not a priority in emerging new business models that monetize data and are facilitated through contract law. But big cities can and should leverage their existing powers to push hard for privacy-by-design in public procurement projects that may jumpstart the market in privacy-preserving 'smart' systems. Yet what we observe across the board in large, cosmopolitan North American cities is a tendency towards data stewardship with a wide spectrum of approaches.

As data stewards, cities sometimes abdicate public power and control over public spaces, behaving more like a commercial actor. Toronto's Quayside project is a harbinger of what we might be seeing more often, albeit to a varying degree, across US cities and elsewhere. Surely the very nature of public spaces—open and accessible to all, without a fee, without government restriction on speech and assembly other than reasonable time, place, manner restrictions, available for community and not privately owned—seems to dictate that public authorities should oversee public spaces. Public power is however hardly a panacea. As demonstrated in the chapter, instead of relying on their police powers as regulators of local-level broadband, housing, and transportation services, some city governments either negotiate data-sharing agreements that may bring them direct revenues or try to deal with street-level problems through collecting ever more data. The robust privacy framework enacted at a higher level of government (in Europe and Canada), but mostly the entrenched conviction of preference for public ownership over public spaces, drives rhetoric on data sovereignty spearheaded by Barcelona. Will the trend of local politicking and the predominance of Voice over Exit[97] signal that more frequent local mobilization can change policies?[98] Since technology firms can gain control over

[96] In 2004, San Francisco brought claims under the California Constitution's Equal Protection Clause, raising state constitutional liberty and privacy protections to challenge statues limiting same-sex marriage. See *In re Marriage Cases*, 43 Cal 4th 747 (2008). Later, the City intervened in the landmark case of *Perry v Schwarzenegger*, 704 F Supp 2d 921 (ND Cal 2010), asserting Due Process and Fourteenth Amendment protections under the US Constitution. These efforts ultimately brought marriage equality to California, and with time, to the rest of the country: see *Obergefell v Hodges*, 576 US 644 (2015).

[97] See, generally, Richard Schragger, 'Federalism, Metropolitanism, and the Problem of States' (2019) 105 *Va L Rev* 1537, 1589–91.

[98] Kate Conger, Richard Fausset and Serge Kovaleski, 'San Francisco Bans Facial Recognition Technology' (*New York Times*, 14 May 2019) <https://www.nytimes.com/2019/05/14/us/facial-recognition-ban-san-francisco.html> accessed 30 September 2021.

a public infrastructure not only through procurement but also over the duration of projects, it remains to be seen whether the promise of Barcelona for a publicly structured smart city will stay merely rhetorical. Or will we see citizens instead of businesses 'vote with their feet',[99] choosing to live in cities with less privacy but more autonomous cars and security cameras? Ultimately, privacy issues in the city need to be treated with caution and, in any case, with an eye towards greater proportionality. The data trust model represents an attractive solution towards precisely such a proportionate solution in tune with city identities and situated in-between possible excessive data power grabs coming from either the public or the private sector as shown in the examples above. When ethically sound and established with a sufficient degree of independence, an intermediary model brokering data privacy questions on behalf of city dwellers holds a lot of promise and is consistent with calls for constitutional recognition for the city voiced in this book.

[99] See Charles M Tiebout, 'A Pure Theory of Local Expenditures' (1956) 64 *J Pol Econ* 416, 419–20.

10

The City in the Future of Federalism

*Richard Schragger**

I. Introduction

As I began to work on this chapter, COVID-19 infections were rising again in the US after a short summer of vaccine optimism. Also rising were conflicts between US states and their cities over local public health regulations. Governors were barring cities or school districts from imposing mask mandates or closure laws;[1] these rules joined existing state legislation or executive orders preventing cities from departing from state law.[2] In other words, the most recent wave of the pandemic was once again highlighting how cities and states in the US are often very far apart as a matter of policy and politics.

This increasing distance has been accompanied by a burgeoning 'preemption' movement across the US.[3] Over the last decade or so, state legislatures have become aggressive overseers of their local governments, in many cases limiting and overriding the authority of cities across a range of policy areas and threatening and punishing city officials and citizens for departures from state policy.[4] Increasingly bitter conflicts between states and their cities have become a feature of America's polarized political life, not just in relation to public health, but more broadly.

I have elsewhere argued that US-style federalism, with its constitutional entrenchment of states, produces weak cities[5]—something that the preemption epidemic (and the COVID-19 pandemic) have only reinforced. I have also argued that cities should be enabled to exercise more power.[6] My sympathies thus lie with the

* Perre Bowen Professor of Law and Martha Lubin Karsh and Bruce A. Karsh Bicentennial Professor of Law, University of Virginia School of Law.

[1] See Ronald Brownstein, '"Breaking Point": Why the Red State/Blue City Conflict is Peaking Over Masks' (*CNN*, 17 August 2021) <https://www.cnn.com/2021/08/17/politics/2020-census-red-states-blue-cities/index.html> accessed 11 October 2021.

[2] Kim Haddow, 'Under the Cover of COVID: A Survey of 2020-2021 State Preemption Trends' (*Local Solutions Support Center*, 2021) 6, 15 <https://static1.squarespace.com/static/5ce4377caeb1ce00013a02fd/t/604faee2e641222b084316ff/1615834855353/LSSC-UndertheCoverofCovid-March2021.pdf> accessed 11 October 2021.

[3] See Richard Briffault, chapter 5 in this volume.

[4] ibid.

[5] See Richard Schragger, *City Power: Urban Governance in a Global Age* (OUP 2016) 78–103 (hereafter Schragger, *City Power*).

[6] ibid.

Richard Schragger, *The City in the Future of Federalism* In: *Cities in Federal Constitutional Theory.* Edited by: Erika Arban, Oxford University Press. © Richard Schragger 2022. DOI: 10.1093/oso/9780192843272.003.0011 contributors in this volume who advocate enlarging the realm of protected city authority, constitutionally or otherwise.[7]

I will say more below about how cities are disadvantaged by state-based federalism. But before turning to that claim, I want to consider and highlight some important themes and questions that have emerged in the previous chapters of this volume. In section II, I consider the odd mismatch between the city's sociological importance and its relative lack of status in constitutional theory—the very mismatch that this volume, which centres the city in the discourse of constitutional law, is trying to correct. In section III, I discuss the use and definition of the term 'city'—a threshold issue that drives much subsequent theorizing about it. And in section IV, I reflect on the various ways institutional designers might go about empowering the city—another theme raised by the contributors to this volume.

Consideration of these questions sets-up section V of the chapter, which explains why state-based federalism is bad for cities. This 'old' federalism presumes weak and ineffectual cities—a presumption that has become self-fulfilling, at least in the US. The conclusion considers how a 'new' federalism that is more attentive to the reality of an urban-based global economy might do otherwise.

II. The Absent City

As Ran Hirschl observes in his contribution to this volume (and more elaborately in his recent book), cities 'have remained largely absent from constitutional law and constitutional thought'.[8] As an American legal academic who writes about cities, I can attest to this absence. US federal constitutional law is actively hostile to assertions of independent city authority or the recognition of cities as relevant constitutional units at all.[9] And while academic federalism discourse in general is becoming more attentive to cities and local governments than in the past, it is still mainly preoccupied with states and state-federal power, mostly subsuming the city within the existing state-based framework.

Thus, a volume dedicated to highlighting this absence and beginning to remedy it is more than welcome, it is necessary. Almost everywhere around the world, cities are the dominant form of settlement. Internationally, urbanization is the driving force of economic, legal, and political development.[10] Municipal government is an entrenched and permanent feature of a multi-tiered government landscape that

[7] See Briffault (n 3); Ran Hirschl, chapter 4 in this volume; Hoi L Kong, chapter 6 in this volume; William Partlett, chapter 7 in this volume.

[8] See Hirschl (n 7); see also Ran Hirschl, *City, State: Constitutionalism and the Megacity* (OUP 2020).

[9] *Community Communications Co, Inc v City of Boulder*, 455 US 40, 53 (1982) (Brennan J): 'ours is a "dual system of government" which has no place for sovereign cities.'). See also *Hunter v Pittsburgh*, 207 US 161 (1907).

[10] See Hirschl (n 7).

is increasingly metropolitan in scope. And the urban–rural divide is arguably the most important political cleavage of the early 21st century.[11] Whatever the doctrinal and political status of state–federal relations, they tend to be parasitic on these more fundamental features of political, economic, and social life.

The central fact and importance of urbanization and metropolitanization gives rise to two mismatches. The first is the mismatch between the increased economic importance of cities and their relative lack of policymaking or constitutionally recognized authority. Globally, cities and megacities are the dominant forces in their regions and nations and are projected to become even more dominant over the next decades.[12] In the US, for example, the National League of Cities has noted that urban metropolitan areas are home to nearly 86 per cent of the nation's population and produce over 91 per cent of the nation's GDP.[13] In 2018, New York City's gross metropolitan product (GMP) of $1.85 trillion exceeded the GDP of the entire state of Texas; Los Angeles's GMP exceeded that of the entire state of Florida.[14] Denver, Atlanta, Phoenix, Houston, and Dallas house by far the bulk of population in their respective states and produce the bulk of economic growth in those places.[15] New York City is now home to over 43 per cent of the state's residents.[16]

Despite their importance, however, cities often enjoy minimal or no recognition in their respective nation's constitutional structures.[17] The US is the most significant and obvious case. Despite the urban resurgence, city power in the US has arguably declined in the last decade, as states take even more aggressive preemptive actions and the values gap between urban and rural becomes even more pronounced. As cities and their surrounding metro areas become increasingly populous and productive, a significant gap arises between the prevailing sites of productive economic activity and the location of the regulation and redistribution of that economic output. That mismatch cannot last long without eliciting a political response.[18]

The second mismatch, also highlighted by the contributors to this volume, is the mismatch between federalism discourse and the relative lack of attention to

[11] Jonathan Rodden, *Why Cities Lose: The Deep Roots of the Urban-Rural Political Divide* (Basic Books 2019).

[12] See Hirschl (n 7).

[13] National League of Cities, 'Principles of Home Rule for the 21st Century' (*National League of Cities*, 2020) <https://www.nlc.org/resource/new-principles-of-home-rule> accessed 11 October 2021.

[14] IHS Markit, 'US Metro Economies: Annual Report and Forecast September 2019' (*The United States Conference of Mayors*, September 2019) <https://www.usmayors.org/metro-economies/september-2019/> accessed 11 October 2021.

[15] ibid.

[16] Compare 'QuickFacts New York city, New York' (*US Census Bureau*, 2019) <https://www.census.gov/quickfacts/fact/table/newyorkcitynewyork/PST045219> with 'QuickFacts New York' (*US Census Bureau*, 2019) <https://www.census.gov/quickfacts/NY> both accessed 11 October 2021.

[17] See Hirschl (n 7). See also Saunders and Arban, chapter 2 in this volume (comparing national constitutions).

[18] See Richard C Schragger, 'Federalism, Metropolitanism, and the Problem of States' (2019) 105 *Va L Rev* 1537, 1544 (hereafter Schragger, 'Federalism').

city power. Protecting some degree of sub-national autonomy is understood to be advisable for a long list of reasons: deconcentrating power and protecting liberty, encouraging innovation and experimentation, preventing unequal treatment, fostering democratic engagement and teaching civic skills, lowering the costs of failure, promoting choice and a diversity of policy responses, increasing accountability, taking advantage of local knowledge, and providing political out-groups with opportunities to govern.[19] These are the functions of federalism or, in some cases, subsidiarity[20]— regularly invoked to justify a vertical division of authority.

As Erika Arban and Cheryl Saunders observe in their chapter, these federalism values apply to cities as much or more than to regional governments, like states.[21] For example, state boundaries in the US are incidental, and even if they once were drawn with some attention to history, geography, and culture, in the main they do not capture highly differentiated cultural, political, or language groups. Thus, a formal commitment to states that fails to recognize the advantages of sub-state jurisdictions does not make much sense in functional terms. As Richard Briffault notes in his chapter, 'if you like states you should love cities'[22]—simply as a matter of scale.

There is an additional reason to treat cities as the more appropriate unit for a system of vertically divided government, however, and it has to do with the urban–rural divide. An argument can be made that the most important political cleavage of the 21st century is urban versus rural—a problem that affects countries globally.[23] If an important purpose of the vertical division of authority is to manage ideological disputes by giving different sub-national communities space to govern themselves, states are mis-scaled. That is because the urban–rural divide happens *inside* states. As recent studies of the US observe, within-state political heterogeneity is greater than between-state heterogeneity, mostly along lines of population density.[24]

The failure to recognize cities or incorporate them into our federalism thus represents a blindness to the primary ideological feature of 21st-century politics. State-to-state and regional differences are much less important than metropolitan-area ones; federalism doctrines that contemplate state-to-state diversity can only

[19] See ibid.; see also Saunders and Arban (n 17).

[20] Cf Maria Cahill and Garry O'Sullivan, chapter 3 in this volume.

[21] Saunders and Arban (n 17). The terms 'federalism', 'subsidiarity', 'decentralization', and 'devolution' are importantly distinct, even if overlapping. See Yishai Blank, 'Federalism, Subsidiarity, and the Role of Local Governments in an Age of Global Multilevel Governance' (2010) 37 *Fordham Urb L J* 509.

[22] Briffault (n 3).

[23] Rodden (n 11).

[24] As one commentator recently stated, 'We're actually near a high point in the contribution of within state variation in partisan voting, in contrast to between state variation, precisely as our attention as a country has increasingly turned to the state level debate of blue states versus red states': 'The Science of Politics, Is Demographic and Geographic Polarization Overstated?' (*Niskan Center*, 19 May 2021) <https://www.niskanencenter.org/is-demographic-and-geographic-polarization-overstated/> accessed 11 October 2021.

serve as crude proxies for the divides that are actually at work in our politics today. Indeed, state-based federalism will only exacerbate those ideological cleavages, pretending to be responsive to diverse sub-national constituencies while allowing states to ride roughshod over important internal political differences—differences that now appear to be characteristic of national politics in many countries.[25] To the extent that the urban–rural divide drives our national political polarization, state-based federalism has little to recommend it.

Centring the city's constitutional status and role is thus overdue not only because of cities' increasing economic and demographic dominance in an urbanizing world. If theories of federalism are to make any sense, they have to contend with the scale questions raised by the assertion of city power and the importance of the urban–rural divide to our present-day politics. The city's power or lack thereof cannot be treated as a form of baby federalism—locally interesting, but not as important to our constitutional politics as the doctrines that govern the state–federal relationship. Instead of being the 'forgotten stepchildren of both federal politics and scholarship',[26] cities should be placed at the centre of both—as this volume does.

III. What is the City?

Placing the city at the centre of constitutional theory requires defining it. That is one of the concepts being worked out in the contributions to this volume (often implicitly): the concept and meaning of the term 'city'. Maria Cahill and Garry O'Sullivan are correct when they observe in their chapter that imprecision over what is meant by 'city' can undermine claims made on its behalf.[27] To be sure, 'city' is used in different ways in these chapters. Here, I briefly note some of those various uses, attentive to the fact that the city has often been used as a placeholder for other values in which those ostensibly writing about the city are more interested.[28]

Consider first the use of 'city' as short-hand for urbanization—the concentration of people and economic activity in larger and denser settlements. As I and several authors in this volume have argued, this sociological fact is and should be highly relevant to constitutional theorists and designers.[29] But the fact of global urbanization itself—like other sociological facts about the world—does not necessarily underwrite any particular form of constitutionalism. Urbanization could

[25] Kirk Siegler, 'Biden's Win Shows Urban-Rural Divide has Grown Since 2016' (*National Public Radio*, 18 November 2020) <https://www.npr.org/2020/11/18/934631994/bidens-win-shows-rural-urban-divide-has-grown-since-2016> accessed 11 October 2021.

[26] Loren King, 'Cities, Subsidiarity and Federalism' in James Fleming and Jacob Levy (eds), *Federalism and Subsidiarity* (New York U P 2014) 295, quoted in Hirschl (n 7).

[27] Cahill and O'Sullivan (n 20).

[28] Cf Joan C Williams, 'The Constitutional Vulnerability of American Local Government: The Politics of City Status in American Law' (1986) 1986 *Wis L Rev* 83.

[29] See Hirschl (n 7).

be akin to a technology, like the internal combustion engine, transcontinental air travel, or instantaneous telecommunications. These technologies are all hugely important and influential in altering and shaping our public and private lives, but that does not mean that they are or should be a direct subject of constitutional theory.

The claim that the city is uniquely relevant to constitutional theory seems to me to run through political geography, which asks questions about how global urbanization, the rise of megacities, and the increasing concentration of wealth and population in metropolitan centres influences politics and political structure. These are important subjects for constitutional theorists, though often ignored.[30] Scholars of federalism, especially those in law schools, are mostly concerned about boundaries and less so about who is inside them, whether those people live in cities, towns, favelas, on farms, or in apartments, or how productive they are. Constitutions tend to flatten cities into jurisdictions and tend to treat those jurisdictions as interchangeable.

This 'flattening' is fairly common; the city-as-jurisdiction is another way that contributors use the term 'city' in these chapters—and also often the conventional way that many non-academics talk about the city. When we report on actions taken by the City of New York, for instance, we are likely talking about New York as a recognizable form of government. So too when people talk about voting, the exercise of coercive authority, or the reach of city authority, they are talking about the jurisdictional city.

Importantly, the jurisdictional identity and reach of the city may not coincide with its sociological identity and reach; indeed, in most cases, it probably won't. For example, those who identify as Chicagoans might actually reside across the border in River Forest, Illinois—a part of what some might call Chicagoland, but not part of the legal city of Chicago. Those who live in sprawling Los Angeles County might not realize they are residents of a county but instead identify with their local town. Economically, the city may not coincide with its jurisdictional reach either. Housing and labour markets tend to be regional, crossing multiple local and state jurisdictional boundaries. Metropolitan statistical areas (MSAs) live only in the imaginations of demographers, but they represent something important—often unified regional economies or commuting zones.[31] People live, work, and play across multiple jurisdictions; the 'city' as they understand it is not defined by its jurisdictional reach. Indeed, there are undoubtedly multiple ways to define the sociological or economic city.

A third way to talk about the city is as a legal personality. The legal city (like the jurisdictional city) is only recognizable through law—it is, in some versions, an

[30] A counter-example is David Fontana, 'The Geography of Campaign Finance Law' (2017) 90 *S Cal L Rev* 1247.

[31] For a definition, see 'Metropolitan and Micropolitan' (*United States Census Bureau*, 8 October 2021) <https://www.census.gov/programs-surveys/metro-micro.html> accessed 11 October 2021.

artificial person, a corporation. The legal city can sue and be sued—though here too there are sometimes ambiguities. For example, by the legal city we might mean the proprietary city—the one that owns its property, utilities, roads, and even the data (as Bilyana Petkova discusses in her chapter[32]) that it gathers from those who use its public spaces and municipal services. Or we might mean the regulatory or governmental city—the city that adopts rules for its residents and those within its boundaries. Both the proprietary and regulatory city are alternative ways of talking about the actions and decisions of certain people (city officials) who act within certain bodies (the city council, the mayor's office, the administrative departments) and who are subject to public oversight (elections, removal). Nevertheless, courts often treat the two cities—proprietary and regulatory—quite differently.[33]

Rebecca Nelson, in her contribution to this volume, talks about the 'victim-city' and the 'villain-city' in relation to environmental harm.[34] What she seems to mean is not the legal city, but the city as a geographical entity that by function of its form or location contributes to or experiences environmental harms, such as global warming, heat islands, or air pollution.[35] Cities (understood as dense agglomerations of people and output) in general might contribute to, ameliorate, or experience these harms, as might a specific city or a specific city neighbourhood. So, too, the city, understood as a government jurisdiction, might adopt rules and regulations that contribute to or ameliorate environmental harm.

In thinking about the city's role in a federal structure, a number of contributors to this volume treat the city in this latter, policymaking mode. Rebecca Nelson, William Partlett, and Bilyana Petkova are interested in what role city governments might play in addressing problems of environmental regulation, criminal law, and data privacy, respectively.[36] These discussions generally assess the relative competence of centralized and decentralized regulation, consider the prevalence of spillover effects or the likelihood of races-to-the-bottom, and weigh the relative political pathologies of different levels of government. In these discussions, 'city' generally means 'local government', though sometimes distinctions are drawn between urban and non-urban forms.

These theorists might also be referring to the city-as-polity—as a democratic political community. Certainly, those scholars interested in elevating the constitutional status of cities (for example, Hoi Kong in his chapter[37]) seem to be using the term 'city' along these lines. But this entails some further elucidation. What are the contours of the city-as-polity and why is it the relevant political unit?[38] The burden

[32] Bilyana Petkova, chapter 9 in this volume.

[33] On the regulatory/proprietary distinction, see Janice C Griffith, 'Local Government Contracts: Escaping from the Governmental/Proprietary Maze' (1990) 75 *Iowa L Rev* 277, 317–18.

[34] Rebecca Nelson, chapter 8 in this volume.

[35] ibid.

[36] ibid. See also Partlett (n 7), Petkova (n 32).

[37] Kong (n 7).

[38] See Cahill and O'Sullivan (n 20).

on those of us who believe that cities are and should be constitutionally salient is explaining why the 'city' is the appropriate unit for any democracy-inspired federal theory. Why isn't the region more appropriate (when cross-border spillovers are endemic), or the neighbourhood (in very large cities)? Is the 'city' in these theories just a placeholder for an entity that is smaller and more democratically accessible than the state? That use of city does not make much sense for global cities, like New York, London, or Tokyo, each of which has more residents than many sub-federal regions, as well as many nations. Invoking the city does not solve the scale problem; one needs to say more about the features that make the city a preferred object of democratic theory and an important subject of constitutional design.

This is not meant as a criticism; the contributors to this volume are engaged in that very task. In doing this work, however, it may be helpful to think about the city in relation to the many different kinds of entities that operate and exercise authority or power in modern society. Scholars thinking about the constitutional status of cities tend to treat cities as what we commonly assume them to be: governmental bodies, ie subordinate components of the state. And they tend to think about federalism as a mechanism for dividing or sharing power between levels of government, ie within the state.

As Gerald Frug argued many decades ago, however, the city-as-the-state (which is again another use of the term 'city') is a fairly recent idea.[39] In medieval political theory, the city occupied a position—like the church and university—somewhat adjacent to the state. The city enjoyed a range of powers and privileges, with some that partook of what we would call sovereignty, some that we would today call property rights, and some that we would characterize as associational. The 'city as a legal concept' (as Frug calls it) is invented in the 19th century when liberal theory divides the world into public entities (the state) and private ones (the association or corporation).[40] With this bifurcation, the city loses its identity as a corporate body; its associational and commercial aspects are eliminated or occluded; and a line that did not previously exist is drawn between business and municipal corporations. The defining feature of this newly bifurcated city is that while it is economically and politically salient, it is wholly constitutionally subordinate.[41]

By contrast, the pre-bifurcated city offers a very different way to understand what is meant by the term 'city'. The medieval city is not only an administrative unit, service provider, and political jurisdiction, but also an association, a corporation, and a market participant. Those aspects of its corporate personality mean that the city may enjoy both powers and rights.

This conception of the city is an abstraction, of course—a combination of legal theory and sociological reality. But it is no more of an abstraction than the

[39] Gerald E Frug, 'The City as a Legal Concept' (1980) 93 *Harv L Rev* 1057, 1118.
[40] ibid.
[41] ibid.

corporate firm, the church, or any other associational entity that exercises powers or rights *vis-a-vis* the state.[42]

And this leads to a final observation. The very idea of divided authority, sovereignty, or power—whether articulated as federalism, subsidiarity, corporatism, or something else—already embodies a conception of the city that is congenial to it. Theories based in popular sovereignty, ie consent-based theories of the state, require that there be a relatively clear demarcation between the state and those who consent to its exercise of authority—the rights-bearing individual in the liberal tradition. Frug observes that the city never quite fits into liberal theory's relevant categories; indeed, he argues that the city has become alienated from those categories.

This problem of 'fit' is perhaps unsurprising; it is appropriate that the city as it is theorized is multi-faceted. And that multiplicity further provides an important reminder that the definition of the city will turn in large part on what purpose the city plays in any given political theory. Whatever one's conception of the city, it is being driven—perhaps especially so in the case of scholars of federalism—by one's democratic theory.

IV. Empowering Cities

This discussion of the concept of the city leads naturally to a consideration of the city's relative power. A number of contributors to this volume argue that cities should be recognized in national constitutions or, in the case of the US, be provided with some level of policymaking freedom through their respective state constitutions.[43] Others argue that cities have an important role to play in specific public policy areas.[44] As already noted, these approaches generally treat the city as a government and understand the exercise of city power as flowing from the devolution of public policymaking authority, often through formal grants. But city power can be understood in other ways. Two distinctions are important. The first is the distinction between cities as power-asserters and cities as rights-bearers. The second is the distinction between the city's formal authority to act and its actual capacity to govern.[45]

As to the first, the conventional way to expand city power is to protect the city's sovereignty, to increase its power to act, and protect it from national or regional intervention. Hoi Kong and Ran Hirschl argue in this volume that cities should

[42] For a discussion of corporate personality, see Richard Schragger and Micah Schwartzman, 'Some Realism About Corporate Rights' in Micah Schwartzman, Chad Flanders, and Zoe Robinson (eds), *The Rise of Corporate Religious Liberty* (OUP 2016).

[43] See Kong (n 7); Hirschl (n 7); Briffault (n 3).

[44] Partlett (n 7); Petkova (n 32); Nelson (n 34).

[45] For a discussion, Schragger, *City Power* (n 5) 1–3.

be constitutionally entrenched so that they enjoy significant regulatory initiative and autonomy.[46] The arguments made in favour of entrenchment vary but tend to combine an appreciation for the unique attributes of cities—their scale, density, and collectivity—with more generic arguments on behalf of participatory or local self-government.[47] On these accounts, the way to give cities more power is for the sovereign to grant them more power.

But there is another way to increase the city's autonomy, already alluded to above. Instead of exercising power, cities could instead enjoy rights. Rights are autonomy protecting when applied to individuals, associations, corporations, or groups; rights are the way we protect these entities from the power of the state. To be sure, the idea of city rights seems alien in a world divided between individuals who exercise rights and governments that exercise powers. But as already noted, the bifurcated city is of recent origin and the fact that corporations of all kinds exercise rights serves as a counter-example. It certainly can be argued that the city is as much an association as is the corporate firm or the homeowners association.[48] Like cities, those entities exercise coercive power over their members, employees, or residents; they regulate in ways that affect third parties; and they can contract, own property, and dispose of it, protected at least in part from state intervention. It is in fact not uncommon to understand the city as a rights-bearer. As also noted above, when the city acts in its proprietary capacity—as owner of its property, data, or resources—it is common to treat the city as any other property owner.

A different and more controversial example is city rights of free speech. In writing about recent controversies over Confederate statuary in the US, Yishai Blank has argued that cities should not be required to maintain symbols of white supremacy in their public parks.[49] Cities have challenged state laws that bar the removal of Confederate monuments either on the theory that the residents of the city enjoy individual speech rights that can be aggregated or on the theory that the city *qua* city—as a municipal corporation—enjoys its own right against compelled speech. Relying on the pre-bifurcated conception of the city, Blank argues that if private business corporations enjoy speech rights (which they do in the US[50]), cities should as well, an argument grounded in both associational autonomy and notions of democratic self-government.[51]

One state supreme court has rejected a city speech right, though the trial court originally vindicated it.[52] Birmingham challenged on First Amendment grounds

46 Kong (n 7); Hirschl (n 7).

47 See also Daniel Weinstock, 'Cities and Federalism' in James E Fleming and Jacob T Levy (eds), *Federalism and Subsidiarity* (New York U P 2014) 269.

48 On this comparison, compare Robert Ellickson, 'Cities and Homeowners Associations' (1982) 130 *U Pa L Rev* 1519 with Gerald E Frug, 'Cities and Homeowners Associations: A Reply' (1982) 130 *U Pa L Rev* 1589.

49 Yishai Blank, 'City Speech' (2019) 54 *Harv CR-CL L Rev* 365, 370–3.

50 See *Citizens United v Fed Election Commission*, 558 US 310 (2010).

51 Blank (n 49).

52 *State v City of Birmingham*, 299 So 3d 220 (2019).

an Alabama law that required the city to maintain a monument to Confederate soldiers.[53] The trial court held that the monument was the city's speech and easily determined that the state law was unconstitutional under conventional free speech doctrine.[54] The Alabama Supreme Court just as easily overturned the trial court, holding that cities—being administrative arms of their states—do not enjoy constitutional rights.[55]

The two decisions are both theoretically plausible; the two courts simply disagreed about what the city *is*, with the Alabama Supreme Court adopting the conventional view. For theorists, the question of whether the city should be afforded a privileged state-like status in a federal system or should instead be treated as a rights-holder remains a live one, however. A rights approach might be attractive under a regime in which any division of power between levels of government is difficult to enforce. But, as illustrated by the Birmingham case, recognizing a city's speech right may also present challenges under existing law.

Either approach to advancing city authority and autonomy—power or rights—has to contend with a second important distinction: the distinction between formal powers or rights and actual capacity. Using constitutional law (presumably enforced by courts) is the formal way to advance city power. But formal powers or rights may not mean very much if the city's capabilities are limited for other reasons. This gap between formal powers or rights and actual capacity is not unique to cities; individuals, groups, or associations may also have a power (to start a business) or a right (to engage in speech), but not have the resources to do so effectively.

For some contributors to this volume, the problem for the city is its lack of power or right to act without interference from regional or central governments. City power is understood to mean the city's freedom to adopt certain policies, like a local minimum wage, a plastic-bag ban, or a mask mandate, and to engage in certain acts, like removing or erecting a Confederate monument.

But a city's agency is limited by more than just the state. When we ask whether cities can govern effectively, we are often asking if the city can weather economic booms and busts, encourage development, foster employment, and provide basic services to its citizens. And this latter meaning of city power might not turn on the city's formal powers or rights but rather on features of a global economy over which the city has little or no control. Even if they have the authority to do so, it is not at all obvious that cities can adopt policies that can stem economic decline, prevent outward migration, or reduce poverty and improve the quality of life for existing residents. In other words, regardless of its formal powers or rights, the city may be

[53] Ian Stewart, 'Judge Throws Out Alabama Law that Protects Confederate Monuments' (*National Public Radio*, 15 January 2019) <https://www.npr.org/2019/01/15/685672038/judge-throws-out-alabama-law-that-protects-confederate-monuments> accessed 11 October 2021.

[54] Order on Cross Motions for Summary Judgment at 1, *State v City of Birmingham*, No CV-17-903426-MGG (Ala Cir Ct, 14 January 2019).

[55] *State v City of Birmingham* (n 52).

unable to influence the most basic preconditions for its existence or its citizens' health and welfare.

If that is the case, the important limitation on cities is not the absence of constitutionally entrenched powers or rights, but rather the constraints imposed on cities by the global market for location. Indeed, the conventional view of cities has long been that they are in a competitive race for mobile residents and capital and that whatever rights or powers they enjoy can only be exercised within a narrow ambit.[56] According to this view, cities are 'limited' by the need to attract and retain people and investment.[57] A city may have the authority or right (in many US states now denied to it[58]) to adopt a local minimum wage, but it may have few workers to apply it to. The city may have the authority or right to tax and spend but may be unable to do so because it has little in the way of valuable land or other economic resources.[59] In fact, it may be that even the most constitutionally entrenched and autonomous city can only weakly counter large-scale economic forces like industrialization, suburbanization, and globalization.

The city's vulnerability points to an important consideration when thinking about how cities should be treated in a federal system: mere independence from central government commands (either through rights or powers) is not sufficient. We might in addition ask central governments that enjoy greater fiscal capacity to adequately support their cities or at least avoid creating conditions that contribute to their fiscal deterioration. An obvious example of the latter is unfunded mandates; the former might include a requirement that national or regional governments provide adequate intergovernmental aid.[60] To be sure, once we begin to assess and evaluate the city's capacity to govern and not just its formal powers or rights, it becomes much more complicated to sort out the appropriate relationship between central governments and their cities. That relationship will undoubtedly entail a balance of independence and dependence.

Constitutionally entrenched protection from central commands is not sufficient for another reason: in the case of the city's fiscal capacity, mobile capital exercises outsized influence. Whatever constitutional powers or rights the city enjoys, urban booms and busts will still occur with all the attendant social ills those cycles cause. Controlling those cycles entails influencing the migration and investment decisions of thousands (and in some cases millions) of individuals, families, and firms, all of which exercise their own kind of power over the city.

[56] See Paul E Peterson, *City Limits* (U Chicago P 1981).

[57] ibid.

[58] See 'Preemption of Minimum Wage' (*Local Solutions Support Center*, 23 August 2021) <https://www.supportdemocracy.org/issuespecific-preemption-guides/preemption-of-minimum-wage> accessed 11 October 2021.

[59] The Detroit bankruptcy is an example. Monica Davey and Mary Williams Walsh, 'Billions in Debt, Detroit Tumbles Into Insolvency' (*The New York Times*, 18 July 2013) <https://www.nytimes.com/2013/07/19/us/detroit-files-for-bankruptcy.html> accessed 19 July 2013.

[60] See, eg, National League of Cities (n 13).

That problem—which might be understood as an imbalance between the market and the city—is less amenable to constitutional reform efforts intended to protect cities from their states or nations.

V. The Old Federalism and the New

This final section turns to that problem. The relationship between mobile capital and the city is central to our understanding of the city's role in federalism. That is because our current federalism assumes for the most part that mobile capital dictates the city's health and welfare. But what if that assumption is wrong? The 'old' federalism, which presumes relatively weak and ineffectual cities, would be wrong too. And a 'new' federalism would be necessary to understand the city's appropriate place in an urban-based global economy.

To understand this claim requires first a short description of the 'old' federalism, which is based on two major premises. The first premise is that capital and labour are and should be mobile across subnational jurisdictional boundaries. The second premise is that in a world of capital mobility, redistributive social welfare policies cannot be effectively pursued at the subnational level.[61] Capital will flee efforts to tax it. In other words, a basic assumption of our current federalism is that sub-national governments, and in particular, territorially limited municipal governments—are highly constrained. This is the conventional 'limited cities' view, previously discussed.

In the US, for example, this federalism is the product of a specific 20th-century history, namely the rapid nationalization of commercial activity, the collapse of local barriers to entry, the rise of large-scale, cross-border corporate enterprise, and the emergence of a centralized administrative state capable of responding to global economic shocks.[62] This is the federalism of the common market, unified currencies, and central banks; it is also the federalism of the modern social welfare state—a culmination of the centralizing impulse of the last long century. In a federal system based on these premises, the national and regional governments provide for the bulk of social welfare provision while sub-national and sub-regional jurisdictions deploy developmental policies in a competitive effort to attract desirable capital and labour.[63]

[61] See, eg, Wallace E Oates, *Fiscal Federalism* (Harcourt Brace Jovanovich 1972) 131–40; Paul E Peterson, *The Price of Federalism* (Brookings Institution P 1995).

[62] For histories, see generally Robert H Wiebe, *The Search for Order 1877–1920* (Hill & Wang 1967); Alan Brinkley, *The End of Reform: New Deal Liberalism in Recession and War* (Alfred A Knopf 1995); David M Kennedy, *Freedom from Fear: The American People in Depression and War 1929–1945* (OUP 1999).

[63] See Michael S Greve, *The Upside-Down Constitution* (Harvard UP 2012).

This account is much abbreviated obviously, but one can see how it accords with a fairly standard view of what cities can and should be doing. The literature on city limits assumes that cities are mostly acted upon by the forces unleashed by open borders and the rapid flow of goods, labour, and capital across the landscape.[64] The city's job is to compete for residents and capital[65] by deploying common strategies of attraction and retention: offering low taxes, limited regulation, a favourable business climate, and desirable amenities.[66] Economically, the unit of analysis is the nation; whether particular cities within the nation grow or decline is less important than overall GDP. The distributional implications of uneven economic growth will be addressed by the central government, which will smooth out inevitable local economic disruptions through national tax-and-spend policies. The city survives by catering to powerful economic interests or by relying on regional or national governments for aid; all those entities are relatively more powerful than the city.

In this way, the conventional theory provides an explanation for city rise and decline and suggests a policy programme that is geared towards the needs and desires of mobile firms and consumer-residents. And it explains why urban politics, regardless of who holds elected office, often privileges business and developmental interests.[67]

This 'city limits' thesis is highly influential, but here I want to argue that it is based on premises that are wrong or at least incomplete. Indeed, there are some good reasons to be sceptical that the 'old' federalism captures the salient features of a global urban-based political economy.

First, and most obviously, it is important to observe that the forces that contributed to nationalization in the last century have not abated but have instead accelerated at a global scale. The nation-state is thus not in a particularly privileged position *vis a vis* global capital. It too seems to be similarly buffeted by the rapid movement of global finance; it too must compete for investment and seek to constrain capital flight.[68] The standard view that nations redistribute and subnational governments compete for development thus needs to be revised. Indeed, the declining capacity of the nation-state to corral and regulate mobile capital—its vulnerability to economic shocks and rapid disinvestment—is a central theme of 21st-century political theory and practice.[69]

64 Peterson (n 56).

65 ibid.

66 ibid. On 'competitive federalism', see generally Greve (n 63).

67 Peterson (n 56); see also Harvey Molotch, 'The City as a Growth Machine: Toward a Political Economy of Place' (1976) 82 *Am J Soc* 309; Stephen L Elkin, *City and Regime in the American Republic* (U Chicago P 1987) 42.

68 See generally Richard Kozul-Wright and Robert Rowthorn, *Transnational Corporations and the Global Economy* (Palgrave Macmillan 1998).

69 See, eg, Dani Rodrik, The Globalization Paradox: Democracy and the Future of the World Economy (W W Norton & Co 2012).

This leads to a second point: in many cases, cities are better positioned than nations to counter capital flight. Large-scale firms operate on a global scale where capital seems largely unhindered by national borders. But global economies are also highly geographically localized, with specialized industries or firms increasingly concentrated in particular cities and metropolitan areas.[70] Urban economists argue that economic growth in modern service- and knowledge-based economies depends a great deal on proximity and that even in an era of rapid telecommunications and transportation, the co-location of firms, industries, and workers in cities has become increasingly important.[71] Cities have thus become desirable locations for firms and residents; their advantages cannot be reproduced elsewhere, at least not easily.[72]

There is an enormous literature on what theorists call the 'agglomeration' advantages of cities; that literature suggests that firms and workers do not choose urban locations so much as urban locations choose them.[73] If that is the case, then capital and labour are arguably less mobile than the old federalism assumes.[74] And this means that cities can engage in more redistribution and regulation of capital than the conventional 'limited cities' thesis would predict. Indeed, cities may be able to corral mobile capital better than nation-states can.

Of course, one can argue that only national governments have the resources to engage in massive redistributive spending. One feature of the old federalism makes that undoubtedly true (at least in the US): the ability for the federal government to engage in deficit spending.

Nevertheless, it is notable that taken by themselves, the largest metropolitan areas have larger economies than many nations. To be sure, cities need assistance from higher-level governments, especially those that can print money. But we should not forget that even when a central city is in decline, it often still generates enormous wealth.[75] The metropolitan areas that have grown up around these places certainly do.[76] Cities are the engines of national economic growth; the national economy can be understood as a way of managing a collection of city

[70] See Mario Polèse, *The Wealth and Poverty of Regions: Why Cities Matter* (U Chicago P 2009); Michael Storper, *Keys to the City: How Economics, Institutions, Social Interactions, and Politics Shape Development* (Princeton UP 2013).

[71] See Polèse (n 70); see also 'World Development Report 2009: Reshaping Economic Geography' (*World Bank*, 2009) <https://openknowledge.worldbank.org/handle/10986/5991> accessed 11 October 2021; Michael E Porter, 'Location, Competition, and Economic Development: Local Clusters in a Global Economy' (2000) 14 *Econ Dev Q* 15.

[72] Edward Glaeser, *Triumph of the City: How Our Greatest Invention Makes Us Richer, Smarter, Greener, Healthier, and Happier* (Penguin P 2011).

[73] Polèse (n 70).

[74] ibid.

[75] The City of Detroit, for example, has an over $1 billion budget: 'Office of Budget' (*City of Detroit*, 2021) <https://detroitmi.gov/departments/office-chief-financial-officer/ocfo-divisions/office-budget> accessed 11 October 2021.

[76] Detroit's metropolitan-area economy is the fourteenth largest in the US: 'Detroit' (*Wayne County*, 2021) <https://www.waynecounty.com/departments/econdev/detroit.aspx> accessed 11 October 2021.

economies, as Jane Jacobs famously argued in her work.[77] Indeed, urban wealth *is* the wealth of the nation, and one can think of national tax and spending policy as a mechanism by which the wealth of cities is distributed—often to other places in the nation that are less productive.

The city's economic primacy leads to a third and final point: the city's subordination to the nation-state and markets is less an economic reality than it is a political one. The old federalism assumed that the primary constraint on city policymaking was economic. In a world of mobile capital, the attract-and-retain strategy seems economically inevitable; one could safely assume that all cities would converge on the same business-friendly strategies. So, too, it has been conventional wisdom that cities have to be restrained from racing-to-the-bottom; the assumption has been that sub-national governments' natural inclination is to under-regulate, thus requiring national standards to ensure a minimal level of compliance.[78]

Ongoing city efforts in the US and elsewhere to regulate and redistribute—and recent state and national efforts to undermine those efforts—suggest the opposite is the case. Cities are racing to the top in many areas, adopting environmental, labour, and employment laws that are not predicted by the traditional account of federalism.[79] Central governments—either state or national—are more likely to object to those efforts, regularly overriding those laws, often in the name of maintaining a statewide or nationwide congenial business climate.

The preemption crisis in the US is a good example. In a functioning federal system, one would expect that the exercise of local power would follow from local competence and that decision-makers would be aligned with the costs and benefits of their decisions. Urban economic and population growth should be accompanied by increased metropolitan responsibility.

State-based federalism, however, has not yet accommodated the new metropolitan political economy. Cities' increased population and productivity has not been accompanied by increased authority and responsibility. Instead, states are reducing city power, through preemptive laws, restrictions on local revenue raising, and policies that impose costs downward[80]—using the system of divided government to off-load fiscal responsibilities without providing off-setting resources.[81]

In this way, the old federalism's presumption of weak cities becomes self-fulfilling. Having weak cities is a political choice, one that favours mobility over

[77] Jane Jacobs was an original proponent of a city-centred theory of national economic growth. See Jane Jacobs, *Cities and the Wealth of Nations: Principles of Economic Life* (New York Vintage 1984) 42–4; see also Polèse (n 70) 110.

[78] See, eg, Daniel C Esty, 'Revitalizing Environmental Federalism' (1996) 95 *Mich L Rev* 570. But see Wallace E Oates and Robert M. Schwab, 'Economic Competition Among Jurisdictions: Efficiency Enhancing or Distortion Inducing?' (1988) 35 *J Pub Econ* 333, 336.

[79] For a discussion, see Schragger, *City Power* (n 5) chs 5–6.

[80] See Briffault (n 3); see also Yunji Kim and Mildred Warner, 'Shrinking Local Autonomy: Corporate Coalitions and the Subnational State' (2018) 11 *Cambridge J Regions, Econ & Soc* 427.

[81] Kim and Warner (n 80).

stability, exit over voice, uniformity over diversity, consumers over citizens, and private economic power over public democratic power.[82] The city is limited, to be sure, but not because it is subservient to mobile capital. Rather, it is limited by a series of political decisions to amass power at the centre and provide cities with few tools to counter the inevitable booms and busts of a spatial economy. Centralization benefits a certain form of economic and political organization—namely one built around large-scale organizations, corporations, and governments.

VI. Conclusion

We could make different political choices. Robert Dahl, in his 1967 Presidential Address to the American Political Science Association, exhorted his audience towards the realization of the 'age of the democratic city within the democratic nation-state'.[83] This city-in-federalism has two important aspects. Dahl emphasizes the first: the need in a democratic political system for a political unit that is small enough to permit citizens to participate in governance and yet large enough to do things that matter. After considering the various possibilities—the globe, the nation, the state, the region, the metropolis, the village, the business firm, the workplace—Dahl concludes that the city is best scaled for democratic participation, learning, and civic education.[84] It is also the scale that matters, where all the difficult and important tasks of the modern social welfare state are joined: education, public order, housing, poverty, healthcare, racial justice, inequality. Dahl is unimpressed with US states, which he dismisses as both too large and too unimportant, 'destined for a kind of limbo of quasi-democracy'.[85]

The second aspect is my own gloss on Dahl: the city-in-federalism as a site for individual and collective economic development and a potential counterweight to the exercise of private economic power.[86] In an era of giant transnational business corporations and highly centralized but increasingly ineffective (and often beset) nation-states, recovering the city as a public alternative to private power is attractive. Too-large political units are not the only contributors to global democracy deficits, so are too-large economic units.

This concern evokes Louis Brandeis's famous 'curse of bigness'—his argument against giantism in both politics and economics.[87] Like Dahl, Brandeis also worried about the immense scale of the modern administrative state, which he argued

[82] See Schragger, 'Federalism' (n 18).
[83] Robert A Dahl, 'The City in the Future of Democracy' (1967) 61 *Am Pol Sci Rev* 953, 964–5.
[84] ibid.
[85] ibid 968.
[86] Schragger, *City Power* (n 5).
[87] See generally Louis D Brandeis, *The Curse of Bigness: Miscellaneous Papers of Louis D Brandeis* (Osmond K Fraenkel and Clarence M Lewis ed, Viking P 1934).

was necessitated by the immense scale of the modern business corporation.[88] Brandeis advocated breaking up those corporations—something current-day anti-monopolists have enthusiastically embraced during this new era of economic concentration.[89] The emerging global municipalist movement, known as 'fearless cities', is also concerned in the main with reforming and dismantling concentrated economic power.[90]

These two strands of the decentralizing tradition—the Dahlian and Brandeisian—make the case for city power. But that case is, of course, older than either of those 20th-century thinkers. As Dahl points out, his account of the city in the democratic state owes much to the ancient Greeks; he argues that even in the modern era the city offers the best opportunity to 'achieve ... what the Greeks did 2500 years ago, to develop an urban civilization founded on the democratic city'.[91]

A large-scale democracy based on a modern urban-based economy must be clear-eyed about the limits of the Greek city-state. But one need not be a romantic or utopian to appreciate the possibilities of the city for democratic governance—or, at least, the necessity of building the city into our constitutional institutions. Urbanization is a fact of the world; democratically governing enormous populations (in enormous cities) is the challenge of our time. So, too, negotiating the urban–rural divide, which has become in many countries the leading political and ideological cleavage of the day, requires a federalism that recognizes the city as a salient constitutional and political unit.

There are many challenges to building robust democratic institutions that can withstand political extremism, dampen polarization, and effectively address a wide range of policy ills that include global pandemics, climate change, and increasing economic inequality. Despite their central importance, cities continue to be under-appreciated and under-powered, in large part because our current federalism assumes them to be relatively ineffectual. The chapters in this volume suggest otherwise. As urbanization continues apace, the gap between urban and rural becomes dominant across political domains, and states and nation-states face increasingly severe crises of legitimacy, the city will by necessity become the future of federalism.

88 ibid.

89 Tim Wu, *The Curse of Bigness: Antitrust in the New Gilded Age* (Columbia Global Rep 2018).

90 See Barcelona En Comú, *Fearless Cities: A Guide to the Global Municipalist Movement* (New Internationalist 2019).

91 Dahl (n 83) 970.

Index

For the benefit of digital users, indexed terms that span two pages (e.g., 52–53) may, on occasion, appear on only one of those pages.